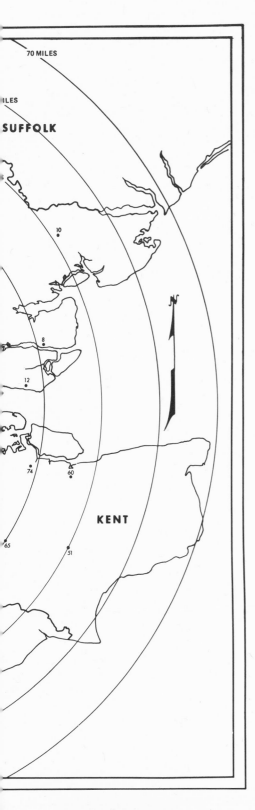

70 MILES

ILES

SUFFOLK

KENT

WOULD
YOU LIKE
TO LIVE
IN ENGLAND?

Mary Spooner Cherry

WOULD YOU LIKE TO LIVE IN ENGLAND?

QUADRANGLE / THE NEW YORK TIMES BOOK CO.

Manufactured in the United States of America.

Published simultaneously in Canada by Fitzhenry & Whiteside, Ltd.,
Toronto.

Book design: Emily Harste

Library of Congress Cataloging in Publication Data

Cherry, Mary Spooner, 1912–
    Would you like to live in England?
    1. Great Britain—Emigration and immigration—Handbooks,
manuals, etc.   2. Americans in Great Britain—Handbooks, manuals,
etc.   3. Great Britain—Description and travel—Guide-books.
I. Title.
JV7674 1974.C47   914.2'04'85   74–77934
ISBN 0–8129–0467–2

TO MATTHEW SEATON

of 14 Twintree Avenue, Minford, Surrey, irresistible hero of the British Consumers' Association, to whom I am indebted for advice on such matters as the purchase of a home and the preparation of a will, and whose portrait was drawn especially for this book by Peter Smith of Essex, England, with permission of the Consumers' Association.

CONTENTS

ACKNOWLEDGMENTS

For supplying me with literature and for patiently answering my many questions, I am deeply indebted to:

In England: Edith Rudinger, Editor, Consumer Publications, London; James G. Parks, of James G. Parks, Ltd., Electrical Contractors and Retailers, Tonbridge, Kent; S. H. Hart, Managing Director of F. Skinner & Son, Ltd., Decorators, Tunbridge Wells, Kent; George Binks, M.B.E., H. M. Customs and Excise, London; T. P. Veitch, The Royal Tunbridge Wells Chamber of Trade; Department of Health and Social Security, London; the Statistics Division, Department of Employment, Watford; N. Morris, Citizens Advice Bureau, London; J. C. Wilcox, of Partridge & Wilcox, Ltd., Pine Nurseries, Rotherfield, Sussex; P. A. Clarke, of The Pet & Garden Centre, Tunbridge Wells; the Department of Education and Science, London; Glyn Davies, of Vauxhall Motors, Ltd., Luton, Bedfordshire; Leonard Jayne, of Wyatt, Powell & Co., Estate Agents, Yeovil, Somerset; A. W. Norman, of Brackett Stokes & Co., Estate Agents, Tunbridge Wells; the Home Office, Department of Immigration and Nationality, London; A. Roberts, of Pitt & Scott, Ltd. (Removals), London; D. B. Smith, Ministry of Agriculture, Fisheries and Food, Surbiton, Surrey; Terence Nowell, of The Granary Quarantine Kennels, Newbury, Berkshire; J. A. Thomas, Department of the Environment, Swansea; T. Loftus of T. Loftus & Co. (Insurance Brokers), Ltd., Tunbridge Wells; Laurence E. Evans, of The Local Government Information Office for England and Wales, London; S. T. Ayling, Estate Duty Office, London; G. Watkin Williams, Institute of Directors, London; Geoff. Forrester, M.N.A.E.A., of Miller & Co., Estate Agents, Truro, Cornwall, and of J. A. Treglown & Sons, Redruth, Cornwall; John

Fuller, Barclays Bank, Ltd., London; and I. G. Emmett, Managing Director of Page Bros., Ltd. (Printers), Norwich, who, when I mistakenly ordered a book published by a different firm, went to the bookstore and bought it for me.

In the United States: C. F. Fisher, British Vice Consul, Washington; The British Tourist Authority, New York; the British Information Services, New York; the Hon. David E. Satterfield III, House of Representatives; Edwin G. Cobb, formerly of the First & Merchants National Bank, Richmond, Va.; Hugh Turner, Internal Revenue Service, Richmond; Anthony Laudari, Vice-President and Manager, BankAmericard Center, The Bank of America, San Francisco; the staff of the Reference Division, Richmond Public Library; and, for her expert assistance with the map of cities within commuting distance of London, Roberta S. Kershaw, Richmond.

WOULD
YOU LIKE
TO LIVE
IN ENGLAND?

Chapter I
WHY ENGLAND?

At the age of 56, I first set foot on English soil and I knew that I had come home. I had gone to London to be with my flautist daughter during her entrance auditions at the Royal Academy of Music and to help her get settled for a year of study. I had exactly one week to accomplish my mission. Looking back, it seems impossible that Ann and I could have done so much in seven days. We opened a bank account, located a hairdresser, rented her room, and decorated it with a new bedspread and curtains. We bought posters and used them to hide the cracks in the plastered walls. We learned how to cross the most dangerous intersections by using the underground tube stations. We had her photographed and registered. We bought boots and an umbrella. We took a sight-seeing bus tour and a boat ride on the Thames and attended four concerts. We went to the Festival Hall complex on the South Bank and bought Ann's concert tickets for the coming month. We located the best music shops and got acquainted with Foyle's bookstore. Not the least important to Ann—we found the way to American-style hamburgers and cold Cokes. And, between times, Ann practiced and took her auditions and arranged for her lessons. Yet, the time was adequate: It was as if we already knew what to do and where to go. We were not in alien territory; we felt no insecurity, no awkwardness, no dread of a misstep. And we fell in love with England.

We are a family of musicians and I could not wait to tell my husband how everyone we met in London knew and understood music—how the shoe clerk described the opera to us, and how the waitress in the department-store cafeteria asked to examine Ann's flute because she, too, had studied at the Royal Academy. I told my husband about the wonderful British college students—hundreds of them—who waited in line for hours to get *standing-room tickets to the prom concerts at Albert Hall; how, before the program started, the students in the balcony promenade sailed paper airplanes to the stage below and drew enthusiastic applause from their fellow students in the ground-level prom circle when there were direct hits on the podium; how, when the orchestra members took their seats and the concertmaster signaled for an "A," a great chorus welled up from the promenade as the students sang "la" along with the oboe; and how, from the moment the conductor raised his baton until the end of the piece, not a sound could be heard from the ten thousand listeners in that enormous hall —no mean achievement when the piece is a Bruckner symphony. I told him with great delight about the two British gentlemen who had walked behind us as we left a recital hall and how one of them had asked, in that charming British accent that I can never get enough of, "I say, did you enjoy that piece for voice and percussion?" and the other had replied, thoughtfully, "Well, not really."*

My husband was intrigued with the thought of a city where interest in music is so prevalent, and soon it occurred to us that England might be a congenial place to live when we retired. Without too many facts to go on, we set about comparing the type of life we imagined we would lead in England with our present life. In Richmond, we had a large house and yard, and we knew we could not acquire a similar "estate" in England. But while our home had served as a source of pride to us, our children were now grown and we no longer needed a place of that size. Besides, with each passing year the lawnmower grew a little heavier and the stairs a little steeper, and we realized that we could not cope much longer with the physical burden of maintaining our home by ourselves, nor would we be able to afford help on a retirement income.

On the other hand, to remain in Richmond in an apartment or a different house was unthinkable. Our home had become too personal, too important: We had waited too long for it. Our married life had begun during the Great Depression, when our only income was my husband's meager salary as a young college instructor. Every summer we lived on borrowed money, and every school year we struggled to pay back the loan so we could borrow again the following summer. Borrow for three months, pay back for nine, borrow for three, pay back for nine: So it went, year after year, with a sort of dirgelike rhythm. Our house was not an easily acquired, taken-for-granted item, as it is with so many young people starting out in today's affluence; it was an acquisition of middle age, earned by years of sweat and worry and deprivation. And, once having acquired it, we had spent untold hours beautifying it with our own hands—building bookshelves and cabinets, hanging wallpaper, planting shrubbery. Don't think it's easy to give up something so hard come by! We knew it would be difficult to let our home go; in fact, we knew it would be a big mistake unless we could replace it with something that would be equally important to us—and we could think of nothing else in our community that would keep us fully occupied and happy. We knew that Richmond could never provide an adequate outlet for our still most consuming interest—music—and we suspected that, as much as we loved our house, our preoccupation with it was really a sublimation of our unfulfilled longing for musical activity. London could offer us our choice of excellent concerts—two or three a day, if we wished—as well as an opportunity to participate in small orchestral and chamber groups. Our time could be fully and pleasantly occupied there.

And then, of course, there was that old, familiar problem—money. A considerable chunk of our retirement pensions would be required just to maintain our home in Richmond: Taxes, utilities, repairs, insurance, even grass seed and turf builder, were all costly items. And we had deliberately built in a secluded area, far from bus lines and shopping centers; a car was a necessity. It was probable, we reasoned, that we could cut down on expenses by living in a flat or a small house near London, and if we chose our location wisely an automobile would not be needed at all, thanks to London's superb public transportation facilities.

We knew that most Britishers were not accustomed to the many luxuries that Americans take for granted. We would not be disgraced if we used a broom instead of a vacuum cleaner and a bottle of Lux Liquid instead of an automatic dishwasher. If we should feel any necessity for keeping up with the London Joneses, it would certainly be easier than keeping up with their American cousins. Our carefully calculated pensions, which, in the face of ever-increasing living costs, were beginning to seem totally inadequate by American standards, began to acquire an air of importance, even abundance, when applied to the British way of life.

Top this all off with a conviction that if you're going to break with something it should be a clean, decisive break—the kind from which there can be no turning back—and you'll see why we began to consider England so seriously.

But there were so many unanswered questions: How much of our pension money would be paid out in taxes to both Britain and the United States? Should we, or could we, become British citizens? Could we buy property in England? What would it cost us to install, in a British home, a heating system that would keep a couple of thin-blooded Virginians warm? Should we try to dispose of all our personal belongings or keep a few favorite items? Would American insurance policies cover us in England? How does socialized medicine work? Would it be possible to call a doctor in the middle of the night? Could we take our dogs with us?

We decided to begin our search for answers to these and dozens of other questions with a sort of trial run, and as we gathered and organized our information we realized that there must be many others who would be interested—not just musicians like ourselves and not just retirees, but people in all walks of life—students, exchange professors, businessmen on assignment in England, military personnel. We determined then to make our findings available to all Americans who may be interested in moving to England.

What started out as a trip to help us formulate our own personal plans thus snowballed into an undertaking to find out for all Americans exactly what might be involved in moving to England. We questioned every British organization and government agency that we thought could provide essential information. We visited furniture stores and supermarkets, clothing shops and appliance showrooms. We consulted with estate agents, solicitors, bankers, accountants. We walked what seemed like hundreds of miles, questioning people and begging pamphlets and literature on pertinent topics; and, as we went along, we kept a sort of ledger in which we listed the advantages and disadvantages of moving to England. On the plus side we listed:

The British people. Shopkeepers, bus drivers, hotel personnel—all were unfailingly gracious and friendly. If we paused on the sidewalk to study our map, someone was sure to stop and offer to help. I recall a day when we were searching for the Royal College of Music: We stopped a British couple to ask directions, but they were uncertain themselves and walked on; a few minutes later, they came back—they had located the school and wanted to show us how to get there. Drivers slowed to let us cross streets, even in places where they weren't required to do so. People in offices, if they didn't know the answers to our questions, telephoned other offices to get the answers for us. We liked the British habit of "queueing" for tickets and bus seats. (Incidentally, after we returned to the States, we learned still more about the importance that the British people attach to queueing. In her book, *Here Is England,* Elizabeth Burton tells how, when throngs line the street to watch a royal procession, an onlooker with a choice spot can leave for a while without fear of losing his place; it will be held for his return. Rudolf Bing, in his memoirs, *5000 Nights at the Opera,* describes the behavior of the queues that formed at the railroad stations during World War II when transportation was disrupted and a train seat was a prized possession: A buzz bomb would drone overhead; suddenly the motor would cut off—the signal that the bomb was on its way down; the queue would scatter; the bomb would explode elsewhere; and the queue would reform in exactly the same order in which it had previously stood.) We found that elderly people are respected and treated with thoughtfulness and deference; we learned that there are organizations of young people whose purpose is to assist the aging in many ways—cleaning and repairing their houses, returning their library books, doing their grocery shopping, taking their clothes to the laundromat, and just listening to them. Add to this courtesy and friendliness the sort of courage and determination that can withstand the blitz, the kind of pride in his city that keeps a Londoner from crushing his cigarette on the sidewalk, and a really great sense of humor: These are the qualities that we found so enchanting in the British people.

The lack of pressure.   Nowhere was there a feeling of urgency; people seemed relaxed and content to do things at a leisurely pace. Occasionally, we found it difficult to adapt to this: We waited until 2:30 for a shopkeeper whose sign proclaimed that he'd be back at 2:00, and when we found we were getting annoyed we realized that our impatience was the result of working at top speed for so long and of the ulcer-making tensions that had built up inside us over the years. We discovered that we weren't really in a hurry after all, and we laughed it off. Frequently, in our persistent quest for information, we wondered if we were using up too much of some busy person's time. We needn't have worried: We were made to feel that our questions were welcomed and that our informant had no more pressing concern than to help us. And it was refreshing to go to a restaurant even at its busiest hours and not have a waiter trying to hustle us out quickly to make room for the next customer.

The feeling of safety.   London is one of the few cities where we don't worry when our daughter walks home alone at night after a concert or show. I am not trying to imply that London is free of crime: Of course it is not, any more than it is free of the many other troubles that plague the world's large cities—pollution, traffic jams, strikes, slums. And, as in all large metropolitan areas, there has been an increase in crime in recent years—an upsurge in juvenile delinquency (witness the wave of "granny-bashing" not long ago by gangs of young girls) and, as we all know, the bombings by terrorist groups. Yet the incidence of crime in London (one of the three largest urban concentrations in the world) is so low that one need not walk in fear. In 1972, there were 1691 murders in New York City; in London there were 113, and approximately three-fourths of those resulted from domestic troubles—the percentage of murder victims who were unknown to their attackers was infinitesimal. In America, we tend to feel that crime is an outgrowth of poverty; but Britain's low incidence of crime seems to have no relation to standards of living. It appears, instead, to result from a combination of attitudes: a basic respect for the law and a swift meting out of justice to those who disobey, combined with a humanitarian approach to drug addiction and a firm, no-nonsense manner of dealing with criminals while at the same time refraining from an antagonistic attitude that serves only to inflame and magnify resentment against law and order. London police do not carry guns while on regular duty; neither do many criminals carry them, because they know much stiffer penalties will be imposed if they are caught with weapons. Sir John Waldron, commissioner of London police, has said, "We do here what practically no other police force in the world does. We are nonprovocative. We wear no protective clothing. We have no riot squads. There is no barbed wire, no water cannon, no tear gas. When we do have a confrontation, the policy is containment —keep close to the chaps and talk to them."

The knowledge that you're being treated honestly. There are countries, I'm told, where everyone has his hand out to get what he can from the tourist. Not so, England. Taxi drivers don't take the long way around. Admission prices aren't jacked up just because the show's a hit and sales are good. If you're not sure how much to tip, you can ask the person you're tipping; you'll get a reasonable figure for an answer—not too much, not too little. I wrote to London before our trip to inquire about concert tickets; the reply was—send us a signed, blank check and we'll get all the tickets we can for you and fill in the proper amount. I never questioned the wisdom of this advice, because it came from England; I would have given a long, hard thought to sending a blank check somewhere else. Surely, to Americans, among the more impressive manifestations of British honesty is that which characterizes the British government. In fact, the setup is such that dishonest campaign tactics could not be used even if anyone would tolerate them. The Prime Minister, unlike our President, is not an elected official; he is the head of the party in power at the moment and is formally appointed by the sovereign. And as for general elections for other Members of Parliament, they occur only when the government says they will, and the government sees to it that there is little time for campaigning. Each candidate is limited in his campaign spending to about 1¢ for each potential voter, and woe be unto him who offers a bribe! Furthermore, an M.P. is not required to live within the area he represents; the government really prefers that he live where he cannot be unduly influenced by his constituents. I expect, too, that because an Englishman cannot get rich by being a Member of Parliament the post is not coveted like one of our Congressional seats. A member of the House of Lords draws no pay at all except for a modest expense account, and a member of the House of Commons earns £4,500 ($11,250) a year.

The beautiful surroundings. The lovely trees, the green, green grass, the spectacular flowers—these pleasures were so surprising to a pair of Virginians who, every April, faithfully seeded, fertilized, planted, and limed, only to reap a brown stubble after a scorching July sun and an August drought, that we used up most of our film in London's parks. Everywhere, there were lawns with immaculately trimmed edges and carefully groomed flower beds. (We discovered one enchanting garden —with ornamental trees, magnificent flowers, and a stream with ducks, turtles, and flamingos—on top of a seven-storey department store!) The English countryside, of course, is acclaimed for its pastoral beauty, and the Cotswolds for their picturesque villages. There are so many varieties of beautiful scenery on this small island that it is impossible to describe them all here. More about that in Chapter V.

The sense of history.   Wherever you go in England, you are seldom more than a stone's throw from the site of at least one historic event, one famous building, one home that housed a person of renown. How could it be otherwise? When you stop to consider that all of the history that has occurred in England in the past two thousand years has been crammed into an area no bigger than the State of Alabama, you realize that it is virtually impossible to set foot in an uninteresting spot. The triumphs, the tragedies, the pomp and elegance, the suffering—it is as if the sound waves created by all these things are somehow still bouncing about and permeating the atmosphere. England's past becomes intensely personal to the newcomer as he learns more and more about his surroundings, about the people who walked on this same ground before him and traveled the same roads and rivers and stood on the same sandy beaches to watch the sun rise over the North Sea. Your boat carries you past the Tower and you weep for Anne Boleyn as she enters Traitor's Gate; you stroll through Hyde Park and you hear the barking of the hounds as Henry and his royal hunting party close in on their quarry; you step out on a pier at Plymouth and you wave good-bye as the *Mayflower* slips out of sight toward the open sea. Everywhere there are reminders of the past and it is useless to feign indifference: One cannot learn about England and at the same time remain casual about being there.

The cultural opportunities.   The British government subsidizes the arts to the tune of over £15 million a year, both through direct allocations and indirectly through such institutions as the Arts Council of Great Britain and the British Film Institute. There is a government minister responsible for the arts, assisted by a Royal Fine Arts Commission, a Standing Commission on Museums and Galleries, and various other advisory groups. In addition, the central government encourages local authorities to use a part of their revenues for promotion of the arts. England has over 900 museums and art galleries, 1500 cinemas, several thousand libraries, and 140 professional theatres. There are regular seasons of opera and ballet and orchestral concerts in all the larger towns, and special exhibits, theatrical performances, and arts festivals all over England. London alone has between 30 and 40 theatres, 5 major symphony orchestras, regular seasons of opera and ballet at

Covent Garden, opera in English performed by Sadler's Wells Opera at the London Coliseum, art galleries with some of the world's most brilliant collections, and museums with famous historical exhibits—including, to name just a few, the manuscript of Magna Carta, the Rosetta Stone, and Shakespeare's First Folio. There were 31,600 new book titles published in England in 1971.

The lower cost of living.   Like the United States and all of Europe, England has been hard hit by inflation in recent years. The saving in living costs is, therefore, not so much the result of a difference in commodity prices; it is more accurately accounted for by a different way of life. There is no reason why you should not have as lovely a home in England as you have in the United States, but it probably won't have an intercom system or a garbage compacter.[1] Market basket prices average out about the same in both countries, though there are many rather startling differences in certain items. Clothing, especially men's clothing, is very reasonable. One of the biggest contributors to a lower cost of living in the London area is the superb transportation system.[2] If you pick your spot carefully, you can do without a car altogether. And perhaps the greatest saving of all, particularly for older people, is in doctor and hospital bills and health insurance premiums: Except for pre-existing conditions, your health care will be free.

The proximity to the Continent.   Although it is possible to fly from New York to Europe in six or seven hours, the cost of transportation has deprived most Americans of more than an occasional trip. But suppose you live in England. As experienced travelers know, you are already in the spot from which most bargain tours originate. London travel agents have gained such a reputation for skillful scheduling of fascinating tours at a fraction of their usual cost that the knowledgeable American traveler, no matter what his ultimate destination may be, goes first to London—and *there* he makes arrangements for the balance of his tour. Once in England, you can have a long weekend in Majorca for $35, two weeks in Morocco for $150, a week in Mayrhofen in the Austrian Tyrol with a side trip to Innsbruck for $70, an eight-day cruise on the Blue Danube for $120—and these are just a few of the bargains available.

The language.   The more we delved into the complexities of moving permanently to a different country, the more we realized the importance of living among people whose language we share. We were

[1]On the other hand, it won't have a property tax. See pp. 114, 159 for an explanation of England's "rates" system.
[2]London Transport's underground trains and its buses cover an area of 1000 square miles, extending 20 miles out into the suburbs. There are 6200 buses and 254 miles of railway lines, and over 2.5 billion passengers a year.

charmed by Germany, but we would hesitate to undertake the purchase of a house there, simply because foreign laws and business procedures are too complex to grasp without a thorough understanding of the language in which they are written. It's true that many people on the Continent speak English well enough to converse about everyday matters—and what difference does it make if you think you've ordered a cup of hot chocolate and you get an ice cream soda instead? But when your life savings are at stake, you don't risk the possibility of a misunderstanding.

On the negative side, we had only two entries in our ledger:

The climate. Many Americans complain bitterly about England's climate; and while the outdoor thermometer on a British house may, in fact, register a temperature no lower than it would register if it were hung outside a Virginia window, the English habit of "heating" houses to a maximum of 65° (55° in the bedrooms) does little to convince Americans that the climate in England is anything other than miserable. Frequent rainy days add to our disenchantment with England's climate, and it does not help much to realize that the amount of water that falls on England each year is about the same as the amount that falls on Florida, because there *is* a difference: Florida rain is likely to fall in heavy, short-lived torrents, leaving ample time for clear weather in between downpours; British rain seems always to seep down from the clouds in slow, misty dribbles—many more wet days are required to get all that dampness down to earth, and consequently there's just not as much opportunity for sunshine. And yet, English weather is not all bad —cool and wet frequently, unpredictable always—but not altogether bad. If you'll study the weather chart, you'll notice that the average

WEATHER CHART

	Jan.	Feb.	March	April	May	June
Low	35°	35°	36°	40°	45°	51°
High	43°	45°	49°	55°	62°	68°
Average	39°	40°	43°	48°	54°	60°
Sunny Days	16	13	17	17	19	18
	July	**Aug.**	**Sept.**	**Oct.**	**Nov.**	**Dec.**
Low	54°	54°	49°	44°	39°	36°
High	71°	70°	65°	56°	49°	45°
Average	63°	62°	57°	50°	44°	41°
Sunny Days	18	18	18	15	14	15

NOTE: Reproduced with the permission of Pan American World Airways, Inc. from *Pan Am's World Guide*, Pan American World Airways, Inc., 1973.

winter temperature (December through February) is 40°; the average
summer temperature (June through August) is 61 2/3°. Compared with
a large segment of the United States, England's climate is really quite
mild. When the dampness gets to us, we can always comfort ourselves
with warm clothing, central heating, and thoughts of the money we're
saving on air conditioning; and we've set aside the wettest month (February) for an annual holiday in Spain, Italy, or southern France—a
holiday that can be accomplished from England with as little expense
and inconvenience as our accustomed annual vacation in Florida.

The effort of moving.   The thing that most nearly caused us to change
our minds about retiring in England was the effort involved: the physical strain of packing and crating, the timing and coordination required
in selling out in the United States and purchasing in England; the
detailed planning necessary for proper handling of personal finances;
the documentation required for entry into Britain as a resident; legal
matters, such as wills and insurance policies. Moving to a different
country *is* a big step to take and a difficult one, but for us it has been
the right step. By writing down what we have learned in the process
and by putting it all together in one volume, I have tried to make the
task easier for those who follow.

Chapter II
BEFORE YOU GO

REQUIREMENTS FOR ENTRY

Many people who want to move to England are under the impression that all they have to do is pack up and go. No country could be more courteous toward tourists than England is—but its hospitality does not extend to an unquestioning acceptance of everyone who might want to make his home there. People who attempt to move to England without first acquainting themselves with the proper procedures are a constant source of worry (and, therefore, irritation) to the British government, and the would-be immigrants are shocked and disappointed to find that Britain may not let them stay. It is one of the aims of this book to inform the reader of the requirements for residence in Britain and to help him make the transition properly and with as little effort and frustration as possible.

Eligibility

You will find that most articles and leaflets about entering Britain name only one requirement: a valid passport. That generally suffices—if all you wish to do is visit Britain for not more than six months. If, however, you hope to stay for a longer period of time, or become a permanent resident, a passport is only the beginning.

The first thing you should do is familiarize yourself with the residence requirements and decide whether *you think* you are eligible to remain in Britain for more than six months.[1] Can you answer "Yes" to the following questions?

Are you in good mental and physical health?

Is your record free of serious criminal convictions?

If you are a retired person (or unemployed for some other reason): Can you produce documentary evidence (e.g., pension and social security certificates, bank statements, letters of credit) showing that you can support yourself?

If you are a student: Can you show that a British educational institution will admit you, that you can pay for your tuition and maintenance while you are studying, and that you have enough money to get back to the United States when your studies are completed?

If you are entering for medical treatment: Can you prove that you have already been accepted as a private patient and that you can pay for the treatments and for your own maintenance without calling on the National Health Service for assistance?

If you are entering to take a job: Have you a work permit[2] issued by the Department of Employment?

If you are planning to set up a business: Have you obtained permission to do so from the Immigration and Nationality Department?

If you are an employee of an American firm or a civilian employee of the U.S. Government: Do you have documentary evidence of your position?

If you are a dependent of someone already living in Britain: Can you produce evidence that your relative can and will support you?

Each case is examined on its own, but you can judge from your answers to the above questions whether your case is good enough to proceed to the next step—its presentation (two to six months before you want to move, and in person, if possible) to a British consul or visa officer.[3] He cannot give you permission to enter Britain (only the immigration officer at the port of arrival has that authority), but he can take your application, submit it for you to the Department of Immigration and Nationality, and obtain a *tentative* approval for you to present to the immigration officer along with your other documentation. This step will allow you to proceed with your plans for moving—with, if not complete assurance, at least a reasonable degree of confidence. (Even if your documentation satisfies the immigration officer at the port of arrival, you will not immediately be given permission to stay indefi-

[1]Members of armed forces assigned to duty or training in Britain, crew members on shore leave, and certain diplomats and their families need not be concerned.

[2]Work permits are not required for doctors, dentists, clergymen, representatives of overseas newspapers, and self-employed people such as artists and writers; but such people should, nevertheless, seek the advice of a consulate before they attempt to settle in Britain.

[3]British consulates are located in the following American cities: Atlanta, Baltimore, Boston, Chicago, Cleveland, Denver, Detroit, Honolulu, Houston, Los Angeles, Miami, Minneapolis, New Orleans, New York, Norfolk, Philadelphia, Portland, St. Louis, San Francisco, Seattle, Washington, D.C., San Juan (Puerto Rico), and St. Thomas (Virgin Islands).

nitely. Your passport will be stamped with a specified time limitation not exceeding 12 months, and you will have to request periodic extensions from the Home Office, Department of Immigration and Nationality, 271 High Holborn, London W.C. 1, until you are finally accepted as a permanent resident and are advised by that office that further extensions are not necessary.)

Illegal entry and overstaying are punishable by fine and/or imprisonment—as are the acts of harboring and assisting illegal entrants.

Passport

To obtain a passport you must complete an application form (DSP–11) and execute it in the presence of either a clerk of a federal or state court having naturalization jurisdiction or an agent of the Passport Office, Department of State. At the time you execute the form, you must present proof of United States citizenship, photographs, and the required fee.[4]

Passport agencies are located in Boston, Chicago, Honolulu, Los Angeles, Miami, New Orleans, New York, Philadelphia, San Francisco, Seattle, and Washington, D.C. Many other cities have branch offices or facilities at the post office for handling your application. (Look in your phone directory under "United States Government" to see if there is a passport facility in your city.) If you have a passport issued within the eight-year period prior to your application, and if you were at least 18 years old when it was issued, you may ask a passport office to send you a form DSP–82. Complete it, return it to the office with your old passport, and obtain a new one by mail.

Acceptable proofs of citizenship are:

A former passport;

A birth certificate showing the United States as your place of birth; or, if not available, a baptismal certificate showing that birth or baptism was recorded shortly after birth; or a statement signed by the appropriate authorities (and accompanied by such evidence as a family Bible, school records, or census records) that no record of birth exists;

A certificate of naturalization, if not born in the United States or to parents who were United States citizens; or parents' certificates of naturalization together with the applicant's foreign birth certificate or evidence of admission to the United States for permanent residence; or

If born abroad to United States citizens, a Consular Report of Birth, a birth certificate issued by the Department of State, or evidence of the parents' United States citizenship accompanied by an affidavit from the parents showing periods and places of residence in the United States and abroad.

---

[4]At present, $12.

Two duplicate photographs must accompany the application. They must be a good likeness, full face, between 2½ in. by 2½ in. and 3 in. by 3 in. in size, and must have been taken within six months of the application. Vending machine photos, snapshots, and magazine pictures are not acceptable. The photographs must be signed on the front along the left-hand side. In most cities there are photographers who specialize in passport photographs and are familiar with the passport regulations; often, their studios are located near passport offices. While you're at it, don't limit your order to two pictures: You may need additional ones in England if your passport requires that you register with the police on arrival there, and you will need two to get an international driver's license before you go; order at least eight.

Vaccination Certificate

Possession of a vaccination certificate is no longer a requirement for re-entry into the United States after visiting Europe, nor is it a requirement for entry into Britain from the United States except when there are outbreaks in the United States of contagious diseases such as smallpox, cholera, or yellow fever. Inquire at your local public health service facility.

A certificate of vaccination against smallpox is valid for three years; yellow fever, ten years; and cholera, six months.

Driver's License

You will be permitted to drive in England for a while under your current U.S. driver's license, but it is wisest to obtain from your local office of AAA an international driving permit before you leave the States. AAA will prepare one for you while you wait if you have with you two passport-size photos, a valid driver's license, and $3. You need not be a member of AAA.

Your international permit will cover you for a period of 12 months if you enter England on a temporary basis. If you enter with the intention of becoming a resident, however, the permit will expire in three months. By the date of its expiration you must either have passed the British driving test or have obtained a "provisional" license (see p. 47).

CITIZENSHIP

U.S. Citizenship vs. British

You have probably by now begun to wonder whether or not you should apply for British citizenship. In general, there is little or no advantage in going through the naturalization process.

Regardless of citizenship, you will have to file income tax returns with both countries as long as you have income from the United States; and you must pay income taxes to one or the other or both countries (though you will be entitled to certain reliefs under the Double Taxation Conventions, see p. 148), depending on the kinds of income you have and the prevailing tax rates.

If you work for a British employer, you will normally be required to contribute to Britain's National Insurance Scheme (Social Security) whether you are a British citizen or not and you will be entitled to share in its benefits. If you have never been a contributor, you will not be eligible for National Insurance benefits even if you become a British citizen.

If you have resided in the United States for ten years or more, *or* if you have at least 40 quarters under U.S. Social Security or have had railroad service that was treated as employment covered by the Social Security Act, you will receive your Social Security pension and lump sum death benefit whether or not you become a British citizen. You will also continue to receive any U.S. Government pension to which you may be entitled.

All residents of Britain, regardless of citizenship, are eligible for benefits under Britain's National Health Service.

If you become a naturalized British citizen, you will forfeit the privilege of voting in United States elections. There is no possibility of acquiring "dual nationality" through the naturalization process.

In any case, you cannot apply for naturalization until you have been a resident of the United Kingdom for five of the previous years, including the year immediately preceding application.

It would appear that the sole advantage of applying for British citizenship lies in facilitating one's ability to move freely among the member countries of the European Economic Community[5] and to seek and accept employment in any of them except Northern Ireland, where the restrictions will not be removed until 1978.

Birth of Child Overseas (Dual Nationality)

A child born in England to American parents is a "dual national." The United States considers him an American citizen just as it would if he were born on American soil; Britain considers him a British citizen because he was born within the confines of the United Kingdom.[6] As

[5]Italy, Belgium, Luxembourg, France, Britain, The Netherlands, Denmark, Irish Republic, and the Federal Republic of Germany.
[6]Unless at the time of the birth the father is a foreign diplomat who possesses immunity from suit and legal process in the United Kingdom.

a safeguard, however, the parents will probably want to obtain documentary proof of the child's U.S. citizenship, even though they are not required by law to do so. This may be done in two ways: (a) by asking the U.S. Department of Justice, Immigration & Naturalization Service, Washington, D.C., to send them a Certificate of American Citizenship for the child; or (b) by obtaining for him, from the U.S. Embassy in London, a Report of Birth, a Certificate of Birth, and a passport. The child will retain his dual nationality and will be permitted to vote in U.S. elections when he reaches voting age unless he voluntarily renounces his U.S. citizenship.

A child born in England to one American parent and one British parent also acquires dual nationality at birth. If *this* child wishes to retain his U.S. citizenship, however, he must return to the United States after his fourteenth birthday and remain continuously and physically present in the United States for a period of not less than two years between the ages of 14 and 28. He may then return to England, and his U.S. citizenship will not be challenged unless he voluntarily renounces it or takes some other action (*e.g.*, the acquisition of a British passport or the acceptance of a job requiring an oath of allegiance to the Queen) that is considered by the United States to be clear and convincing evidence that he wishes to divest himself of U.S. citizenship.

FINANCIAL ARRANGEMENTS

Exchange Control

"Exchange Control" is the term applied to certain regulations administered jointly by the British Treasury Department and the Bank of England and designed primarily to promote sound management of Britain's gold reserves.

Exchange Control is an extremely complex subject, but its most apparent effect on British residents may be stated quite simply: It's a lot easier to take money into England than it is to take it out. (British residents are permitted to exchange *reasonable* amounts of British money into foreign currencies if they wish to visit other countries, but they may find it difficult to exchange more than £300.)[7]

When you move to England, you will be allowed a sort of "trial"

---

[7]The £300 may be exchanged into foreign currency upon application to a travel agency or authorized bank and does not include the cost of fares and travel services such as hotel accommodations for which payment is made in British money to a travel agency in advance of the trip. In addition, a traveler may take along £25 in United Kingdom notes to cover expenses incidental to departure and return and on board British ships or airlines, and may, within certain specified limits, use his credit cards and check guarantee cards for travel expenditures while he is abroad.

period of three years, during which time you can make up your mind whether or not you wish to stay there permanently. During this trial period you are permitted to hold, in a British bank, an "external" account to which you may deposit money in any currency and from which you may pay out money in any currency to anyone anywhere in the world. At the end of three years, however, you automatically become a resident "for Exchange Control purposes" and can no longer maintain an external account.

When you first arrive in England, whether you intend to remain there or not, it is advisable to establish one of these external accounts and, if you decide to buy a home in England, have your U.S. bank transfer to that account a sufficient number of *dollars* to cover the purchase price. Then, if you should decide, before your three-year trial period is up, to move back to the States, you will be permitted to sell the house, convert the proceeds back into dollars, and take the money with you. When the transaction is thus piloted through the British bank, you should have no difficulty; but make certain that the bank understands exactly what you are doing when you buy the British house and that it establishes some record whereby it can be proved later that you paid for the house in dollars.

U.S. Bank Accounts

There are a number of reasons why you should continue to maintain checking and savings accounts in the United States even if your intention is to reside permanently in Britain:

1. In general, "earned" income (and this includes U.S. Social Security and other pensions whether or not the employee has contributed to a retirement fund) is liable to United Kingdom tax only insofar as it is remitted to or received in any way in Britain.[8] You should therefore try to arrange for all such money to be paid into a U.S. savings account and instruct your banker to transfer to your British bank only so much as you require for expenses in England. Since Social Security pensions are not taxable by the United States but *are* taxable by Britain if remitted to Britain, it makes sense to leave as much Social Security money in the United States as you can spare. You may find, however, that after you have been in England for six months the Social Security Administration will try to insist on mailing your checks to your British address, where they will immediately become liable to United Kingdom tax. You can avoid this by having an understanding with the Social Security Administration before you leave and by filing an SF–233 ("Power of Attorney

[8]But see footnote 4, page 150.

by Individual to a Financial Organization for the Collection of Checks Drawn on the Treasurer of the United States") with your bank. There is no legal justification—either British or American—for the Social Security Administration's policy of mailing pension checks to overseas addresses (see p. 204). You should encounter no difficulty in arranging for *other* pensions (including U.S. Civil Service pensions) to be paid to a U.S. bank for an unlimited period of time, and those portions that are not taxable by the United States (*i.e.,* the amounts that are not in excess of your contributions) should certainly be left in the United States if you can get along without them. (Interest earned on pension money, whether or not it is left in the United States, *is* liable to United Kingdom tax.)

2. You will not want to take with you enough money to pay in full for a house. Take only enough to cover a down payment and arrange with your U.S. banker to send you the rest when you determine the exact amount needed. The transaction can be handled by cable, usually within 24 hours, and transfer of funds through normal banking procedures rather than by actual physical transfer need not be reported to the Bureau of Customs (see p. 23).

3. You will want to keep enough money in the United States to pay your U.S. taxes. This will be especially important after you have become a British resident "for Exchange Control purposes" at the end of three years. The U.S. Treasury will not accept payment in any currency but dollars. Therefore, if your income is blocked by Exchange Control regulations you will have to request deferment of your U.S. tax payment by filing a tentative return with an explanation of your situation and a report of blocked income. To this tentative return, you must attach a regular return on which you report any income that has become unblocked during the year. Since any blocked income used for personal expenditures or disposed of through gifts or bequests is regarded as having become unblocked and is reportable, it's much simpler to pay the U.S. tax each year when it falls due than to file two returns and attempt to defer a portion of it. Write a check on your U.S. bank account and be done with it.

4. You may want to make a loan or a gift to someone in the States, or you may want to order some commodity from a U.S. business house, or pay dues to fraternal or professional organizations, or subscribe to U.S. newspapers and magazines. After you become subject to Exchange Control, you may find it more difficult to do these things without a U.S. bank account.

Keep only a minimum in your checking account, of course, and instruct your banker by letter to transfer sums from your savings account to your checking account as the need arises. In any case, do not permit your savings account to remain inactive for as long as a year. If no withdrawals or deposits are being made, and if your bank does not send periodic statements, submit your passbook at least once a year for posting of interest earned.

For reasons of estate settlement, it is generally advisable for married couples to have checking and savings accounts in the names of both husband and wife (the "either/or" arrangement). Check with your banker on this, because laws differ in the various states.

Arrange for your banker to send your monthly statements by airmail.

U.S. Safe Deposit Box

If you are entering Britain as a temporary resident with the intent of returning eventually to the States, you will probably not want to take all of your valuable papers and records with you. The checklists at the end of this chapter will help you determine which items should properly remain in a U.S. safe deposit box.

Traveler's Checks

You will need a sufficient sum in traveler's checks to cover your expenses until you are settled and have established your external account in a British bank. Traveler's checks are available at most banks and at some travel agencies. The usual fee is 1 percent, but shop around before you buy. Some of the issuing agencies have periodic sales. For example, it has become the practice of one of the issuing banks to offer, during the month of May, up to $5,000 in traveler's checks for a fee of $2—a saving of $48.

Letters of Credit

Another way to have money available in England—though perhaps a bit more inconvenient than traveler's checks because it involves going to a bank to collect, whereas traveler's checks can be cashed at many kinds of establishments—is with a letter of credit issued by your U.S. bank against money you have on deposit. The usual charge for a letter of credit is $10 plus 1 percent of the face value. You draw against it at an English bank as you need money.

Tip Packs

Before you leave the United States, buy several "tip packs" to cover cab fares, tips, and other incidentals when you arrive in England. Tip packs are available at most U.S. banks and cost $10.25 for approximately $10.00 worth of British coins and bank notes.

Credit Cards

Credit cards that are valid only in the United States should be canceled before you leave. Advise the issuing companies by certified mail of your wish to cancel and keep carbon copies of your letters. Don't return the cards; cut them up and discard the pieces.

Other cards are, of course, as valuable in England as they are in the United States—more so, perhaps, before you have established your new bank account. The various credit card companies differ in their recommendations to card holders who plan to move out of the United States, but there is one course of action that works well with all of them during that period when you have given up your U.S. address but have not yet established a permanent English address: Estimate as closely as possible, before you leave the States, the amounts you expect to charge, and remit in advance. Look on your cards solely as a convenience—a quick way to pay for meals and lodging, rent a car, and make purchases without the bother of cashing traveler's checks or drawing money from a bank against a letter of credit—*not* as a way to defer payment. Keep a running account of your expenditures against each card, and before your advance remittance is entirely used up send the company another check drawn on your U.S. checking account. It is not a good idea to withhold your remittances until you receive bills: By the time the bills find their way to you, your credit may have suffered a blow that will be a severe setback when you attempt to establish credit in England.

Below are suggestions made by some of the major credit card companies. Other companies with which you have accounts should be contacted for their specific recommendations.

AMERICAN EXPRESS is probably the most flexible of the credit card plans in that the customer may pay his account in dollars or in any one of eight European currencies and has the privilege of choosing which currency he wants to be billed in. If you so request, American Express will continue to service your account from its U.S. Operating Center but recommends that, to save mailing time and possible loss through currency conversions, you transfer your account to its English Operating Center (33 Cavendish Square, London W1M OBA) as soon as you have a permanent mailing address in England.

DINERS CLUB charges are billed in the currency of the country that services the account. If you wish, Diners Club will continue to service your account from its U.S. office after you become a resident of England, but all charges will be converted to dollars and all payments must be made in dollars. To obtain a British card, you will have to apply to the London office of Diners Club (214 Oxford Street, W. 1); all charges will then be converted to British pounds sterling and all payments must be made in British pounds sterling.

MASTER CHARGE is affiliated with Eurocard Limited (34 Craven Street, London WC2N 5NP). Although Master Charge cards tendered by tourists are accepted freely at establishments that accept Eurocards, a person who becomes a resident of Britain should discontinue his Master Charge account and apply for a Eurocard at one of the following banks:

Midland Bank
National Westminster Bank
Coutts Bank
Royal Bank of Scotland
Clydesdale Bank
Williams & Glyn's Bank

BANKAMERICARD can and does handle accounts of Americans residing abroad but finds that mail delays resulting in late receipt of statements and late payment of accounts are a major problem. BankAmericard therefore recommends that customers who move to England apply for Barclaycards. Application may be made in advance of your move by writing to Barclays Bank, Ltd., Juxon House, St. Paul's Churchyard, London E.C. 4. It will help to enclose a letter of recommendation from the U.S. bank that is now servicing your BankAmericard account, and—if you are on assignment in England for a U.S. company—a letter from your employer.

Sale of U.S. Home

If you plan to become a permanent resident of Britain, you will probably want to sell your U.S. home before you go. In fact, if you are like most of us, you will need the money from the sale of your home in order to buy a new home in England. There's another reason for selling your U.S. home: By doing so, you remove all traces of "residence" from the state in which you are now living and are thereafter immune from a state income tax. (Don't leave the United States before the sale is completed. Something *could* go wrong, *e.g.*, the buyer's loan application could be disapproved.)

There is no need to go into the procedure for selling U.S. property, since this is easily ascertainable; however, before you put your house on the market take careful inventory of the capital improvements you've made since you purchased it and of the fix-up costs you incurred for the purpose of making it marketable, and gather together all supporting documents. Because of inflationary trends in the real estate market, you will probably realize a substantial profit on the sale, and you will need a strong defense to avoid paying a heavy capital gains tax. The following paragraphs will show you how the tax works.

Capital Gains Tax on Sale of U.S. Home

When you sell your U.S. residence—and a "residence" can be anything from a houseboat to a condominium—you become liable to the U.S. Government (though payment may, under certain circumstances, be postponed) for a tax on any profit you may realize.

Simply stated, profit is the sale price of the residence minus (a) its adjusted cost (meaning its original cost plus capital improvements and minus depreciation) and (b) selling expenses (meaning agent's commission, legal fees, advertising, and "points").

"Fix-up" costs, *i.e.*, noncapital expenditures within the 90-day period preceding the date of sale for work performed to put your home in salable condition, are not deductible in determining the actual profit but *are* considered in determining the amount of profit on which payment of tax may be postponed.

One of the conditions that permits deferred payment of the capital gains tax is the purchase of a new home at a cost (purchase price plus settlement fees) equal to or in excess of the adjusted cost of the old residence. To take advantage of this opportunity for deferment, you must purchase and occupy your new home within a period of a year after you sell the old one, unless (a) you build (in which case you're allowed 18 months), or (b) you are a member of the armed forces on extended active duty (in which case you may wait as long as four years to purchase or build a new home without forfeiting the postponement privilege). Don't let anyone try to tell you that you can't get a postponement if your new house is outside the United States; you can get one anywhere.[9]

If you have two homes to sell—for example, a town house and a summer home—capital gains tax may be postponed only on the principal residence.

You report your capital gain by attaching Schedule D (Capital Gains & Losses) and form 2119 (Sale or Exchange of Personal Residence) to your form 1040. It works like this:

Line 4 (of form 2119) – Selling price of old residence	$32,500
Line 5 – Less selling expenses	− 2,000
Line 6 – Amount realized	30,500
Line 7 – Less adjusted cost of old residence	− 24,000
Line 8 – Gain on sale	6,500

[9]Revenue Ruling 54–611, cited in *Commerce Clearing House Tax Service*, Regs. 1.1034–1.

Line 9 – Fix-up expenses	500
Line 10 – Adjusted sale price (Line 6 minus Line 9)	30,000
Line 11 – Cost of new residence	24,500
Line 12 – Gain taxable this year (Line 10 minus Line 11)	5,500
Line 13 – Gain on which tax may be deferred (Line 8 minus Line 12)	1,000

The amount on Line 12 is transferred to Schedule D, where it is halved before being added on form 1040 as a part of your income.

On the face of it, it looks simple—but this is a simple example; and there are so many ramifications that you will be wise to seek professional assistance in preparing these forms.[10]

Bureau of Customs Report

You must report to the Bureau of Customs the amount of money you remove from the United States on any one occasion *if:*

The amount is $5,000 or more;
It is physically transported, mailed, or shipped;
It is in the form of currency (U.S. or any other) or negotiable monetary instruments such as traveler's checks, money orders, and investment securities in bearer form.

If you ship or mail the money, you can obtain form 4790 from any Customs office and file in advance of shipment by mailing the completed form to: Commissioner of Customs, Attention: Currency Transportation Requests, Washington, D.C. 20226. If you carry the money with you, you will file with the Customs Officer at the port of departure.

There are several important points to remember here:

The regulation says that "each person" transporting $5,000 or more must make a report; and although the legal definition of "person" in respect to this particular regulation includes corporations, business partnerships, and "all entities cognizable as legal personalities," it does not include married couples. Therefore, an individual and his spouse may each take up to $4,999.99 without filing.
Transfer of funds through normal banking procedures, *i.e.*, without actual physical transfer, is not reportable.
Don't overlook the words "on any one occasion" in the first sentence of this section.

CHECKLISTS

The following four checklists were designed to help you organize and execute the necessary paper work for moving to England. Not all of the items on them will apply to everybody, but many of them will.

---

[10]For special provisions applicable to older people, see pp. 206–208.

The first list is a list of items that you should leave in a U.S. safe deposit box *if* you plan to return eventually to the States. The second is a list of things you should keep in a metal, fireproof lockbox to be carried with you as handluggage and kept under constant surveillance until you can store the contents safely in Britain. The third is a list of items to be carried on your person. The fourth is a list of things you should enter in a "journal" (or notebook, or ledger, or whatever you choose to call it) and carry with you.

CHECKLIST #1

(U.S. Safe Deposit Box)

1. Stocks, bonds, and other certificates of investment ___
2. Papers pertaining to real estate you still own in the States:

   Tax receipts ___

   Deeds ___

   Mortgage papers ___

   Title insurance policies ___

   Title abstracts ___

   Surveys ___

   Closing statements ___

   Building cost figures ___

   Hazard insurance policies ___

   Leases ___
3. Inventory of all personal property remaining in the States ___
4. Written appraisals, if you have them, of valuable items left in the States ___
5. Insurance policies on any personal property left in the States ___
6. All records on the sale of U.S. real estate ___
7. Income tax returns (with supporting papers) for the past three years ___
8. Important canceled checks (past U.S. transactions) ___
9. A signed statement giving name, address, and phone number of the person who will take care of your U.S. affairs in case you die or become incapacitated (Make a duplicate to put in your metal box) ___
10. Burial instructions (Make a duplicate for your metal box) ___

When you sign the contract for your safe deposit box, see that the person you have designated to handle your U.S. affairs (Item 9) has authorized entry to the box, and give him one key. Take the other key with you.

CHECKLIST #2

(The Metal Box)

1. Signed statement giving name, address, and phone number of the person designated to handle your U.S. affairs (Item 9 of Checklist #1) ___

2. Burial instructions (Item 10 of Checklist #1) ___

3. Birth certificates—your own, your spouse's, and copies of your children's, whether they live with you or not (Include adoption papers, if you have adopted children) ___

4. Proof of U.S. citizenship, if not by birth ___

5. Death certificates for members of your immediate family ___

6. Military records ___

7. Your will (and your spouse's) ___

8. Marriage license and/or certificate ___

9. Pension papers, and Social Security forms SSA–1425(f) ___

10. Divorce and alimony papers ___

11. Insurance policies:

    Life (and records of any loans against life insurance) ___

    Hospitalization ___

    Travel accident ___

    Floater policies on property taken with you (*e.g.*, jewelry, musical instruments, coin and stamp collections) ___

12. Records and warranties on equipment and appliances taken with you ___

13. Contracts or notes you hold (money owing you, money you owe), including memos of verbal agreements and moral obligations ___

14. Proof of membership in fraternal, professional, or union organizations ___

15. Canceled checks relating to current income tax deductions, payments relating to moving expenses, etc. ___

16. Diplomas and transcripts ___

17. List of all items to be shipped to England, with written appraisals of valuable items ___

18. The key to your U.S. safe deposit box ___

19. Letters of importance and sentimental value (Weed these out carefully and destroy any that could embarrass or incriminate anyone) ___

20. Savings account passbooks or statements ___

21. List of traveler's checks ___

22. Supporting data accumulated for your next income tax return ___

23. Medical records, if you have them, list of prescription medications by generic names, and immunization records ___

24. Everything in Items 1 through 8 of Checklist #1, if you plan to stay in England permanently   ___

25. A memorandum to the effect that you have at your residence a "journal" that will be helpful when your estate is settled   ___

When you select your home town in England, rent a safe deposit box there and put Items 1 through 14 in it, as well as Items 1 through 8 of Checklist #1, if you're staying in England permanently. Add a signed statement giving the name, address, and phone number of the British solicitor who will handle your affairs in England. If he will permit you to do so, authorize his access to the box and give him one key. The other key, as well as the remaining items on the checklist, can stay in the metal box in a safe niche of your new home.

CHECKLIST #3

(Carry on Your Person)

1. Passport   ___
2. Vaccination certificate (if applicable)   ___
3. U.S. or international driver's license   ___
4. Traveler's checks and cash   ___
5. Credit cards   ___
6. Record of current bank balances; checkbook   ___
7. Documents required for entry (Home Office approval, work permit, evidence of financial independence, etc.)   ___
8. Name and address of person(s) to be notified in case of illness or accident   ___
9. Car title, if you're shipping your American car over, plus evidence of its use in the U.S. and proof of purchase date[11]   ___
10. Papers relating to shipment of car   ___
11. Confirmation of hotel reservation, if any   ___
12. Your plane or boat ticket   ___
13. Papers relating to shipment of personal property   ___
14. Papers relating to shipment of pet   ___

CHECKLIST #4

(Journal)

1. Names and addresses:
   Person(s) to notify in case of illness or accident   ___

[11]A duty is levied unless you have owned and used the car for at least 12 months.

All other relatives and friends —

Banker —

Lawyer —

Real estate agent —

Doctor —

Dentist —

Minister —

(Leave space to add their British counterparts)

2. Inventory of all household goods and personal property to be removed to England. Include estimated value of each item, date, and place of acquisition (if known), and memos giving the history of inherited items and items of sentimental value —

   (Leave space to add items acquired in England)

3. Inventory of all personal property remaining in the States and its exact location. Include the same type of information as in Item 2 —

4. A list of the contents of your safe deposit box, with a memorandum giving the name and address of the bank in which it's located and the name and address of the person holding your duplicate key —

   (Leave space for adding the same information about your British safety deposit box)

5. A list of pensions payable, with sources, due dates, names and addresses of the persons you should contact in case payment isn't received or you wish to make a change —

   (Leave ample space to keep a running account of amounts received and dates of receipt)

6. Inventory of all other assets (real estate, notes receivable, stocks, bonds, and other certificates of investment) —

   (Leave space for changes)

7. Inventory of all liabilities (including moral and verbal obligations) —

   (Leave space for changes)

8. A list of all places where you have money (e.g., bank savings and checking accounts, credit unions, savings and loan associations). Include account numbers —

   (Leave space for changes)

9. Inventory of insurance, including names and addresses of companies, policy numbers, types and amounts of coverage, records of loans against life insurance, instructions for filing claims —

   (Leave space to add insurance purchased in England)

10. Record of tax-deductible items for the current year —

11. Record of taxable income for the current year —

12. List of credit cards and all other active accounts, including account num-

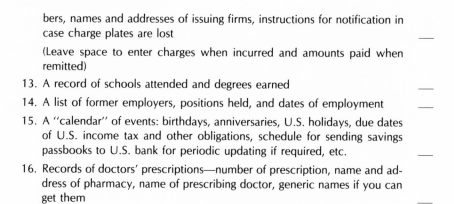

bers, names and addresses of issuing firms, instructions for notification in case charge plates are lost _____

(Leave space to enter charges when incurred and amounts paid when remitted)

13. A record of schools attended and degrees earned _____

14. A list of former employers, positions held, and dates of employment _____

15. A "calendar" of events: birthdays, anniversaries, U.S. holidays, due dates of U.S. income tax and other obligations, schedule for sending savings passbooks to U.S. bank for periodic updating if required, etc. _____

16. Records of doctors' prescriptions—number of prescription, name and address of pharmacy, name of prescribing doctor, generic names if you can get them _____

Don't let this section scare you. The majority of the items on these checklists should be attended to whether you move to England or not. You can accomplish most of them quickly and easily and, believe it or not, it can even be fun to get organized.

Since transportation of your pet, your automobile, and your household goods—as well as your own passage—are matters that require not only "before you go" arrangements but also some knowledge of what happens en route and at the other end, I have saved these topics for Chapter III.

Chapter III
GETTING THERE

SHIPPING YOUR HOUSEHOLD EFFECTS

The question of whether or not you should take your furniture to England depends on so many factors that no pat answer can be given. I can tell you only what I found out when I was faced with the problem, and the conclusions I drew:

Cost estimates vary, and so do the attitudes of moving companies. Some agents are cooperative and helpful regardless of the size of the shipment; others appear to lose interest unless you consent to their removal of your entire household. It is advisable to ask at least three agents to visit your home—not only to have them make estimates of your costs, but to give yourself an opportunity to make estimates of the agents.

Now is the time to dispose of things you don't need. Have a yard sale or a garage sale, or, better yet, an auction sale. An auctioneer will probably charge you a 10 percent commission for his services if you make all the advance preparations yourself—the advertising, the gathering together of the items that are to be sold, and so forth. But for 25 percent he will handle everything: You can go away for the weekend and leave the whole messy business in his hands; and because he is not in the least reluctant to sell an item for as much money as possible—as you might be, if you handled the sale—he will probably bring in more than you could hope to get on your own.

Shipping furniture to England is expensive, even from the East Coast. From our home in Virginia, only a hundred miles from a port, estimates averaged about $1,000 per room. I think, therefore, that unless a person has already purchased a home in England and knows exactly what his needs are, it is not wise to take much furniture. Most English houses in a middle price bracket have very small rooms; American sofas and carpets are likely to be too large.

Heirlooms and other items to which a person has deep sentimental attachment *should* be shipped. While it is not financially feasible to take everything, there is certainly no need to deprive oneself of the items one really treasures. Have the moving company pack and crate these pieces for you; it doesn't make sense to pay the freight if there's a chance the items may be damaged in transit.

Let the mover hold in his U.S. warehouse any furniture that you decide to take but don't yet have a place for in England. Storage charges are less in the United States. You can send for your furniture when you acquire your new home, and you should receive it within a month.

Despite the fact that most electrical appliances cost considerably less in the United States than they do in England, it is not advisable to take them. The standard house current in British domestic premises is 240 volts, AC, 50 hertz (cycles per second). Most American motor-driven appliances can be made to run on British current by the use of transformers, but they will run at only five-sixths their designed speed. When plugged into British outlets, your electric clock will cover only 50 minutes in an hour, your refrigerator will take an hour and 12 minutes to replace the ice cubes it used to make in an hour, and your stereo will probably play the Mozart A Major Violin Concerto in G Major. British repair shops don't like to work on American appliances, and spare parts are hard to come by. One British electrician tells me he's been waiting two years for a replacement part to go in an American dishwasher.

Don't even consider taking your television set. This isn't a matter of electrical supply: British and American transmission systems are totally incompatible.

If you travel by ship, make full use of your free baggage allowance (see p. 37). You will be agreeably surprised at the number of articles you can cram into 25 cubic feet of "hold" space and in your cabin. Except for shoes (it may take a while to find properly fitting ones in England), don't allot much space to clothes; they are better and less expensive in England. Try to use most of your space for items that are more expensive in England or not easily replaced there. Here are a few suggestions:

Favorite books and phonograph records
Favorite paintings and other art objects
Linens
The family silver
American cookbooks
Favorite kitchen gadgets

American measuring cups and spoons
A Fahrenheit oven thermometer
Photograph albums
Home town telephone book
Your typewriter, if it's a manual one

Mark each piece of luggage to indicate whether it is to be stored in the hold or kept in your cabin.

You can take into England, without payment of duty, any household effects that you have owned and used for at least a year, any item or set of items worth no more than £5, and most antiques (see p. 156). To facilitate the handling of your shipment and to speed it through customs, list, in duplicate, the contents of each box as it is packed, and put an estimated value opposite each item. Attach one copy of the list to the applicable box and keep the duplicate lists in your metal box. You will have to declare everything at the port of entry in England, and you will also be required to file an Export Form 7525–V with U.S. Customs. If you engage the services of a mover, he will supply you with the necessary forms and help you with their completion.

If you expect to return to the United States, register foreign-made items (watches, cameras, typewriter, and so forth) with the U.S. Customs Officer when you leave for England. This will insure your not having to pay duty on them when you return.

SHIPPING YOUR CAR

There are two conditions that you must meet if you wish to import your present car free of customs duty, car tax, and value added tax, and without an import license: (1) you must have owned and used the car for at least twelve months before you import it or before you arrive in England (whichever is earlier); (2) you must not dispose of it in any manner within two years after you import it or after you arrive in England (whichever is later).

If you cannot prove—by producing a bill of sale, an insurance policy, or some other acceptable evidence—that you have owned and used the car for at least a year, you must pay a customs charge upon its arrival; and if you do not keep the car for at least two years after importing it, you must pay the customs charge when you dispose of it. If you bought your car on the installment plan, the date of your initial deposit is accepted as the date on which your period of ownership began. The twelve months of prior ownership and use need not be in one continuous period; but any time that you spent in the United Kingdom before importing the car does not count toward your 12-month requirement.

If your car does not qualify for duty-free entry under the above conditions, you must be prepared to pay a car tax of 10 percent, a value added tax of 10 percent, and an import duty of 11 percent of its value if it is an American car, 8.8 percent if it was manufactured in the European Economic Community,[1] or 7.5 percent if it is of British Commonwealth origin with Commonwealth labor and materials making up at least 50 percent of its cost. A car manufactured in the European Free Trade Association area[2] or Ireland may be admitted duty free.

The above charges are payable to the Collector of Customs and Excise at the port of entry. If you want immediate possession of the car, be prepared to pay with cash, sterling traveler's checks, or a certified check on a bank approved by Customs and Excise. Further details can be obtained by writing in advance to HM Customs and Excise, Vintry House, Queen Street Place, London, E.C. 4.

You need not apply in advance for permission to import your car, but make certain that you have all the necessary papers when you claim possession. The Customs official will ask you to produce your evidence of ownership (*e.g.*, receipt, installment contract) and of use (insurance policy, foreign license, and registration card) and to fill in a declaration. If an agent is handling the shipment in your behalf, he can supply you with the necessary declaration forms in advance; if not, be sure you have the following information at hand:

Make of car and model name or number
Chassis or frame and engine number
Cubic capacity and number of cylinders
Description of body (sedan, coupe, number of doors and seats)
Whether it's left-hand or right-hand drive
Year of manufacture and date of first registration when new
Total mileage to date
Description of "extras" (automatic transmission, power brakes, and so forth)
List of defects that may affect value
If applicable, evidence to support claim for preferential or duty-free entry by virtue of its having been manufactured in a Commonwealth Preference area or in a European Free Trade Association area

For purposes of establishing the 12-month ownership qualification, the British government considers husband and wife to be joint owners of an automobile. Therefore, a wife may, if she arrives in England in advance of her husband, secure the car's release at the port, even though the bill of sale and other evidence of ownership and use are in her husband's name.

[1]The import duty on cars from the European Economic Community is being decreased at the rate of 20 percent a year and will be eliminated entirely by January, 1978. See p. 15 (footnote 5) for a list of EEC countries.
[2]Austria, Sweden, Denmark, Finland, Lichtenstein, Norway, Portugal, and Switzerland.

The cost of shipping a car is based on its weight. If you ship by passenger liner, transportation of a small car (1501 to 2500 lbs.) from New York to London will cost about $340; a medium car (2501 to 3500 lbs.), about $390; a big car (3501 to 4500 lbs.), $465. But shop around before you make any commitments. A broker may be able to find space for your car on a freighter at a far more reasonable fee. He can also help you obtain marine insurance for your car while it's in transit.

One final word of caution: Think long and hard before you take a car with left-hand drive to England. It's not illegal, but when you drive on the left side of the road, a car with right-hand drive is safer and easier to manipulate.

SHIPPING YOUR PET

At least two months before you ship your pet to England you must request from the Ministry of Agriculture, Government Buildings, Hook Rise South, Tolworth, Surbiton, Surrey, form ID–1, Application for a License to Import a Dog or Cat for Detention in Quarantine. Upon approval by the Ministry of the completed form, a license will be issued and sent to the authorized carrying agent (the person whose job it is to meet the pet when it arrives in England and take it to the quarantine kennel), and a notification will be sent to you, advising you of the license number and authorizing you to ship.

Granting of the license is contingent upon your having made certain advance arrangements and upon your acceptance of several other conditions laid down by the Ministry.

In advance of your application for an import license, you must:

Determine which airport (or seaport)[3] will be the point of landing for your pet;
Determine the approximate date of landing;
Book accommodations for your pet for the entire period of quarantine at a kennel approved by the Ministry, and obtain confirmation of the booking;
Engage an authorized carrying agent and obtain confirmation of your arrangements with him.[4]

The other conditions to which you must agree when you apply for your import license are:

That the animal will remain in quarantine for a period of six calendar months from the date of landing and, if there is an outbreak of rabies at the kennel, for as much longer as the Ministry directs;
That the animal will be vaccinated against rabies by the kennel's veterinarian as soon

[3]All cost estimates in this chapter are based on air shipment.
[4]A list of approved kennels and authorized carrying agents is given in Appendix A.

as possible after arrival (whether or not it has been previously vaccinated) and again four weeks later;

That the animal, in transit, will be confined in an approved crate or box bearing an approved label;[5]

That the animal will be landed on or before the landing date shown on the license and that no one other than the authorized carrying agent shall attempt to remove it from its landing place;

That the animal may be transferred to another kennel during the period of quarantine if the Ministry determines, for any reason, that it is not practicable or desirable to keep it in the kennel originally selected.[6]

The authorized carrying agent is responsible for the safe delivery of the animal to the kennel. He is charged with clearing it through Customs, taking it via the shortest available route to the kennel, and making certain that it does not come in contact with any other animal en route. He must have with him, when he meets the plane or boat and at all times while the animal is in his care, the license that has been forwarded to him by the Ministry, and must be able to produce it readily if he is required to do so by Customs officials, Ministry representatives, or the police.

The United States also makes certain requirements of you when you ship your pet abroad. You will have to obtain a Shipper's Export Declaration 7525–V and submit it in quadruplicate to the Bureau of Customs.

It is not necessary for you to provide the British Ministry of Agriculture with certificates of health or of vaccination (though your shipper may require them). The Ministry is going to insist on the two rabies vaccinations in England regardless of any certificates you may provide testifying to the state of your pet's health and to the number and dates of vaccinations in the United States.

Ministry regulations require that all animals must be separately kenneled; however, if you have two pets, most kennel owners will try to house them in adjacent kennels.

One of the most frustrating things you may run into is the acute shortage of quarantine space throughout England, particularly in the south. Early booking (six months to a year in advance, if possible) is essential. If your inquiries turn up a vacancy, grab it immediately by phone or cable. The Ministry will not grant an import license if a kennel is not available.

The shipping crate should be just large enough for the pet to stand up in, turn around, and lie down. It should have a peaked or domed top so that baggage cannot be piled on top of it and should be well con-

---

[5]If you have more than one pet, each must be separately confined.
[6]If *you* wish to change kennels, you will have to notify the Ministry of your wishes and obtain a license for removal. You may remove the animal from Britain at any time.

structed of wood that does not splinter easily. Typical sizes available from the airlines are:

22"l × 12"w × 15"h—for cats and toy breeds of dogs
26"l × 18"w × 19"h—for dogs with shoulder height of not more than 15" (beagles, cockers, miniature poodles)
36"l × 22"w × 26"h—for dogs with shoulder height of not more than 22" (dalmations, spaniels)
43"l × 25"w × 30"h—for dogs with shoulder height of not more than 25" (collies, dobermans)

If you obtain the crate in advance, accustom your pet to it by placing him in it for a short while each day. Put his own blanket, a favorite toy, and his regular eating bowl in with him.

Try also to accustom your pet to dry food. Personnel who must care for him while he is in transit will be more willing to open a package of dry food than a can. Tie a cloth bag to the outside of the crate and attach feeding instructions in plain view. (Be sure to mention the need for water.) Put individual sealed, plastic bags of dry food, each holding enough for one meal, inside the cloth bag. Include enough extra food for two or three days.

There are very real risks involved in shipping a pet. Airlines are subject to late takeoffs and unscheduled stops, and not all planes have proper temperature controls in the baggage compartments while on the ground, nor are they all careful to avoid overcrowding and to provide proper ventilation. Try to book your pet's passage on a DC-10, a DC "Stretch 8," or a plane of the 700 series (747, 727, or 707). Perhaps the greatest hazard is neglect by ground personnel: That is why it is so important to have a carrying agent waiting for your pet's arrival.

Typical costs are:

Kenneling (in England): Cat or small dog, $200 for 6 months; large dog, $300–$375
Kenneling (in U.S. prior to shipment): $2–$7 per day
Vaccination, laboratory test fees, parasite treatment (in England): $20
Insurance (in English kennel): 6 percent to 9 percent of the sum for which the pet is insured
Flight insurance: $3 per $100 of coverage
Crate: $15–$25
Shipping charge: $150–$250, depending on weight and distance (divide the number of cubic inches in the crate by 194 and multiply the answer by the rate per pound from point of departure to point of arrival)
Carrying agent's fee: Dependent on agent's time required and length of journey, but never less than $25
Dog license (in England): About 80¢

There are no restrictions on the importation of pigeons, doves, and most cage birds such as parrots, budgies, and canaries. Your shipper may require a certificate of health, but the British government will not.

The regulations governing importation of all animals other than cats, dogs, and birds are, however, very strict; and there are only two quarantine facilities authorized for their accommodation: the Ravensden Zoological Company, Bedford Road, Rushden, Northamptonshire, and Banham Zoo, Ltd., The Grove, Banham, Norwich. Both of these have limited space for privately owned animals.

Rabbits may not be imported at all, unless they are of the European species.

YOUR OWN PASSAGE

By this time you have probably begun to wonder whether or not you made the right decision. You've had to arrange the sale of your house, decide which of your belongings to dispose of and which to pack, and do a great deal of paper work. You've been racing along at fever pitch, so busy that there hasn't been time for doubt to creep in. But now, you suddenly feel tired and you're becoming a little depressed at the thought of giving up a familiar way of life. For years, you've been chatting with the same friends and shopping in the same stores; now you're faced with the prospect of house hunting in a strange country and making friends with new neighbors. You must even learn to drive on the wrong side of the road. The enormity of your decision hits you, and there's no turning back because at this point it would be more trouble to reverse your plans than to proceed.

What you are experiencing is fatigue, and all the fears and worries and feelings of depression that are assailing you are nothing more than the normal results of fatigue. The antidote lies in the realization that the hardest part is over and in the pleasure of scheduling your passage to a life that can be as quietly relaxing or as excitingly new as you choose to make it. It is time to buy your ticket.

By Air

There is generally no need for a lot of advance planning if you want to travel by commercial airline. Transatlantic flights are frequent and space is readily available on short notice. Try to book passage on a 747 for a truly comfortable trip.

Charter flights are a little more tedious because space must be reserved well in advance, takeoff time is never quite so accurately scheduled as on commercial flights, and the aircraft itself may not be as comfortable as a regularly scheduled aircraft or the meals as good. Nevertheless, it is possible to save considerable money by taking a charter flight. Perhaps you are already a member of some organization that sponsors charter flights—the Department of Defense, for example, or a retired persons' association, or a student group. Make sure that the sponsoring organization is a legitimate one with full legal authority to operate charter flights for its members. Don't get involved with an organization whose sole purpose is the operation of charter flights.

If you are in a hurry to get to England, flying is the only way to go. But there are disadvantages, too. For one thing, free transportation of luggage is limited to 44 pounds per person, and excess baggage charges are exorbitant. For another thing, the traveler is deposited precipitously in his new country before he's had a chance to rest or to become adjusted to the change. If you go by plane, I suggest that you reserve hotel space before you leave and spend your first week in England resting.

By Water

The beauty of boat travel lies in the opportunity it affords for complete relaxation. Passenger liners have social directors and facilities for swimming, deck games, dancing, and movies. Freighters don't provide planned entertainment, but you will enjoy dining and chatting with the ship's officers, strolling, napping in your cabin, sprawling in a deck chair with a good book, basking in the sunshine, thinking without interruption, and, in general, catching up with yourself. By the time you arrive in England, you will be ready and eager to get started on your new way of life.

You will also have the advantage of being able to take a lot of luggage at little or no cost. Most ships will allow you 25 cubic feet of baggage space in the hold in addition to the space in your cabin, and excess baggage charge is seldom more than $1.25 per cubic foot. You can probably take your car on the same boat for a reasonable fee.

If you choose a passenger liner, have a travel agent arrange the trip for you. His commission is paid by the steamship company, and the cost to you is no more than it would be if you booked your own passage. You will be able to avail yourself of the agent's knowledge about such things as tipping and suitable clothing aboard ship and of his expert assistance in arranging travel to the port and in making hotel reservations at destination.

Fares on passenger liners from New York to London range from approximately $350 for a tourist-class, inside double cabin to well over $1,000 for a first-class outside deluxe cabin. Children under 12 sharing their parents' accommodations travel at greatly reduced fares.

For a really delightful voyage at a reasonable price, try to book passage on a freighter. It will be more difficult than booking on a regular passenger liner, but it is well worth the extra trouble. You will get first-class accommodations for no more than you would pay for tourist class on a passenger ship. Meals are delicious and bountiful, and the service is excellent and more personal because there are generally not more than a dozen passengers. Cabins are usually situated amidships where you won't hear or feel propeller vibrations, and the weight of the cargo causes the ship to ride low in the water, enabling it to plow through rough seas with less pitching and rolling than a high-riding passenger liner. (Incidentally, if you are leery about seasickness anyway, take along some Bonamine. It can be purchased without a prescription, and a tablet a day will keep you well and happy.) Life on board a freighter is casual, and sports clothes serve for all occasions; there is no need for formal attire. For extra enjoyment, take your camera, binoculars, and sunglasses.

Unfortunately, like the American railroads, freighter lines are finding it more and more bothersome and costly to cater to passengers. With the new containerized method of shipping, they find it more profitable to allocate their entire space to cargo. Because of this, your travel agent is not going to be eager to help you get freighter accommodations; you will probably have to find your ship for yourself and book your own passage. Begin making your freighter plans well in advance of your trip. A year is not too soon.

You will have to reconcile yourself to certain inconveniences if you choose to travel by freighter. If you are over 65, for example, you may have to furnish a medical certificate attesting to your good health. (A ship with not more than 12 passengers is not required to have a doctor aboard.) Some freighters will not take children. You can't be certain about departure and arrival times; you may have to engage a hotel room near the port and wait several days for your ship to finish loading, and your uncertainty about arrival time will make it difficult to schedule reservations at a hotel in England. You may very well be put off at the first port of call; even though your ship may be scheduled eventually to dock in London, it may stop first in Germany or France or Ireland —and off you go. But don't let these inconveniences deter you: With a luxurious ten to twelve days of fun and relaxation at less than half the cost of comparable accommodations on a passenger liner, you will still be way ahead of the game.

For information on freighter lines to England, address your inquiries to:

From East Coast and Gulf ports:
Bowerman Shipping, Ltd.
Dock Square
Warrenpoint, Co. Down
N. Ireland

Marchessini Lines
c/o Freighter Travel Service, Ltd.
201 E. 77th Street
New York, N.Y. 10021

From West Coast ports:

Johnson Line
General Steamship Corp., Ltd.
400 California Street
San Francisco, Cal. 94104

French Line
Balfour Guthrie & Co. Ltd.
530 W. 6th Street
Los Angeles, Cal. 90014
            or
Maritime Plaza
San Francisco, Cal. 94119

Alien Registration

If you are permitted to enter England for the purpose of employment
for a period of more than three months (unless you are in one of the
permit-free categories),[7] or if you enter for any other reason for a period
of more than six months, you must register with the police upon arrival.

You may ask the Customs officer where you should register, or, if you
are in London, you may go to the Aliens' Registration Office at 10
Lamb's Conduit Street. You will be asked to produce your passport,
your work permit (if any), two passport-size photographs, and a 25-
pence registration fee; and since you will be queried about the purpose
of your move, you should take with you any other pertinent documentation. The office on Lamb's Conduit Street has a photo machine that you
may use if you failed to have extra passport pictures made.

[7]See footnote 2 on p. 12.

Chapter IV
YOUR AUTOMOBILE

Owning a car in England is an expensive business, just as it is in the United States. In England, however, it is easy to do without a car if one resides in the vicinity of London or in a town readily accessible to London by train or bus. London's transport system is the largest urban passenger system in the world and the easiest to understand. Maps of London transport services are available free at Travel Enquiry Offices (Piccadilly Circus, Victoria, Oxford Circus, St. James's Park, King's Cross Station, and Euston). A few minutes spent studying the underground maps will convince anyone that he is perfectly capable of finding his way from station to station; but if there remains any doubt, he need only dial the Transport Headquarters (222–1234) and ask directions. There is someone on the other end of that line at all hours of the day and night.

Underground and bus fares vary according to distance, with a minimum subway fare of 13 cents and a minimum bus fare of 8 cents. For longer distances, second-class rail fare is about 5 cents per mile and bus fare about 2½ cents per mile. London taxis charge about 39 cents for the first 900 yards (about a half-mile) and 15 cents for each additional 900 yards. There is a slight surcharge for each additional passenger and for travel between midnight and 6:00 A.M., and the rate is doubled for journeys of more than six miles. Rental of a small car costs about $5 a day, plus 5 cents to 8 cents per mile, and the renter pays for the petrol (gasoline) and the insurance. But let's assume that ease of transportation is not one of your primary goals in selecting your place of residence. Or perhaps you simply don't want to be without a car of your own, even though you could get along very well without one.

The business of importing an American car has been discussed in Chapter III. This chapter will deal with the purchase of a car in England and with your ownership and use of any car in England irrespective of how or where you acquired it.

BUYING A CAR IN ENGLAND

If you have decided to buy in England rather than take your American car with you, your best buy will probably be a British car. It will depreciate in value less rapidly than a foreign car, you will be assured of spare parts availability and of more competent mechanical service, and you will avoid an import duty.

Most Britishers drive small cars because of the high cost of petrol (87 cents to $1.26 per gallon in the London area). The initial price of a British car is comparable to the price of an American car of similar size. Typical current prices of small sedans ("saloons," in England) are: Ford Cortina 1600E, $2,350 to $3,100; Hillman Super Imp, $1,530 to $2,000; Rover 2000 TC, $3,750 to $4,850; Vauxhall Viva 1256, $1,850 to $2,500. A car tax of 10 percent and a value added tax of 10 percent are added to these basic prices. (Car tax and VAT also apply to imported cars purchased in England.)

The slack period between November and February is generally the best time to buy; and there are sales from time to time, so it may be worth your while to study the newspaper advertisements for a week or so before you make a purchase.

If you can determine in advance of your trip what make of car you wish to buy, you can order before you go and have your car ready and waiting for you. The factories will send you brochures and price lists and will either sell to you direct or furnish you with the names of distributors with whom you can place your order.[1] Keep in mind, though, that there is no price advantage in buying direct from the factory: You will still have to pay list price, car tax, and value added tax; and if you place an order in advance of your move, either with a factory or a distributor, you will not be in a position to bargain. (A British car dealer—though he probably won't volunteer this information—expects you to ask for a discount if you pay cash and don't have a car to trade.)

It *is* possible to trade in your American car before you leave the United States, to a dealer who handles British cars of the make and model you wish to buy in England. Don't look for a particularly good bargain, however, because your American dealer will have to share his

[1]Some of the principal makes of British cars and the names and addresses of their manufacturers are listed in Appendix B.

commission with a British dealer. You will probably do better to sell your American car outright. A person who knows several years in advance that he is going to move to England at a certain time (*e.g.,* someone who plans to retire in England when he reaches a certain age) is fortunate: He can time the purchase of his last American car to give him maximum value and minimum loss through depreciation.

INSURANCE

When you buy a car in England (or secure the release of your American car at the port), you cannot drive it away until you have a British insurance certificate. Don't assume that you're covered for liability insurance because you have a U.S. automobile policy with an unexpired term: Your U.S. policy is no longer valid.

In your readings about travel abroad, you may have come across an occasional reference to a "green card" (an international insurance card), and you may think that possession of such a card will solve your automobile insurance problems. It won't. "Green cards" may be issued by only a few large insurance companies who, because they are members of a motor insurers bureau (which is, in turn, a member of the international Council of Bureaux) have authority to provide worldwide coverage and facilities for handling claims abroad. The "green card" is designed only for visitors traveling from country to country on a temporary basis and will not serve as a substitute for the liability insurance that Britain requires of its residents.

If you have shipped your own car across, you will normally be able to obtain a temporary British certificate at the port; ask the Customs Officer how to go about this. If for any reason the certificate is not available at the port facilities, however, you must wait until a nearby insurance office is open and get one there. *You must not drive in England without British liability insurance.*

Few laws in England are more detailed and precise than road traffic laws. The Road Traffic Act has 271 sections of its own; and, in addition, it empowers the Secretary of State for the Environment to make additional regulations (which have the force of law) and the Minister of Transport to draw up a Highway Code which, though not a law in itself, should be obeyed since a breach of Code can help prove a charge of careless driving. It is well to remember that although the motorist who is involved in an accident is most likely to come in contact with civil law, dangerous driving—whether or not an accident results—is a criminal offense.

Compulsory insurance was introduced in 1930, and since the only way to get out of it is to deposit £15,000 with the High Court, "compulsory" is a pretty apt term for it. Compulsory insurance is sometimes referred to as "RTA" (Road Traffic Act) insurance; or "Act-Only" insurance (if the policy has no coverages in addition to compulsory insurance); or "third-party liability" (the first party—car owner—obtains a policy from the second party—insurance company—to pay for damages to a third party). Driving without third-party liability insurance is a criminal offense, but the law requires only bodily injury coverage to the third party, excluding private passengers in the policyholder's car; property damage to the third party and medical payments coverage to protect the insured's own passengers are not mandatory. Of course, limiting one's policy to Act-Only insurance is not advisable if one can afford additional liability coverages, since there are many types of accidents for which a driver may be held legally and financially responsible even though they are outside the area of compulsory insurance. You can, and should, widen the scope of your liability insurance to cover legal liability for damage to the third party's property and injury to passengers in your own car, as well as lump-sum payments in the event of your own accidental death or disability or that of your spouse.

As in the United States, the policy can be further broadened to cover fire, theft, broken glass, and collision. This "comprehensive" coverage will be required by the lending institution if you buy an English car on the "hire purchase" (installment) plan.

When you apply for automobile insurance, the agent will ask you to fill in a proposal form and give him a part of the premium. In return, he will give you a short-term binder, good for perhaps fifteen days. He then submits your proposal form to the insurance company, which decides whether to accept or reject you and, if it accepts you, calculates the balance of the premium from the information furnished on the proposal. There are two things that may work against you: your place of birth and—if you are a retiree—your age. A British insurance company is not going to consider you a good risk until you've been driving in England for several years without mishap; and if you are over 65 you may have to furnish a medical report. If you succeed in getting the insurance, consider yourself lucky and pay the high premium cheerfully. Later, after you've proved yourself a capable driver, you may be entitled to a lower rate.

It is impossible to cite exact costs of automobile insurance in England since there are too many variables in type of coverage and amount of deductible. Rates are also dependent on the age and accident record of the driver, the type of car, the use to which the car is put and the area in which it is principally garaged.

You can save money during the initial high-premium years by taking out liability insurance only and forgoing the comprehensive coverage —unless, of course, there is a lien on the car. If you do wish to carry comprehensive insurance, you can reduce the premium by carrying a high deductible—"excess," as it's called in England. A further saving can be achieved by limiting the coverage to the owner-driver only. As time passes without accidents, you will be allowed "no-claims" discounts; after four years, you may get as much as 60 percent off.

After an insurance company has accepted you and you have paid the full premium, you will receive a policy and a certificate of insurance. It is advisable to keep the certificate on your person; you may have to show it to the police to prove that you have the liability coverage required by law, and you must be able to produce it when you renew your vehicle license.

LICENSING

Vehicle License

As soon as you have a temporary insurance certificate you must obtain a motor vehicle license. If you imported your American car, the Customs Officer will provide you with a form (C. & E. 386) that you must take to the Motor Taxation Office of the nearest County Council— though, if that office is closed because of a holiday or odd hours, you are permitted to drive on to your first stopping place in Great Britain. At the Motor Taxation Office you must show your form C. & E. 386 and your certificate of British liability insurance, and you must produce a British vehicle test certificate if the car is more than three years old or file a declaration of exemption from the testing requirement if it is not more than three years old. The vehicle test certificate, if required, may be obtained from any authorized examiner and is issued after inspection of brakes, steering mechanism, tires, headlights, and taillights. Its cost is £1.25 and it must be renewed each year. (If you have brought your American car, ask the Customs Officer to direct you to the nearest Motor Taxation Office and examining station; if you buy a car in England, your dealer will help you with these things.)

A vehicle license is in the form of a small paper disc and must be displayed in the lower corner of the windshield ("windscreen" in England) on the passenger side. The £25 a year that you pay for this license is sometimes referred to as "road tax." (If you don't have £25 handy, you can ask for a four-month license—£9.15.)

Along with the license you will be given a registration or logbook. Every time the license is renewed or the car changes hands, the logbook must be produced. Keep it in a safe place at home or in the bank—not in the car.

The office providing you with the license will assign a registration number that stays with the car as long as the car is in use, even if ownership changes.

Driver's License

Although you will be permitted to drive under your international permit or your regular U.S. driver's license for three months,[2] put the booking of your driver's test at the top of your list of things to do. You may have to wait longer than you anticipate for your testing appointment.

You can pick up an application form for a driving test (DL 26—or DL 26 [M] if you plan to take the test in a metropolitan traffic area) at any general post office. Be sure to answer every question on the form or it will be returned to you for correction. Send the completed form to the Traffic Area Office in the region where you wish to take the test (the address will be on the back of the form) and enclose a check or money order, payable to "The Department of the Environment," in the amount shown on the application form. (It is a good idea to request, on your application, a specific date for the test—preferably four to six weeks after date of filing the application. This will give you time to prepare yourself for the test while you are waiting for the appointment.) You will receive in return a receipt and a notice of appointment. Testing appointments are run on a very tight schedule, so don't be late. Allow yourself plenty of time for parking, because the testing areas are often crowded. If you can't be present at the exact time for which you are scheduled, notify the Traffic Area Office as soon as possible and in no case give less than three days' notice or you will forfeit the fee.

To help yourself prepare for the test, obtain and study the following literature:

Highway Code—available at most bookstores, or from the Ministry of Transport or the Central Office of Information, 6p;
Driving—available at most bookstores or from the Department of the Environment or the Central Office of Information, 62½p;
Your Driving Test and How to Pass—available from the Driving & Motor Licenses Division of the Department of the Environment, no charge.

It will also be helpful to take a few lessons from a registered driving instructor. You may be a skilled driver in the United States, but this may work against you in England. In fact, the longer you have been driving the harder it may be for you to switch to right-hand drive. Driving on the "wrong" side of the road and negotiating turns into the "wrong" lane will require constant presence of mind, and it will be helpful to

---

[2]The three-month limitation is for people who intend to become permanent residents. Visitors may drive for 12 months under U.S. or international permits.

have someone beside you for a while to prevent the occasional lapses that are almost certain to occur until you become accustomed to the change. The minimum charge for driving instruction is about £1.50 for an hour's lesson. Twelve lessons should suffice, but if you feel you will need more, bargain for a reduced fee. You may get it, if you pay in full in advance. Every Traffic Area Office has a list of registered instructors.

You will be throwing your money and time away if you attempt to take the test before you have learned the Highway Code from A to Z. Your examiner will question you orally on the Code and observe whether you can put it into practice. Your test will include, among other things, exercises such as backing into a narrow opening, stopping in an emergency situation, maneuvering in a restricted space, stopping and starting on hills. Your use of signals, including hand signals, will be noted and your actions when entering a crossroad observed. You will have to pass an eye test in which you must read without glasses (or with glasses, for a restricted license) 3½-in.-high digits on an auto license plate 75 feet away or 3–1/8-in.-high digits on a plate 67 feet away.

If you use an automobile with automatic transmission for the test, you will not be licensed to drive a car with manual gear shift. If you pass the test with a manual shift, however, you will be permitted to drive either type.

Here are a few tips that may help you pass the test:

Be courteous and considerate of other drivers.
Be silent. The examiner is not permitted to discuss your driving, either to encourage or criticize, and he may consider that your talking is an indication that you are not giving full attention to your driving. Furthermore, he cannot permit any delays that will make him late for his next appointment.
Before you start the motor, apply the handbrake and be sure the gears are in neutral.
Don't look at the controls when you shift gears.
Try to accelerate and brake smoothly.
Don't coast.
Don't rest your arm on the window ledge. Keep both hands on the wheel except when you need one hand to signal or shift gears.
Suit your speed to the traffic flow.
Before you move off, look around. Don't be satisfied with just a look in the mirror.
Buckle your seat belt.
Above all, do not attempt to bribe the examiner. Attempted bribery is a very serious offense for which you can be prosecuted.

If, despite all your precautions, you fail the test, you may try again after a one-month waiting period. During that month, take to heart the form D.L. 24 (Statement of Failure) that will have been presented to you and brush up on the areas in which your performance was not satisfactory. These areas will have been checked on the statement.

After you have taken the test, pick up a form D.L. 1 (Application for a License to Drive a Motor Vehicle) at a post office and ask at the post office where the completed form should be sent. If you passed the test, you may apply for a "substantive" license (good for three years) and you must send your test pass certificate along with your application. If you failed, you may apply only for a "provisional" license (good for one year). The same form is used in applying for either type of license and the fee is £1. Follow the instructions on the form carefully and answer every question truthfully.

Plates

Plates may be obtained from a garage or dealer. Have your vehicle license with you when you go to buy them.

The cost of plates varies, depending on the type you choose, from £2.50 a pair to £4.50 a pair. The cheapest plates are black metal with aluminum digits; the most expensive are reflectorized plates—an effective safeguard at night, particularly if one headlight should burn out.

If you did not pass the test, you must buy "L" (Learner) plates, and you must not drive unless you are accompanied by someone who holds a current British driving license.

The steps required to become a licensed driver in England are outlined in Appendix C.

Chapter V
CHOOSING YOUR LOCATION

In England there is so much variety of landscape within a small area—such ease of transition from wooded hill to marshy fen, from city to village, from old to new—that anyone who has been accustomed to traveling hundred-mile stretches along the New Jersey Turnpike or through the midwestern plains of Kansas and Nebraska begins to feel as though he's looking through the wrong end of a telescope. To help the newcomer get his bearings and catalog in his mind's eye with some semblance of order this abundance of scenery, the English Tourist Board has divided the country (excluding London) into ten geographical regions, about which I hope to give you some idea in the following pages.[1] Many of these regions are not close enough to London for daily commuting but none is too far away for frequent trips to the capital—and all have something to offer the prospective resident.

One of the first things you will want to do in England is choose the region that you will call your own. (If you are going over to take a job or attend a school, your general area is, of course, already established; but, even so, you will still have a choice of city or suburb.) There are many factors that will influence you in making your choice, and you should take time to consider them all very carefully. A retiree should be particularly choosy, because, unless he has a great deal of energy and is not overly concerned about money, his new home will probably be the home in which he will spend the rest of his life.

[1]Addresses of Regional Tourist Boards (from which you may obtain detailed information after you arrive in England) are given in Appendix D. If, before you leave the United States, you want more information than is given in this book, you may write to the British Tourist Authority, 680 Fifth Avenue, New York 10019.

Consider, first of all, the way you expect to occupy yourself in your leisure time. If you are an ardent theatregoer, for instance, you will want to be in London or at least within commuting distance of London, whereas if you enjoy hunting and fishing, a country environment will be more to your liking. Some of you have grown up in large cities and may dream wistfully of small quiet villages. If possible, sample small-town life before you sign a contract to buy in such an area: It may be that you will not be able to sleep without noisy parties going on next door and police sirens wailing in the streets, or you may want your days filled with more excitement than you can find at a church supper or a Thursday afternoon bridge club.

Plan to spend at least a month or two in England before you make your final decision. Give yourself a taste of British big-city life and at the same time an opportunity to visit smaller cities and the lovely English countryside by establishing temporary headquarters at a small, inexpensive hotel in London and using this as a base from which to go exploring. Map out an itinerary to save yourself the time and money that can be wasted in haphazard, hit-or-miss traveling.

There are many small family-type hotels in London where you can set up headquarters. Most of them are clean and have courteous and helpful proprietors, and many are easily accessible to subway and bus lines. A month's stay in such a hotel will cost two people between $300–$450 (including a huge English breakfast), and you will find that this investment will pay you handsome dividends in future satisfaction. The hotel that we chose—and it was a happy choice—was the Trevose at 70 Queensborough Terrace, opposite Hyde Park, one block from a bus stop and two blocks from an underground station. The rates at this hotel, as with all such hotels that do not have elevators, depend on which floor you are housed on. (Don't forget that in England the bottom floor is called the "ground" floor, and their first floor is our second floor. We made advance reservations for a second-floor room and found ourselves puffing and wheezing up an unexpected extra flight.) On the same street with the Trevose are at least half a dozen similar hotels costing about the same, and there are many others scattered throughout the city. This stay in a hotel can coincide with the period during which your household pets are in quarantine—when you don't have a home for them anyway—and during which your household goods (if you decided to bring them) are being prepared for shipment to England.

Once established at your hotel, unpack and arrange your clothes in neat and easily accessible order, then stash away your luggage, keeping only a small bag available for a change of clothing, night clothes, and film. If you've acquired your car, taken your driving lessons, studied your Highway Code, and are ready to tackle driving on the left side of the road, by all means do your traveling by automobile: You will see much more of the countryside and be in a better position to investigate housing. Photograph everything, and as you snap the pictures keep an exact listing of the things you've photographed. You may think you'll remember everything, but don't rely on it. Buy newspapers wherever you go and save them for future reference. Keep a notebook for jotting down your impressions.

It won't be long before you'll be able to decide whether you wish to settle in a large city, a small town or village, or a rural area. Before you choose a rural area, however, give some thought to the fact that when you are older and perhaps in poor health you may need neighbors. You may also need, if you plan to live in England permanently and there comes a time when you find it difficult or unsafe to drive, easy access to grocery stores, pharmacies, and a laundromat. And think twice before you choose a hilly location: Some day you may want to swap those scenic hills for a level place to walk. Consider what the weather will be like in other seasons; a seashore site may be great in summer but damp and uncomfortable during the winter months.

Because of our interest in music, we narrowed our own choice to the area within a 60-mile radius of London. We drew a circle on the map and then set about investigating all the small towns within the circle—that is, all that were readily accessible to London by train. We settled on a small city in Kent called Tunbridge Wells, mainly because it has a fine amateur symphony orchestra in which we can play. The city itself is beautiful—an old "spa" town, once patronized by the royal family as a health and pleasure resort; and, in addition to its symphony, Tunbridge Wells has excellent small shops, good housing, many lovely parks, a high rate of sunshine, and courteous and cooperative townfolk. There are many such charming places—not all with symphonies, but with other areas of interest. You will find, I'm afraid, that unimproved land is scarce and hard to come by and that the cost of housing in all of England has taken a tremendous jump in recent years. Now, at last, there appears to be a leveling off; hopefully, the market has reached the point where it can tolerate no further increases. Of course, the closer a place is to London the more attractive it is to commuters—and the more expensive it is. The type of house for which we are paying £ 12,000 ($30,000) in Tunbridge Wells could probably be purchased for £10,000 ($25,000) if it were situated north of London and 20 miles farther out from the city.[2]

After you have made a tentative choice, spend another week in a

---

[2] At the current rate of exchange, the English pound is worth approximately $2.50. To make the conversion, multiply the number of pounds by 2½—or divide by four and add a zero.

hotel in the area you've selected. This will give you a chance to price food and clothing and other commodities, as well as an opportunity to visit local "estate agents" and investigate properties for sale. You will have time to meet and talk with your prospective neighbors and make certain that this is really the place that suits you best. You might talk to a local doctor and a local solicitor, both of whom may be assisting you at some time in the future. Buy the local newspaper, study the classified ads, and read every word of the news items to get the "feel" of the community.

THE TEN GEOGRAPHICAL REGIONS

The most northerly of the English Tourist Board's ten regions, at the Scottish border and with the North Sea to its east, is NORTHUMBRIA —five hours from London by automobile and three and a half hours by train. There are two counties in the region (*Northumberland* at the top, and *Durham* at the bottom); and several important rail centers (Darlington, Sunderland, and the city of Durham in Durham County; Berwick and Newcastle-upon-Tyne in Northumberland). Northumbria's major industry for years was the mining and exporting of coal (hence the phrase about "carrying coals to Newcastle"); today, the steel and petrochemical industries, shipbuilding, and electrical and marine engineering have acquired more importance than coal in Northumbria's economy. It would be a mistake, however, to think that all of Northumbria is an industrial region. The cities named above are all on or near the East Coast: In between them and to the west is some of the most magnificent scenery in England—fairy-tale castles (more than in any other area of England); forests of spruce and pine; woodland paths bordered with anemones, primroses, and foxglove; tumbling rivers and waterfalls; an abundance of wildlife, including the "wild white cattle of Chillingham"; and Hadrian's wall, the 2000-year-old northernmost boundary of the Roman Empire. This is a land of legends—of dragon-slaying heroes and murderous barons, of haunted abbeys and headless kitchen boys who still seek revenge by breaking the crockery in the middle of the night. The people of Northumbria are convivial, self-sufficient, and fiercely proud of their ancestors, who, for centuries, battled the marauding Scots and finally won.

To the west of Northumbria, and extending not quite so far north and a little farther south (but still bordering on Scotland) is the ENGLISH LAKES REGION (*Cumberland* and *Westmoreland* counties). Its coastline is on the Irish Sea; and the Isle of Man, where the famous Manx homespun is made and Manx cats dream wistfully of having something to wag, lies offshore. Two thousand years ago, the Romans left their marks here—their roads, their forts, Hadrian's Wall; but the deepest impression on the Lake District's culture was made by the Vikings, who came over from Iceland to the Isle of Man a thousand years later and from there invaded England, probably almost unopposed after a few minor skirmishes with the Anglicans on the beach. The Vikings farmed and built fences and sang of their adventures and named the rivers and mountains and left an indelible imprint on the language and dialect of the area. The District is famed for the beauty of its tree-lined lakes, its golden sands, its trout and salmon streams spanned by narrow stone bridges, its quiet meadows, the rock cliffs sloping to the Wastwater, the magnificent coastline, and the tiny sparkling pools ("tarns") hidden among the mountain crags. This part of England is very beautiful in autumn colors, and the snow-clad mountains provide a stunning backdrop for winter sports; but it is in the early spring, when sudden showers dampen the fields and trees and depart just as suddenly to leave them glistening in the sunshine, that the Lakes Region is at its loveliest. This is the area that has been depicted so vividly in the writings of Coleridge, Tennyson, Scott, Keats, Shelley, Charlotte Brontë—the place where Wordsworth came upon his "host of golden daffodils."

YORKSHIRE occupies a rather large portion of north-central England. Directly below Northumbria, its coastline is on the North Sea. The region designated by the Tourist Board covers only the one large county of *Yorkshire*, which is subdivided into three Ridings—North, East, and West. (The word "Riding" is of Scandinavian derivation and means "one-third.") Vast areas of Yorkshire (768,000 acres in all) have been set aside as national parks. Because Yorkshire is so large and its topography so varied, it has something to interest everyone. The 100-mile stretch of coastline has a number of resorts (Saltburn, Scarborough, Filey, Bridlington, Hornsea, Withernsea), especially popular with young families for their sandy beaches and sailing and lively night life. Three of Yorkshire's coastal cities are of special interest for additional reasons: Hornsea, because of its pottery; Hull, because it is Britain's third largest seaport; and Robin Hood's Bay, because of its onetime association with smugglers. Older people are more likely to delight in the high wolds, an inland area of chalk hills dotted with farms and charming villages. Here is York itself, a medieval walled city of winding cobbled streets and ancient timbered buildings. To the north are the North York Moors—wild, lonely, gray, but with an occasional hamlet or inn where the traveler can stop for a bite to eat and a cup of hot tea. In the southern part of West Riding are the wool towns (Huddersfield, Halifax, Bradford) and the town so famous for its cutlery—Sheffield; and between these cities and the lovely dales of northwest Yorkshire, where rivers wind through wooded glens and pasture lands and the massive walls of a Norman castle keep watch over the enchanting old market town of Richmond, lie Wuthering Heights and Ponden Hall, with the lonely, windswept moors of the Brontë sisters.

The NORTH WEST REGION lies below the English Lakes, west of Yorkshire and on the Irish Sea, and includes the predominantly industrial counties of *Lancashire* and *Cheshire*. In 1852, a notice was posted on the bulletin board of a Lancashire cotton mill: "Now that the hours of business have been drastically reduced," it read, (meaning from 12 hours per day to 11 hours per day, six days a week), "the partaking of food is allowed between 11:30 A.M. and noon, but work will not, on any account, cease." The clerical staff was exhorted to bring four pounds of coal each day during winter and their own pencils (the mill would magnanimously provide the stove and the sharpener), and a distinct increase in output was expected "to compensate for these near-Utopian conditions." But England weathered the Industrial Revolution and the subsequent years of upheaval and adjustment as it has weathered so many changes; and—notwithstanding the severe setback 35 years ago from the bombings of World War II— Lancashire is today one of England's richest and most densely populated counties. The North West's two major cities, Manchester and Liverpool, are enormously important commercial centers. As in most big cities, there is a movement away from the centers of the towns and a rash of building in the suburbs. Housing is modern and convenient, cultural activities thrive, and there is not much similarity to the "near-Utopian" living conditions described on the cotton mill bulletin board. The area is noted for its schools, art galleries, and fine libraries; and Manchester, in particular, is a favorite with music lovers. The surrounding terrain is varied and much of it is lovely—the Pennine Range, the unspoiled Ribble Valley, and the sandy beaches (Blackpool is one of England's most popular coastal resorts). And despite the ravages of war, much remains of the old: Cheshire's black-and-white half-timbered houses; Lancaster's castle; Manchester's cathedral. The people of the North West are noted for their friendliness and hospitality.

The EAST MIDLAND counties *(Lincolnshire, Nottinghamshire, Derbyshire, Leicestershire, Rutland,* and *Northamptonshire)* are often "put down" because of the preponderance of industry in them. Granted, some of the land is pockmarked and pimpled with mines and slag heaps; and Sherwood forest, once a handsome 200-square-mile royal hunting preserve, has now shrunk to a tiny corner of Northamptonshire, the rest of it swept away and replaced by the city of Mansfield and surrounding villages, making it appear as though Robin Hood and his Merry Men stole the very trees from the rich and gave them to the poor for firewood. Yet I still think the general lack of interest in this area is not altogether justified. The Nottingham countryside has many lovely streams and parks and interesting villages, and the steep streets of Nottingham city sloping sharply to the River Trent are a fascinating mixture of nineteenth- and twentieth-century architecture. On the outskirts of the city is spectacular Newstead Abbey, the ancestral home of Lord Byron, the poet. Neighboring Derbyshire offers a variety of scenery from meadows to moors; two stately mansions, Haddon Hall and Chatsworth, in the lovely Wye River Valley; and, in the north and northwest portions, the Peak District—a national park, rugged and dramatic, so carefully protected that its trustees have placed, next to one of its living trees, an old stump bearing the message, "Carve Here." Eastern Leicestershire, with its abundance of grassland and its neighboring small county, Rutland, are both famous fox-hunting areas. Rutland is particularly noted for its stone houses; and the ancient city of Leicester, although it is now an important manufacturing center, has an impressive number of exciting Roman ruins. Northamptonshire, despite its rather disfiguring quarries, has many beautiful churches, fine estates, and an intriguing history (see p. 60). Lincolnshire, divided into three "Ridings," is an important agricultural county, but it, too, has many beautiful churches and an exciting past: This was the home of Alfred Lord Tennyson, of John Wesley, and of Sir Isaac Newton.

The WEST MIDLANDS, one of the two regions without a seacoast, borders Wales and includes *Staffordshire, Shropshire, Herefordshire, Worcestershire, Warwickshire,* and *Gloucestershire.* This delightful area is perhaps the most romantic, the most historically interesting, and the most "typically English" of the ten regions. Here are the Cotswolds, where rambler roses and honeysuckle climb over cottages of mellow stone, where lilies, phlox, and blue delphinium grow in tiny gardens, where the waters of the Evenlode and the Windrush wind lazily among rolling hills and the villages have names as picturesque as their settings: Chipping Campden, Birdlip, Stow-on-the-Wold, Bourton-on-the-Water. Here, too, are the ancient and beautiful towns of Gloucester, with its magnificent cathedral; Cheltenham, with its Regency elegance still very much in evidence; and Cirencester, which has not forgotten its Roman origin and has preserved, in its Corinium Museum, relics of its exciting past. A bit to the north lies Shakespeare country—Stratford-upon-Avon; and Shottery, where Anne Hathaway lived. (If the world equates "typical England" with the West Midlands, it is probably because Shakespeare's vivid imagery has created an indelible impression on all of us.) Not far from Stratford are the towns of Warwick, with its glorious castle on the Avon; Coventry, where the cathedral's architectural style is a matter of controversy but the excellence of its music is disputed by none; Worcester, with its great cathedral and fine timbered houses; and Kenilworth Castle, now a red sandstone ruin but with a romantic past that is still very much alive in the minds of Sir Walter Scott's readers. To the west is the remote county of Hereford, where the River Wye, coming in from Wales, flows slowly and unsuspectingly through meadows, then gathers excitement as it enters a narrow gorge on its way to meet the Severn. At the Welsh border are mountains and to the east are peaceful villages and apple orchards, spectacular at blossom time. North of Herefordshire is Shropshire—hilly, wild, and lonely in its southern region, rolling and gentle in the north. Staffordshire, the northernmost county of the West Midlands, is where the River Trent (the traditional dividing line between North and South) originates. To the north are rocky hills; to the south are farms and villages. The scenery is magnificent and diverse, with Cammock Chase, Needwood Forest, Peak Park, and Dovedale providing some of the most delightful views in England. Here are the five towns known as the "Potteries" (Stoke, Burslem, Longton, Hanley, and Tunstall), immortalized by Arnold Bennett and famous for their exquisite china and porcelain—Wedgewood, Spode, Minton, Copeland. Turning southward again, back toward the Cotswolds, is Birmingham—the center of England and its second largest city—beautiful, modern, rich, and surpassed only by London in the importance of its cultural activities.

The top of EAST ANGLIA juts into the North Sea; its southern part is on the English Channel at the Thames estuary. East Anglia includes the counties of *Essex, Cambridgeshire, Suffolk, Norfolk*, and *Huntingdonshire*. Almost all of Essex is within commuting distance of London, from the quiet beauty of Epping Forest, through pastoral villages and the ancient market towns of Braintree, Halstead, and Colchester (did you know there *was* an old King Cole—some authorities say his real name was Cunobelin and others say it was Coel—and this is where he reigned from A.D. 10 to 40?) to the holiday beachside resorts. To the north of Essex, the Cambridgeshire Fens provide miles of quiet waterways—some natural, others man made for drainage purposes and dating back to the Romans. The city of Cambridge is often referred to as the "Gateway to East Anglia" and of course its most revered landmark is its great university. Huntingdonshire, an incredibly fertile land with rich, peaty soil, is one of England's most important agricultural areas—but it is described as being "permanently waterlogged," and with each harvest a little more of the damp earth is removed and a little more water seeps in; before long, the land of Oliver Cromwell and Samuel Pepys may have sunk out of sight. In northern Huntingdonshire, however, founded on the site of a great monastery, lies Peterborough—still prospering, and still expanding. The coastal towns of Norfolk and northern Suffolk are fine holiday resorts, noted for their sunshine and sand-and-shingle beaches. South of Lowestoft, the Suffolk coast becomes wild, lonely, a place for the person who enjoys solitude; yet in the midst of this remote and little-used stretch of coastline lies Aldeburgh, the setting for Benjamin Britten's *Peter Grimes;* and since that opera was first performed in 1945 Aldeburgh has become a very famous music center, the home of what is now perhaps the most renowned music festival in England. Inland Norfolk and Suffolk are both loved for their serene pastoral beauty, portrayed so vividly in John Constable's landscapes, and the Norfolk Broads are a favorite holiday area and a paradise for sportsmen.

In south central England, to the immediate northwest of London and embracing *Oxfordshire, Berkshire, Buckinghamshire, Bedfordshire,* and *Hertfordshire,* is the inland region known as the THAMES AND CHILTERNS. The Chilterns, a range of flint and chalk hills rising to a height of 900 feet, run through several of these counties and, in addition to enhancing the beauty of the area, provide an interesting and convenient way for a Member of Parliament to resign his seat. The only way he can do so is to accept an office for which he is paid by the Crown; he therefore applies for the position of "Steward of the Chiltern Hundreds," and the Crown pays him a nominal salary in return for his services in warding off the bandits whose sinister leers have not peeked out from behind the beechwoods for several centuries; then, feeling no immediate threat and therefore no great sense of responsibility, he immediately resigns from that post also and leaves an opening for the next M.P. who wants to get out. The River Thames, originating in the Cotswolds, cuts through the southern part of the region before it finds its way to London and on to the sea. A boat trip on the Thames from Kingston Pier to Oxford—past Windsor, Maidenhead, Marlow, Henley-on-Thames, Reading—is a journey through history. Today the river is busy with steamers and private pleasure boats, but the past is so much in evidence that I cannot help finding it more reassuring to travel the Thames from east to west than from west to east, lest the current carry me on to the Tower and drop me off at Traitors' Gate. Great, sprawling London has begun to spill out over the easternmost edge of the Thames and Chilterns just as it has over its other neighboring regions, but there are still plenty of gently rolling pasture lands and grassy plains, unspoiled villages in peaceful valleys, deep woods and willow-bordered rivers, where one can live quietly, away from the city and yet close to it.

The WEST COUNTRY, most of which has a coastline (and most of that on the English Channel) is a long, narrow region, adjoining the Thames and Chilterns and South East regions on its eastern border and the West Midlands on its northern border, and separated from Wales by the Bristol Channel. It includes the counties of *Wiltshire, Dorset, Somerset, Devon,* and *Cornwall.* This is an area of enchantment and excitement—made so by its natural beauty, its climate, its history, its legends, and its writers. Wiltshire is a county of chalk downs, of stone villages beside clear streams that flow through the valleys, and of magnificent estates (including Wilton House, home of the Earls of Pembroke). It includes the town of Salisbury, with its glorious cathedral, and that 4000-year-old enigma, Stonehenge. Dorset, another county with chalk hills and fertile valleys, is Thomas Hardy's "Wessex." Its Eggendon Hill is "Norcombe Hill" in *Far from the Madding Crowd;* its Dorchester is Hardy's "Casterbridge"; its Puddletown Heath is Hardy's "Egdon Heath"; the manor house at Wool is the Wellbridge House in which Tess of the D'Urbervilles honeymooned. Dorchester was the scene of the "Bloody Assize" of 1685, when the infamous Judge Jeffreys found 292 men guilty of treason and sentenced them to death (though he got around to hanging only 74)—his "proof" being that they had been absent from their homes "att the tyme of the Rebellion"; and it was in Dorset that the six Tolpuddle martyrs were sentenced to seven years' exile for forming what was perhaps the first trade union after they asked for a raise from nine shillings per week to ten and in return were cut first to eight shillings and then to seven. Somerset is the land of the Mendips, a crescent-shaped range of pink-brown hills—untamed and windswept in places but with charming villages nestled in the valleys. This is the land of Exmoor—the setting for Blackmore's *Lorna Doone.* Devon, into which Exmoor National Park extends, is renowned for its lush woodlands with wildflowers and ferns, its winding lanes and picturesque cottages, its spectacular coastline (tranquil sands and blue waters in the south, rugged cliffs and heavy surf in the north), and its mild climate. The town of Bideford in Devon's northwest corner was the setting for Charles Kingsley's *Westward Ho!;* in Manaton, high up in the moors, John Galsworthy lived for many years and began work on *The Forsyte Saga;* and Sir Arthur Conan Doyle's hound of the Baskervilles roamed the Dartmoor area—now a national park. Cornwall, the peninsula in the extreme southwest, has 360 miles of beautiful coastline, some of it with sandy beaches and peaceful coves, some of it with precipitous cliffs pounded by rough seas that have spelled disaster for countless ships. Here is the land of King Arthur, the legendary sixth-century hero of whose existence everyone—except a few spoilsport scholars—is quite certain. Land's End—the wild and craggy tip of England—does indeed look as though it is the end of everything: It is hard to believe that 30 miles offshore palm trees flourish on the Isles of Scilly and daffodils bloom in mid-December.

The SOUTH EAST REGION lies below London. Its southern and eastern coasts are on the English Channel; its northeast corner is at the Thames estuary; and its western and northwestern boundaries adjoin the West Country and the Thames and Chilterns. Its counties *(Kent, Sussex, Surrey,* and *Hampshire)* are among the most popular in England for several reasons: Travel to the Continent is convenient and economical; rail service between London and many southeast towns is fast and frequent; the seaside resorts provide pleasant holidays; the weather is mild; and the scenery is unsurpassed. Kent is a county of oasthouses, hop fields, orchards, beaches, and sunshine. It is also, you might say, the county through which history entered England: It was here, in 54 B.C., that the Romans first landed—and later, the Saxons and the Danes; even Christianity entered England through Kent when St. Augustine landed at Ebbsfleet. Neighboring Sussex, to the west, has 75 miles of coastline with attractive, well-kept beaches, lovely gardens, and an abundance of entertainment—opera at Glyndebourne, drama at Chichester, star-studded night life at Brighton. Sussex, too, has its fascinating reminders of the past: among them, Battle Abbey, site of the historic battle of Hastings in 1066, and Arundel Castle, where the Dukes of Norfolk have lived for 500 years. Surrey, which lies between London and Sussex, is perhaps the most beautiful of all the southeastern counties—and certainly the most convenient: All parts of Surrey are easily accessible to London. The Surrey countryside is magnificent; most of it lies at least 500 feet above sea level, and the North Downs climb to 1000 feet. There are pine forests and heathland, charming villages and gracious, elegant towns, beautiful gardens and fine estates. Hampshire, still farther to the west, is predominantly rural; but it, too, offers a diversity of scenery—chalk downs, sandy beaches, marshland, trout streams, and the woodlands and heathlands of the New Forest (England's finest plant and animal preserve, dating from the days of William the Conqueror). Here, too, are Winchester, capital of England under Alfred the Great; Portsmouth, so important in England's great naval history and the resting place of Nelson's flagship, the HMS *Victory;* Portchester Castle, where Henry V assembled his army before invading France; Hambledon, where cricket originated; and, offshore, the beautiful, diamond-shaped Isle of Wight.

THE TEN GEOGRAPHICAL REGIONS

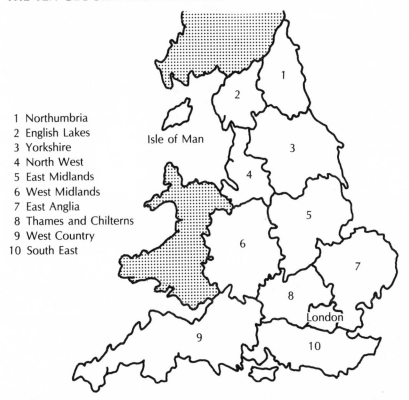

1 Northumbria
2 English Lakes
3 Yorkshire
4 North West
5 East Midlands
6 West Midlands
7 East Anglia
8 Thames and Chilterns
9 West Country
10 South East

THE TOWNS

To write in detail about every town in England—though it would be fun —is obviously impossible; a line has to be drawn somewhere. I shall act on the premise that most of you, like my own family, want to be fairly close to London; and I shall therefore limit my notes about towns and villages to those within a radius of approximately 60 miles—or not more than an hour and a half by train—from the capital. I am skipping London itself, not only for the obvious reason that it would take up the whole book, but because there is already more written about London than you will ever have time to read and also because property is very expensive in the city and rents are high.

The towns named below in capital letters all have rail service into London. The list is not complete: only the more important (and useful to readers of this book) have been included. A few lesser villages—those with some special charm—are listed immediately below their nearest neighbors. Some of these less important villages also have rail service; the ones that do are asterisked. Those of you who are enchanted with the small villages off the beaten track may ask for Green Line bus schedules at any London Transport office. It would be difficult, indeed, to pick a town of any size in this populous area of England where there is not adequate transportation of one kind or another.

Within this commuting area, four of the Tourist Board's regions are touched upon: the *East Midlands* (a few towns in Northamptonshire); *East Anglia* (most of Essex and a little bit of Cambridgeshire); the *Thames and Chilterns* (parts of Oxfordshire and Berkshire, all of Buckinghamshire, Bedfordshire, and Hertfordshire); and the *South East* (most of Kent and Sussex, all of Surrey, and a little bit of Hampshire).

EAST MIDLANDS

Northamptonshire

KETTERING   (London terminal: St. Pancras)

Kettering, a commercial area for more than 700 years, is now a manufacturing center for clothes and boots. There are good schools (including institutions of further education and special schools for handicapped children) and well-equipped recreation areas. Although the capital can be reached in about an hour and ten minutes by a mainline train, houses are much more reasonably priced than in the more southerly areas.

NORTHAMPTON   (London terminal: Euston)

In 1675, a fire destroyed most of Northampton's old buildings. As a result, the city appears to be quite modern. That is, in a way, sad— because Northampton's history is fascinating. This was, at first, an ancient Saxon town; then it became a favorite of the Norman kings. Thomas à Becket was tried and condemned here, and Henry VI was taken prisoner outside the city walls during the Wars of the Roses. Today, the population numbers 121,000, and there are many industries, the chief one being shoe manufacture. Look for moderately priced homes here.

WELLINGBOROUGH   (London terminal: St. Pancras)

Wellingborough is a neat and attractive market town, well planned with wide streets and orderly rows of trees. It is not as large a city as Kettering and not quite as far north, though house prices are still lower than in the other directions from London. Wellingborough has a good park with a small zoo, and numbers among its many schools an excellent grammar school for boys and a technical college. St. Luke's Church has some interesting misericords.

EAST ANGLIA

Essex

BENFLEET/CANVEY ISLAND   (London terminal: Fenchurch Street)

Canvey Island, about five miles long and three across at its widest point, is a rapidly developing residential area near the mouth of the Thames. A bridge crosses over to the mainland at Benfleet, where commuters can get fast train service into London. There are a few old buildings on the island (*e.g.*, the 1618 octagon-shaped dwelling that now houses the Canvey Island Dutch Cottage Museum), but most of the houses are new. Nine primary schools, one comprehensive school, and a smattering of good shops make it unnecessary for the Canvey Island housewife or child to cross the bridge to Benfleet unless something special arises.

BILLERICAY   (London terminal: Liverpool Street)

Billericay is the site of Chantry House, where the Pilgrims assembled when they prepared to embark for America on the Mayflower. In 1952, Billericay was designated as one of the towns that would be expanded —and since that time a great many modern houses have been erected. High Street, however, still boasts a number of interesting old buildings.

BRAINTREE   (London terminal: Liverpool Street)

Braintree, in central Essex where two old Roman roads (Staine and Icknield) meet, was noted in medieval times for its woolen cloth. Today, weaving is still an important industry, but the materials woven are mostly silk and nylon. Agriculture and seed growing—industries that enhance rather than detract from the natural beauty of the pleasant river valleys—are also important to Braintree.

THE BELCHAMPS: Three tiny villages with great manor houses and picturesque cottages.

CASTLE HEDINGHAM: A marvelous, typically old-English village on a riverside, with a fine church and a great castle.

COGGESHALL: A weaver's village, site of an interesting merchant's house.

*CRESSING: Two large fifteenth-century barns built by the Knights Hospitallers.

FINCHINGFIELD: A village green, a duck pond, a Norman tower—one of the loveliest of all Essex villages.

GESTINGTHORPE: Charming cottages and one of the most interesting churches in Essex.

GREAT DUNMOW: The place where the annual Flitch Trials are held. (The "court" awards a "flitch" of bacon to the most happily married couple.)

GREENSTED: The oldest Saxon church in existence; walls made of split tree trunks.

HALSTEAD: A few miles north of Braintree, also important for its weaving industry.

THE RODINGS: Rolling country, medieval buildings, timbered houses.

SAFFRON WALDEN: A very ancient town with an earth maze—a series of con-
centric circles cut into the turf, believed to be of pre-Christian origin and
connected with fertility rites. The town's name comes from its cultivation of
the Saffron crocus (used as a dye, a medicine, and a condiment).

THAXTED: A truly lovely village with picturesque homes, a Guild Hall, and one
of the most magnificent churches in the county.

BRENTWOOD   (London terminal: Liverpool Street)

In Brentwood's High Street there is a fine old inn that was the first
staging post out of London on the old coaching road. Here, also, is
Brentwood School for boys, founded in 1557. Barely outside of the
capital, Brentwood has become another of London's bedroom communities. The population is already over 54,000 and is growing. There
are excellent schools, including a college of further education, and fast
and frequent trains into London.

*ROMFORD: A fast-growing town with a large shopping center, between Brent-
wood and London.

*SHENFIELD: Almost a part of Brentwood; has a particularly interesting old
church.

BURNHAM-ON-CROUCH   (London terminal: Liverpool Street)

Burnham lies in southeast Essex at the mouth of the River Crouch. It
is a lovely, quiet town of 4500 inhabitants. A dry, sunny climate adds
to its charm and attracts the boating enthusiasts, who have turned
Burnham into Essex's most popular sailing center. Despite its small size,
Burnham has several fine schools.

*SOUTHMINSTER: Site of a fine perpendicular church; a quiet village at the end
of the train line.

CHELMSFORD   (London terminal: Liverpool Street)

Chelmsford is the county town of Essex—an old town built on the site
of a Roman settlement and mentioned in the Domesday Book, but with
a modern appearance that belies its antiquity. The cathedral (St. Mary's)
dates back to 1424—but even that is no longer very old because it
collapsed in 1800 and had to be rebuilt. The Shire Hall is of interest
because it is where Marconi developed his wireless. (Fittingly, Chelmsford now has a large electronics industry.) Schools are good and include
a technical college and school of art and—one of the town's few remaining links with the past—the Edward VI Grammar School for Boys,
founded in 1551.

DANBURY: An interesting village atop a hill, with a church built in 1402 and a

Tudor Palace that has housed (but not at the same time) the Bishops of Rochester and St. Albans.

MALDON: One of the most ancient and picturesque towns on England's east coast. Its history dates back to the Romans; and in 1171 Henry II granted it a charter that required it to provide a ship for the King's defense. There are a number of interesting buildings, including a church (St. Peter's) in which there is a library containing a first edition of Milton's *Paradise Lost*. This charming town is built on a steep hill overlooking the Chelmer and Blackwater rivers.

COLCHESTER   (London terminal: Liverpool Street)

For more than 2000 years, Colchester has been a town of importance. There was a Bronze Age settlement here in 1100 B.C. In A.D. 43–44, Claudius stormed in and established the first Roman colony—and the town then remained a Roman stronghold (except for a short period after the warrior Queen of the Iceni, Boadicea, devastated it with sword and fire and a just indignation) (see p.74) until the Romans departed. In the third century, the city walls (still standing but no longer a full 20 feet high) were built. The castle was the work of William the Conqueror in the eleventh century, and the fourteenth century marked the beginning of Colchester's prosperity as a weaving center. Today, Colchester is renowned for its beautiful roses and fine oysters, and its walls are stormed only by well-meaning tourists. This is a truly beautiful and fascinating city, with treasures of the past and present too numerous to recount. A superb road (two hours) and a fast train (56 minutes) lead to London.

DEDHAM: A village of sedate charm and quiet dignity.

MANNINGTREE: At the mouth of the River Stour, called the "Gateway to Constable County" because it has been so beautifully portrayed in the works of the famous painter.

WEST MERSEA: A resort and yacht-building center on Mersea Island, with good bus service across to Colchester's fast trains.

WIVENHOE: On the bank of the Colne, with a notable church. The University of Essex is at Wivenhoe Park, midway between Wivenhoe and Colchester.

RAYLEIGH   (London terminal: Liverpool Street)

Rayleigh, like all towns in southeast Essex, is fast becoming a residential center for London commuters; and as it grows, the quality of its schools and local shops improves. In spite of its expanding population and new housing developments, however, High Street remains a typically picturesque "old world" street. The Rectory was built in medieval times, and many fine old houses enhance the city's charm.

SOUTHEND-ON-SEA   (London terminal: Fenchurch Street)

At the mouth of the Thames, Southend-on-Sea is best known as a holiday resort. It is a large city (166,000) with two parts, contradictory and complementary in atmosphere, so that everyone may find something to his liking. Southend proper is lively, festive, crowded with people bent on entertainment. From here protrudes the world's longest pier—a city in itself, with restaurant, theatre, bowling alley, exhibition hall, even an electric railway to carry those who may be too done in from merrymaking to walk the mile and a half to its end or older folks who may want to skip the intervening attractions and get on with the more serious business of angling or watching the ships on their way to and from the Port of London. The other part of Southend, known as Westcliff, is quiet, reserved, more select, with peaceful parks and gardens, two good theatres, and a concert hall. Southend has a municipal airport with regularly scheduled flights to other cities in England and to the Continent.

*HADLEIGH: Norman church and castle (a residence of Edward III), immortalized by the painter John Constable.
*LEIGH-ON-SEA: Fishing boats, pleasure boats, sandy beaches, rock gardens, artists.
*ROCHFORD: Site of a Tudor mansion associated with Anne Boleyn's family.
*SHOEBURYNESS: Traditionally a fishing village, but now developing as a commercial center and resort.

WICKFORD   (London terminal: Liverpool Street)

Like its neighbor, Rayleigh, Wickford is expanding rapidly into a London "dormitory" town but somehow manages to retain its original character. There is a large industrial area here, as well as a busy shopping center and new housing developments. The open countryside surrounding Wickford helps the town maintain its reputation as a pleasant place in which to live.

Cambridgeshire

Train service between London and points in Cambridgeshire is not exceptional, and for that reason only the most important town—Cambridge (54 miles, 76 minutes)—is described here. This is not to say that most Cambridgeshire towns are beyond commuting distance—if one has an automobile. And everything has its good points: Presumably because of the rather slow and infrequent train service, the recent inflationary trend in real estate prices has not been so pronounced in Cambridgeshire as in other counties near the capital.

CAMBRIDGE   (London terminals: King's Cross, Liverpool Street)

Seat of one of the world's great universities, Cambridge is a city of towers and courtyards and beautiful stone bridges spanning the River Cam. Its favorite sport is punting on the river; its second favorite sport is sitting on the bank watching for the occasional punter who is left clinging in a state of perplexed embarrassment to his stuck-in-the-mud pole while his boat passes on without him. The oldest of Cambridge's many colleges was founded in 1284, and the town itself was an important trading center long before that.

THAMES AND CHILTERNS

Oxfordshire

BICESTER   (London terminal: Paddington)

Bicester, pronounced "Bister," is in northeast Oxfordshire near the borders of Buckinghamshire and Northamptonshire. It is an ancient market town with many interesting churches and the remains of an Augustinian priory (1182). On a direct rail line from London, its popularity as a residential center for commuters is growing. New houses are being built, and there is a good shopping center. Bicester's population now numbers over 12,000.

BRACKLEY (in Northamptonshire): Site of Magdalen College School (1447).

GORING   (in Oxfordshire) and **STREATLEY** (in Berkshire) (London terminal: Paddington)

These two delightful spots, served by the same station, lie on the Oxfordshire-Berkshire border. Goring's church has a Norman tower and the ruins of an Augustinian nunnery. Streatley, a pretty village on the Berkshire bank of the river, lies at the foot of the Berkshire Downs, from which the views are magnificent.

HENLEY-ON-THAMES   (London terminal: Paddington)

In the southeast corner of Oxfordshire, at the boundaries of Buckinghamshire and Berkshire, Henley (the county's oldest town) is a pleasure spot where picnics and rowing regattas and outdoor evening parties are the principal leisure activities during June and July. Very close to London (as well as to Oxford and Reading), Henley is an attractive spot for commuters. Nearby are two beautiful Elizabethan mansions—Gray's Court and Mapledurham House. Mapledurham provided the background for much of *The Forsyte Saga* and *The Wind in the Willows*.

HAMBLEDEN (in Buckinghamshire): A charming village two miles from Henley, reached by road or footpath.
NETTLEBED: A fine takeoff point for exploring the Chiltern countryside.
*WARGRAVE (in Berkshire): A lovely riverside town, favorite spot for artists.

OXFORD   (London terminal: Paddington)

The "City of Spires," with its world-renowned university, lies between the banks of the Cherwell and Thames rivers. The first recorded mention of the university was in the twelfth century, though "Gown" was not granted immunity from "Town" until the early thirteenth century. The city itself is first mentioned in the *Anglo-Saxon Chronicle* of 912. Oxford now has a population of well over 100,000; and the university, made up of 39 colleges, has approximately 11,000 students. Oxford's High Street (called "The High") is justly acclaimed as one of England's most splendid architectural vistas; and equally renowned are the Bodleian Library, housing 3 million books and 50,000 manuscripts, and the Sheldonian Theatre, built by Christopher Wren in 1668. In Broad Street (called "The Broad") a cross marks the spot where, during Mary Tudor's reign, Bishops Cranmer, Latimer, and Ridley were burned at the stake. Today, a lot of restoration is taking place in Oxford, and new development homes are available.

ABINGDON (in Berkshire): Delightful old town on the banks of the Thames; site of a seventh-century Benedictine abbey.

*CULHAM: Church of England college for schoolmasters; atomic-energy research laboratories.

DORCHESTER:[3] An ancient Saxon town, the cathedral city of Wessex from 634 to 705.

SUTTON COURTENAY (in Berkshire): A charming old town across the river from Culham.

WITNEY: Industrial area, especially blanket manufacturing.

WOODSTOCK: Site of Blenheim Palace, home of the Duke of Marlborough and birthplace of Sir Winston Churchill.

Berkshire

BRACKNELL   (London terminal: Waterloo)

Bracknell is in one of the most beautiful areas of Berkshire. There are royal forests, mostly pinewood, and places of historical interest. Most of Bracknell (headquarters of the Meteorological Office) is fairly new and expanding rapidly.

*ASCOT: Scene of the famous Gold Cup race in June (see also VIRGINIA WATER, in Surrey County).

*SUNNINGDALE: An expensive suburb in the "stockbroker area"; fine golf course.

MAIDENHEAD   (London terminal: Paddington)

Maidenhead, a town of 45,000 people, is one of the liveliest of the

---

[3]This is not the same Dorchester that is mentioned on page 57 in connection with the "Bloody Assize" of 1685.

Thames River resorts. Its location, in the northeast corner of Berkshire, marks the beginning of the prettiest and most popular stretch of the river. With trains departing for the capital every thirty minutes, Maidenhead has become a London bedroom community, but—with light industry, good schools, and a well-developed shopping center—still maintains its identity as a town in its own right.

BRAY-ON-THAMES: A picturesque town of 4000 inhabitants where, in the sixteenth century, lived the infamous Vicar of Bray, who suffered convenient changes of heart about his religious beliefs every time his job was in peril.

*COOKHAM: A riverside town with an old timbered inn and a monument to Fred Walker, noted English artist who illustrated some of Thackeray's books.

NEWBURY   (London terminal: Paddington)

Newbury, granted its town charter by Elizabeth I in 1596, lies on the banks of the River Kennet in southwest Berkshire. Its most famous character was a weaver, John Winchcombe ("Jack of Newbury"), to whom is attributed the establishment of England's first factory. Donnington Castle lies two miles to the northwest. New homes are available in Newbury.

READING   (London terminal: Paddington)

Reading, headquarters of the Danes in their invasion of England during King Alfred's reign, has had a very exciting history and is still one of the most important towns to the immediate west of London. Here the Thames joins the River Kennet, reputed to offer the best trout fishing in England. Reading is both an industrial center (noted especially for its biscuit making) and a beautiful residential center with an excellent university, splendid parks and sporting grounds, and a wealth of cultural activity.

*PANGBOURNE: Location of Pangbourne College.
*THEALE: A small town with a large church modeled after the Salisbury Cathedral.

STREATLEY   (See GORING in Oxfordshire)

WINDSOR   (London terminal: Paddington)

Windsor is an elegant and prosperous town of 31,000 inhabitants, and its majestic castle has been the chief residence of the British royal family since the days of William the Conqueror. The town lies on the bank of the Thames, with bridges connecting it to Eton and Datchet in Buckinghamshire. Its parks and gardens are magnificent, and its houses—some old and quaint, some new and luxurious—present an interesting assortment of architectural styles. Horse racing and golf are the principal sports.

*DATCHET (in Buckinghamshire): Faces Windsor's Home Park; fine golf course.
*ETON (in Buckinghamshire): Site of famed Eton College, founded in 1440 by
 Henry VI.

WOKINGHAM   (London terminal: Waterloo)

With good schools at all levels, churches of many denominations, excellent shops, and numerous amateur groups and societies with a variety of interests ranging from sports to music and from youth activities to hobbies for the elderly, Wokingham makes an excellent residential area both for young couples and for retirees. The surrounding countryside (including a National Trust area known as "The Ridges") has abundant pine woodland and gorse.

*CROWTHORNE: Site of Wellington College.

Buckinghamshire

AMERSHAM   (London terminal: Baker Street)

Amersham, like Chesham (see below), can be reached on the fast Metropolitan Line subway without changing trains. It is an old town, studded with interesting landmarks: the King's Arms Hotel; the seventeenth-century market hall and almshouses; Shardeloes, the Drake home; and many fine eighteenth-century houses. Amersham's population is now 69,000, and modern housing is available.

*CHESHAM: A few miles to the north of Amersham, in the lovely Chess River
 Valley. A pleasant town with a population of 20,000.

AYLESBURY   (London terminal: Marylebone)

Aylesbury is the county town of Buckinghamshire, situated in the county's center. The ancient part of Aylesbury has a typically old-world square surrounded by seventeenth- and eighteenth-century houses. In recent years industry has crept in, displacing the poultry and dairy farming for which the area was once noted. Places of historic interest include the County Hall, the King's Head Inn, the Bull's Head Inn, and the County Museum.

WADDESDON: Site of Waddesdon Manor, a magnificent "French chateau" with
 fine paintings and furniture on display.
*WENDOVER: Picturesque village on the Icknield Way (Britain's oldest road).

BEACONSFIELD   (London terminal: Marylebone)

Beaconsfield, a little to the east of High Wycombe, is interesting historically because of its association with Disraeli (Earl of Beaconsfield), G. K.

Chesterton, Edmund Burke, and Edmund Waller. The town is a pleasant one, with a wide Georgian brick street. Bekonscot Gardens, with a miniature railway and a model village, are in Warwick Road, north of the station.

*DENHAM: Picturesque street and site of Denham Place, an interesting seventeenth-century house.
*JORDANS: Quaker meeting house, burial place of William Penn (founder of Pennsylvania) and his family.

BLETCHLEY   (London terminal: Euston)

Bletchley is in northern Buckinghamshire, close to the Bedfordshire border. An ancient market town with twelfth-century landmarks, its population has tripled in recent years (now 30,000) with the introduction of large industrial developments. Modern housing is available here.

BUCKINGHAM: On the River Ouse in the northern part of the county. A small, quiet town (population 5100) built around a marketplace with a Georgian town hall. Its recorded history dates back more than a thousand years.
*FENNY STRATFORD: On the church grounds there are funny little cannons called "Fenny Poppers," which are fired at Martinmas.
NEWPORT PAGNELL: Ideal residential town—shopping center, churches, schools, parks, boating and fishing on the Rivers Ouse and Lovat.
OLNEY: A pleasant town on the Ouse, famous for its bootmaking and for its renowned clergyman, John Newton, who wrote the hymn "Amazing Grace."
STONY STRATFORD: Where the yarn swapping of Edward V and Richard of Gloucester at two coaching inns led to the phrase "cock and bull story."

CHALFONT ST. GILES   (London terminal: Marylebone)

Chalfont St. Giles, in southern Buckinghamshire near the Hertfordshire border, is a most attractive village, to which John Milton fled during the Great Plague of London (1665) and where he completed *Paradise Lost* and began *Paradise Regained*. Milton's cottage is now a museum.

HIGH WYCOMBE   (London terminals: Marylebone, Paddington)

High Wycombe, a thriving market and manufacturing town famous for its furniture making, lies along the Wye Valley of the Chiltern Hill region amid beechwoods and lovely fields. Educational facilities are excellent and include a famous girls' school (Wycombe Abbey) and a College of Technology and Art. Nearby are Hughenden Manor (home of Benjamin Disraeli) and Penn, the ancestral home of Pennsylvania's founder.

MARLOW-ON-THAMES   (London terminal: Paddington)

Marlow is a pleasant town with old houses and fine old hotels where guests stay when they come to fish and boat on the river. Some famous writers (Shelley, T. S. Eliot, Jerome K. Jerome) have found Marlow a quiet and peaceful place in which to work.

*BOURNE END: A favored residential area across the river from Cookham (see MAIDENHEAD, in Berkshire).

PRINCES RISBOROUGH   (London terminal: Paddington)

The town was named "Princes" Risborough to designate it as a royal possession and thus distinguish it from Monks Risborough (see below), which belonged to the Archbishop of Canterbury. The Prince referred to was the Black Prince (Edward, Prince of Wales, father of King Richard II). Although there has been some development on the edge of town, the center looks just as it did several centuries ago.

BLEDLOW: Pleasant village; Norman font in the church.
*MONKS RISBOROUGH/WHITELEAF: Early English and perpendicular church; site of Whiteleaf Cross cut into a chalk hillside to mark the intersection of the Oxford road and the Icknield Way (the oldest road in Britain).

SLOUGH   (London terminal: Paddington)

Slough is an industrial city of 87,000 inhabitants, across the county line from Windsor.

Bedfordshire

BEDFORD   (London terminals: St. Pancras for Bedford Midland Road; Euston for Bedford St. Johns)

In 1566 William Harpur, a tailor and Lord Mayor of London, endowed a grammar school in Bedford with income from properties in Bedford and Holborn. In the first years of this endowment, the total sum was £40 (£28 from Bedford and £12 from Holborn); but with income from these sources increasing each year, more and more money has gone into the Bedford schools. Thus from a humble beginning, Bedford's educational system has grown into one of the finest in England. Bedford attracts many holiday visitors and tourists, not only because of its river and parks and superb recreational facilities, but also because of its association with John Bunyan, who wrote a part of *Pilgrim's Progress* while he was in prison for "devilishly and perniciously" refusing to attend church services and for holding "unlawful meetings and conventicles." Bunyan Meeting, a house built on the site where Bunyan used to preach, contains personal relics of the "Immortal Tinker."

AMPTHILL: Charming place to live. A cross marks the site of the "faire castle" where Catherine of Aragon stayed while awaiting her divorce from Henry VIII.

ELSTOW: John Bunyan's birthplace.

OAKLEY, PAVENHAM, STEVINGTON, CARLTON, and HARROLD: All nice villages on the river and with rare flowers, butterflies, and birds.

SHARNBROOK: Picturesque village, but with modern housing available.

TURVEY: One of the attractive limestone villages of northwest Bedfordshire.

WILLINGTON: Royal stables.

BIGGLESWADE (London terminal: King's Cross)

The point at which the Romans crossed the River Ivel when they built the Great North Road became Biggleswade. There was a day, remembered by the oldest townspeople, when the river was navigable and could be used for transporting coal and wood and locally grown produce; now it is used only for fishing and the operation of two mills. It was here that the host of "The Ongley Arms" manufactured England's first practicable bicycle—the excellence of which he demonstrated by traveling 20 miles on a cinder track near Paddington in an hour and six minutes.

ICKWELL: Beautiful village, famous for its Maypole dancing.

NORTHILL: Birthplace of Thomas Tompion, "father of English clock-making."

SHEFFORD: Ancient and pretty market town.

SOUTHILL: Site of the finest Regency-style mansion in England.

LEIGHTON BUZZARD (London terminal: Euston)

Situated on the River Ousel, Leighton Buzzard is an ancient marketplace dating back to the days of the Saxons and mentioned in the Domesday Book. Its fine Early English parish church, with its handsome spire rising to a height of 191 feet, is built on the order of a cathedral. In North Street there are almshouses, the money for which was bequeathed in 1630 by Edward Wilkes; and on Rogation Monday—the day on which, for 15 centuries, it has been customary to ask God's blessing on the fruits of the earth—Wilkes's gift is commemorated in a rather startling fashion: An almshouse trustee reads aloud passages from the benefactor's will while the town crier, his staff adorned with flowers, stands silently by and a choirboy is stood on his head.

WING (in Buckinghamshire): Site of Ascott House, which contains the famous Rothschild collection of paintings.

WOBURN: Site of Woburn Abbey, the county's showplace.

LUTON (London terminal: St. Pancras)

Luton, in the southeast corner of Bedfordshire, is a large industrial city where straw hats, vacuum cleaners, and Vauxhalls keep many of its 161,000 people employed. Luton is so well planned that its factories do not detract from its beauty. There is an abundance of green open space. Wardown Park, in the center of the city, has a large boating lake, a cricket ground, and a mansion housing a museum and an art gallery. On the outskirts of the city is a new 256–acre park with formal gardens. Luton has a stately church (one of its few remaining links with the past) and a new Town Centre housing a large library and a well-equipped theatre.

DUNSTABLE: Where Britain's first theatrical performance (the twelfth-century Miracle Play of St. Katherine) was performed.

TODDINGTON: Attractive village green, old town hall, fine Early English and perpendicular church.

TOTTERNHOE: Site of famous quarries that supplied the stone for Windsor Castle and St. Alban's Cathedral.

SANDY   (London terminal: King's Cross)

Sandy is a small town (about 5000 people) in east central Bedfordshire on the River Ivel and the Great North Road. The district around Sandy is a truck-farming area, and most of the produce is shipped to London. Remains of two Roman camps and a Danish one attest to the town's antiquity. The Royal Society for the Protection of Birds owns a 100–acre preserve at Sandy, where many species of birds enjoy the freedom of natural surroundings in perfect safety.

COCKAYNE HATLEY: Church containing fine Flemish wood carvings; burial place of the poet W. E. Henley, whose daughter Margaret was the "Wendy" of James Barrie's *Peter Pan.*

POTTON: A very old market town; traditional annual fairs.

TEMPSFORD: A place of considerable historical importance, occupied alternately in the tenth century by Danes and Saxons. John Donne, the poet, was a church rector here.

Hertfordshire

BISHOP'S STORTFORD   (London terminal: Liverpool Street)

Bishop's Stortford is on the eastern border of Hertfordshire on the River Stort. It is a town of about 22,000 people and has excellent schools and shops. Three miles to the east is Hatfield Forest, a 1000–acre tract of National Trust woodland with a boating lake. An interesting museum occupies the old vicarage which was the birthplace of Cecil Rhodes, the statesman and financier who bequeathed most of his fortune for the endowment of scholarships at Oxford University.

HARPENDEN   (London terminal: St. Pancras)

Harpenden offers superb commuter service into London—trains at 30–

minute intervals and extra ones during rush hours. Although Harpenden is not a particularly old city, it has a population of 22,000, a number of light industries, and good educational facilities (including a well-known coeducational school, St. George's). Harpenden is noted for its Rothamstead Experimental Station, a 527–acre farm engaged in agricultural research.

HATFIELD (London terminal: King's Cross)

Twenty-one miles from the center of London, Hatfield lies on the old "Great North Road" south of Welwyn. It is an ancient market town that has developed into a thriving city of 45,000 people. Hatfield House, a splendid Jacobean mansion, stands in a beautiful park in the old part of town. In the West Gardens of the park is Hatfield Palace, where Elizabeth I spent her childhood and where she received the news that she had succeeded her half-sister Mary to the throne.

HEMEL HEMPSTEAD (London terminal: Euston)

Hemel Hempstead is one of the most rapidly expanding towns in western Hertfordshire with a population now numbering 70,000. The last 20 years have witnessed the building of many roads and shops and thousands of new homes. There is a fine new Town Centre linking the old and new shopping centers, and trains into the capital are fast and frequent. Despite the bustling atmosphere of the city, however, the surrounding countryside, in the valleys of the Gale and Bulbourne rivers, is serene and idyllic.

ALDBURY: An exceptionally charming village, one mile east of Tring (see below).

*BERKHAMSTED: Ruins of the castle where Edgar Atheling surrendered to William the Conqueror in 1066. Three miles north is Ashridge Park, where Princess Elizabeth (later Elizabeth I) was arrested at the command of her half-sister, Queen Mary.

*KING'S LANGLEY: Burial place of Edmund de Langley (Duke of York and brother of Richard II) and his wife, Isabella of Castile.

*TRING: A few miles to the northwest of Berkhamsted, seat of the Rothschild family.

HERTFORD (London terminals: Liverpool Street for Hertford East, King's Cross and Broad Street for Hertford North)

Only 24 miles due north of London's center, Hertford somehow retains the appearance of an ancient rural market town. It borders the River Lea and is surrounded by meadows and woodland. Hertford is the site of Christ's Hospital School and of Hertford Castle, one of Elizabeth I's favorite residences.

HODDESDON: A splendid Georgian High Street with good houses and a fine old inn (The Golden Lion).

*WARE: Attractive homes on the River Lea, and many fine old buildings. One of the vicars of the local church was Charles Chauncey, who later became president of Harvard College.

HITCHIN   (London terminal: King's Cross)

Hitchin lies at the base of the Chiltern Hills in the Hiz River valley. It is a beautiful town, and beautifully placed in a bowllike area ringed with hills. Thanks to the natural defenses of its topography, its ancient buildings are well preserved. The 35-mile trip into London takes only 39 minutes by British Rail.

*STEVENAGE: One of the new "satellite" towns—32 miles into London in 29 minutes. Three miles south of Stevenage is Knebworth, a Tudor mansion built in 1492, ancestral home of the Bulwer-Lyttons.

LETCHWORTH   (London terminal: King's Cross)

Letchworth is one of those rare sights in England—a twentieth-century city. Founded in 1903, it was laid out as a "garden city" and is therefore a pleasant and conveniently arranged town. Of course, as in all areas of England, some of the old is present: A hotel (Letchworth Hall) was a Jacobean manor house. Local industries employ many of Letchworth's 31,000 people, and fast commuter trains provide excellent service for others.

*BALDOCK: An ancient town of 6300 inhabitants, founded by the Templars and situated at a crossing of the Icknield Way.

RICKMANSWORTH   (London terminal: Baker Street)

Near the confluence of three rivers (the Gade, the Chess, and the Golne), the marshy area around Rickmansworth is famous for its watercress. The recorded history of the town itself goes back several centuries before the Domesday Book, but Stone Age artifacts have been found in the gravel pits. Rickmansworth is primarily a residential center, with good shops and schools and excellent transportation into London.

*CHORLEYWOOD: An elite suburb, almost entirely residential, which has been the home of many celebrities.

ROYSTON   (London terminal: King's Cross)

In northern Hertfordshire at the Cambridgeshire border, Royston has recently become a commuter town (for everyone except some hooded birds called Royston crows who, the townsfolk will tell you, have steadfastly refused to fly south of the city). Royston is in the midst of an agricultural area and has two interesting street markets where farmers from outlying areas bring their poultry and produce. Educational facilities are good, and modern houses are appearing on the scene.

*ASHWELL: Picturesque main street with good houses, one of which is the Town House (now a museum); fourteenth-century church with fine tapestries by a local craftsman.

BUNTINGFORD: Long, attractive street of old houses, and a seventeenth-century church.

ST. ALBANS   (London terminal: St. Pancras)

St. Albans is a cathedral city on the River Ver with a long and stormy history. Two thousand years ago, it was the capital of the Belgic King Tasciovanus, then later became a Roman stronghold (Verulamium). In A.D. 61, Boadicea, a British tribal queen, became so incensed at the public indignities dealt her and her daughters by the Romans (she was publicly flogged and her daughters were made to submit to the lust of the Romans' slaves) that she destroyed London and its neighboring towns, including St. Albans; but the Romans rebuilt the cities during the next century, and their remarkable theatre and "hypocaust" (heating system) at St. Albans may be seen today. St. Albans derives its name from England's first Christian martyr, who was beheaded here in A.D. 303 for offering refuge to the priest who had converted him. Modern housing is available in St. Albans; though, because of the city's proximity to London, prices are somewhat higher than in the more northerly towns of Hertfordshire.

LONDON COLNEY: Site of Salisbury Hall, a moated manor house built by Henry VIII and remodeled by Charles II for Nell Gwynn. Churchill spent a part of his childhood here.

WELWYN and WELWYN GARDEN CITY   (London terminal: King's Cross)

Welwyn (pronounced "Wellin") and its satellite town, Welwyn Garden City, have separate railway stations, although they are only a few miles apart. The older Welwyn is a small rural town, close to Ayot St. Lawrence (George Bernard Shaw's home) and to the interesting Lullingstone Silk Farm. The satellite town is a well-planned, attractively laid-out residential center. Both towns have quick and easy access to London.

THE SOUTH EAST

Kent

ASHFORD (London terminals: Charing Cross, Cannon Street)

New industries are springing up in east-central Kent, though agriculture and the cattle market are still important businesses in Ashford. Many new homes are being built, and older homes are available at still-reasonable prices. All along the eastern coast of Kent, in fact, real estate prices are not as inflated as in western Kent or the other counties adjacent to London. Ashford itself is only an hour from the capital; but the coastal towns east of Ashford (*e.g.*, Broadstairs, Deal, Ramsgate, Margate, and Dover), though they have a high rate of sunshine and are excellent vacation spots, are too far for daily commuting.

AYLESFORD (London terminals: Charing Cross, Cannon Street)

Aylesford, one of Kent's loveliest villages, with ancient cottages lining the banks of the Medway, is a few miles north of Maidstone on the road to Rochester. Nearby Allington Castle, a thirteenth-century building with Tudor additions, was the home of Sir Thomas Wyatt, the poet; and it was from here that the younger Sir Thomas set out on his fateful journey to protest Queen Mary's marriage to Philip of Spain. The castle is now a Carmelite retreat.

BOROUGH GREEN (See **WROTHAM/BOROUGH GREEN**)

CHATHAM (London terminals: Charing Cross, Cannon Street, Victoria)

Chatham is one of the three Medway towns, so called because all are grouped within a few miles of each other at the mouth of the Medway River. Chatham's educational facilities are excellent: There are many primary and secondary schools, a Medway College of Technology, the Chatham Girls' Grammar School (between Chatham and Gillingham), and a girls' technical high school (between Chatham and Rochester). The biennial Medway Arts Festival is held here. Chatham has been a naval base since the time of Henry VIII. Of particular interest are the Sir John Hawkins Hospital (founded in 1596) and the Royal Navy Dockyard. Modern housing is available in all the Medway towns.

DARTFORD (London terminals: Charing Cross, Cannon Street, Blackfriars)

Dartford, 16 miles south of London's center, is a busy town on the River Darent. Since it is an important British Rail junction, it is ideally situated for commuters. This is an industrial town with engineering and chemical works and it offers fine educational opportunities, including two colleges of higher education. Dartford has two historic inns and a church with a Norman tower.

*SUTTON-AT-HONE: House of St. John's Jerusalem (twelfth to eighteenth centuries).

EAST MALLING/WEST MALLING   (London terminals: Blackfriars, Victoria)

East and West Malling, both pleasant villages, lie two miles apart to the northwest of Maidstone and are joined by an old road on which there is an attractive park where Clare House (built in 1793) stands. East Malling has a church dating from the fourteenth century; West Malling is a newer (eighteenth-century) village but is the site of St. Leonard's Tower (c. 1100) and of a Benedictine abbey founded by Bishop Gundulf of Rochester in 1090. Nearby Offham has the only quintain on the green (a device used in the sport of tilting) in England.

EDENBRIDGE   (London terminals: London Bridge, Victoria)

Edenbridge is a small, attractive town in western Kent at the Surrey border. It is built on the banks of the Eden River, and its main street, with buildings spanning four historic centuries (fifteenth to nineteenth), is particularly interesting. Edenbridge is about three miles upstream from Hever Castle.

EYNSFORD   (London terminals: Blackfriars, Victoria)

Eynsford is in western Kent, about midway between Sevenoaks and Dartford. A stone bridge across the Darent at this point leads to Lullingstone Roman Villa, one of the most exciting archaeological finds in England, with mosaic pavements and a painted wall plaster revealing that these fourth-century settlers were Christians. A bit farther on is Lullingstone Castle, home of the Hart Dyke family since 1500; it was here that the first game of lawn tennis (1873) was played.

FAVERSHAM   (London terminals: Cannon Street, Victoria)

Faversham, an historic town of about 15,000 inhabitants, is ideally situated in northeast Kent within easy commuting distance of London and also close to the coast. The countryside is dotted with oasthouses and hop gardens, and local buses operate among the neighboring towns and villages. There is a quaint Guildhall in the market place, as well as a very ancient parish church, a grammar school dating from 1567, and a tastefully restored sixteenth-century thoroughfare (Abbey Street).

*TEYNHAM: Across the Swale from the Isle of Sheppey; location of Kent's first cherry and apple orchards.

GILLINGHAM (London terminals: Charing Cross, Cannon Street, Victoria)

Gillingham (with the G sounded like J) is one of the three Medway towns (Chatham, Gillingham, Rochester—combined population 200,-000). It is an industrial town (paper mills) and has exceptionally fine educational facilities: 28 primary and 7 secondary modern schools; a technical high school for boys; and, shared with Chatham, the Girls' Grammar School on the boundary between the two towns. Gillingham has a particularly fine perpendicular church with a Norman font.

GRAVESEND (London terminals: Charing Cross, Cannon Street)

Gravesend, at the mouth of the Thames, is the pilot station for vessels using the Port of London, and its dockside inns and frame houses give it the weatherbeaten appearance of a typical seaport. The views of the Thames from the Gravesend piers are magnificent. Leonard Calvert, founder of the State of Maryland, sailed from here when he left for America—as did John and Charles Wesley and the Quaker George Fox. Pocahontas is buried at Gravesend. The city's population is now about 55,000. There are good schools and good shopping facilities, and modern homes are available.

*NORTHFLEET: Fourteenth-century church on a bluff.

GREENHITHE (London terminals: Charing Cross, Cannon Street)

Greenhithe, between Dartford and Gravesend, on the south bank of the Thames, was Sir John Franklin's port of departure when he left England in 1845 for an expedition to the polar regions, where he and his crew perished in 1847. Greenhithe's Ingress Abbey, built originally in 1772 and later enlarged with stones from the old London Bridge, is now a training school for Merchant Navy cadets. The town has a quaint and interesting waterfront.

GROOMBRIDGE (London terminals: London Bridge, Victoria)

Groombridge, to the west of Royal Tunbridge Wells, is a lovely village lying partly in Kent and partly in Sussex. It has an enchanting village green surrounded by charming old houses and cottages, a chapel dating from 1625, and an ancient moated mansion (Groombridge Place) set amid lovely gardens.

HEADCORN (London terminals: Charing Cross, Cannon Street)

Headcorn is important because of its central Kent location and its proximity to a number of especially interesting surrounding towns, most of which are not on a main line to London. Headcorn itself has some splendid old timbered houses. Good and reasonably priced homes are available in the area.

BENENDEN: Elizabethan-style building housing a famous public school for girls.
BIDDENDEN: Charming main street.
CRANBROOK: Steep High Street; largest working windmill in England; perpendicular church; 1576 grammar school.
HIGH HALDEN: Splendid timber belfry.
SISSINGHURST: Castle with beautiful gardens.
SUTTON VALENCE: Boys' public school (1578).
TENTERDEN: Lovely village, broad High Street, perpendicular tower.

HEVER   (London terminals: London Bridge, Victoria)

Hever is one of the most charming of England's small villages. It is dominated by Hever Castle, home of Ann Boleyn before her marriage to Henry VIII. The tomb of Ann's father, Sir Thomas Boleyn, is in the ancient church; and the inn—though you would think care would be taken to avoid the name here, of all places—is known as "The Henry VIII."

MAIDSTONE   (London terminals: Charing Cross, Cannon Street, Victoria, Blackfriars)

Maidstone, the county town of Kent, lies midway between London and the East Coast on both sides of the River Medway. It is a bustling, congested rail and road center with paper mills and breweries and topnotch shopping facilities, set in the midst of an agricultural area characterized by oasthouses and hop gardens. To preserve the appeal of its older and more historic neighborhoods, certain streets in the vicinity of High Street have been closed to traffic. Interesting landmarks include a fourteenth-century church (All Saints); a sixteenth-century manor house (Chillington); the eighteenth-century Town Hall; the fourteenth-century Tithe Barn; and, nearby, Boughton Monchelsea Place, a fine Elizabethan manor house with battlements and splendid views over the Weald of Kent.

MEOPHAM   (London terminals: Blackfriars, Victoria)

Meopham (pronounced "Meppam") is a village of 7000 people, many of whom are commuters living in modern housing developments. It is situated halfway between Gravesend and Wrotham, just west of the Medway towns. Meopham is famous for its cricket matches (the first of which was a match against Chatham in 1778) and for its cricket green, which is reputed to be the best kept in the county. There is a village school for children of primary school age; older children attend secondary schools in Hoo, Gravesend, and the Medway towns.

ORPINGTON   (London terminals: Charing Cross, Cannon Street, Victoria, Blackfriars)

Orpington is just outside London on the Kent border. Its beautiful old homes and its proximity to the capital make it an expensive residential area.

PENSHURST   (London terminals: Charing Cross, Cannon Street)

Penshurst is a delightful Tudor village, seven miles northwest of Royal Tunbridge Wells. The town is dominated by Penshurst Place, a fourteenth-century mansion that has belonged to the Sidney family since 1552. The most striking feature of the house is its hall—64 feet long with an open timber roof and a central hearth. Penshurst Place has been noted for its gracious hospitality for centuries and has been praised by many visiting poets, the first of whom was Ben Jonson.

ROCHESTER   (London terminals: Charing Cross, Cannon Street, Victoria, Blackfriars)

Rochester is the oldest and most interesting, historically, of the three Medway towns (Chatham, Gillingham, Rochester). The Romans called it Durobrivae; the Saxons called it Hroffeceaster. It has been an Episcopal See since the early seventh century. Rochester's cathedral, dating from the twelfth to fourteenth centuries, is one of England's most renowned; and the twelfth-century Castle Keep, with walls 12 feet thick, is regarded as one of the finest examples of Norman architecture in England. Dickens's novels lend a special flavor to many Rochester buildings: Restoration House, a Tudor mansion, was the Satis House of *Great Expectations;* Eastgate House, now a museum, was the Nuns' House of *Edwin Drood;* the gabled Tudor building across from the museum was occupied by Uncle Pumblechook in *Great Expectations* and also by Mr. Sapsea in *Edwin Drood;* and the College Gate was Jasper's Gatehouse in *Edwin Drood.* Rochester is an excellent shopping center, and modern housing is available.

STROOD: A suburb of Rochester, across the Medway.

ROYAL TUNBRIDGE WELLS   (London terminals: Charing Cross, Cannon Street)

Royal Tunbridge Wells (the "Royal" is generally omitted in conversation) is one of England's loveliest towns. It is situated in southwest Kent at the Sussex border and is about halfway, in point of train time, between London and the coast. For 350 years royalty and other famous and fashionable people have walked its world-renowned promenade, "The Pantiles," to sample its medicinal waters and enjoy its warm sunshine. Today, Tunbridge Wells is still a popular resort and a stylish retreat for wealthy retirees. (Anyone who thinks Americans have a monopoly on deluxe living should read the newspaper notices of estate duties levied on those who have left Tunbridge Wells for something still better.) The community has a well-balanced program of opera, ballet, drama, and solo recitals, and a fine resident orchestra that performs monthly during the winter.

BRENCHLEY: Lovely row of Tudor cottages.
BURWASH: Rudyard Kipling's home.
CHIDDINGSTONE: Beautiful village; name comes from the Chiding Stone where the townsfolk reprimanded women whose noisy gossip displeased their neighbors.
GOUDHURST: Fifteenth-century church, splendid views of the Weald of Kent.
MAYFIELD (in Sussex): Old convent and school, at one time a palace of the Archbishops of Canterbury.
ROTHERFIELD (in Sussex): Twelfth-century church on a 600-ft. hill.
SPELDHURST: Thirteenth-century inn ("The George and the Dragon").

SEVENOAKS   (London terminals: Charing Cross, Cannon Street)

Sevenoaks, a town of 18,000 inhabitants just 25 miles from the center of London, is both pleasant and expensive. Its elegance is enhanced by the stately baronial mansion Knole, built in the fifteenth century by Archbishop Bourchier, home of the Sackville family, and now owned by the National Trust. Sevenoaks has some fine seventeenth-century houses, a thirteenth-century church, and the oldest cricket ground in England.

IGHTAM: Picturesque village with a moated manor.
*OTFORD: Ruins of a sixteenth-century manor house that belonged to the Archbishops of Canterbury.
*SHOREHAM: Late perpendicular church.
WESTERHAM: Former home of Sir Winston Churchill.

SITTINGBOURNE   (London terminals: Cannon Street, Victoria)

Sittingbourne, an industrial town (paper, brick, cement), adjoins the ancient borough of Milton Regis in north central Kent. London is easily accessible, as are the better shopping areas of Kent—and now Sittingbourne is to have its own large shopping center. Modern housing is available at reasonable prices.

TONBRIDGE   (London terminals: Charing Cross, Cannon Street)

Tonbridge, a market town on the Medway with a population of 31,000, lies halfway between London and the coast. In addition to its ancient landmarks (Chequers Inn, fifteenth century; a Norman castle; Tonbridge School [1553], where Jane Austen's father taught), there are parks and pleasure gardens, good shops, modern housing developments, and ample opportunities for boating and other water sports.

WEST MALLING   (See **EAST MALLING**)

WROTHAM/BOROUGH GREEN (London terminal: Victoria)

The same railway station serves both these charming villages. Wrotham (pronounced "Rootam") has an interesting fourteenth-century church. Nearby is Oldbury, a large hill fort dating from the first century A.D.

Sussex

BILLINGSHURST (London terminals: London Bridge, Victoria)

Billingshurst, in the north-central part of West Sussex, has been gaining popularity as a residential area with modern housing and a rapidly developing shopping center. Its present population numbers 3000. In addition to its name, which probably derives from that of a Saxon tribe (the Billings), its ties with the past include a sixteenth-century half-timbered inn and an Early English and perpendicular church.

BRIGHTON (London terminals: London Bridge, Victoria)

Brighton is the largest and liveliest resort on England's coast. Since the days of George IV, for whom the extravagant pavilion—an elaborate Indo-China-Moorish out-of-context-in-England atrocity—was built, Brighton has swung and glittered with night life. To many people, however, Brighton's chief attractions are not its promenades and piers, its race courses, skating rinks, cinemas, and waxwork exhibitions—but its old quarter, with narrow, tortuous alleys ("The Lanes") where smart tearooms and fascinating antique shops nestle cozily among seventeenth-century cottages.

*HOVE: Regency-style houses; King Alfred Sports Centre (bowling, golf, swimming)

BURGESS HILL (London terminals: London Bridge, Victoria)

Burgess Hill, 11 miles north of Brighton in south-central Sussex, is a growing residential town surrounded by rolling, wooded, Wealden countryside. There are a number of major industries here, including a large brick and tile works and, to the southwest, an "industrial estate" employing 2000 people in 40 factories.

*HASSOCKS: Another developing residential town.

CRAWLEY (London terminals: London Bridge, Victoria)

Conveniently situated in the northeast corner of West Sussex, on the London-Brighton road, Crawley has been designated as one of those areas that may be permitted to expand into one of England's "new towns." The area so designated is only 3½ miles across, so that no part of the city will ever be far from open country. Crawley's expansion is evidenced mainly in the growing number of self-contained (schools, shops) residential areas. Population is now approximately 66,000, and development is two-thirds complete.

EAST GRINSTEAD   (London terminals: London Bridge, Victoria)

East Grinstead lies just inside the Sussex border at the southeast tip of Surrey. An ancient town, inhabited by Anglo-Saxons almost a thousand years ago, it is high above sea level at the edge of a forest. This is a quietly pleasant town, with timbered houses in the High Street. Shops and schools are adequate for a population of 16,000. East Grinstead's most notable landmark is Sackville College, a Jacobean almshouse built in 1619.

GROOMBRIDGE   (See Kent County)

HAYWARD'S HEATH   (London terminals: London Bridge, Victoria)

Hayward's Heath, in central Sussex on the London-Brighton railway, has become one of the most popular residential areas within commuting distance of the capital. There are excellent schools, fine shops, and several outstanding recreational facilities. Modern housing is available.

HORSHAM   (London terminals: London Bridge, Victoria, Waterloo)

In the northern part of West Sussex, due south of Dorking in Surrey and only 38 miles from London, Horsham is very popular with commuters. This is a town that has something of interest to everyone—a skillful blend of the old and the new. In West Street there are many interesting old houses, a museum with stocks and whipping post, and an Early English church with a shingled spire. In other parts of town, modern houses are being built and good shops abound. The 56-acre park has a swimming pool, and there are adequate facilities for all types of outdoor activities. Horsham has many schools, including an Evening Institute and an Art School, and two miles away is Christ's Hospital—a widely renowned school (once attended by Lamb and Coleridge) where the students still wear the traditional blue gowns, knee breeches, and yellow stockings. Sussex roofs are made of the easily split Horsham stone.

LEWES   (London terminals: London Bridge, Victoria)

Lewes, a picturesque and ancient town on the banks of the River Ouse, is one of the most historically important towns in Britain. A Norman castle still stands on a hill not far from its center; William de Warenne built a priory here in 1075 that was destroyed five centuries later by Thomas Cromwell; Henry III built the town walls and then, despite them, was defeated here in 1264 by Simon de Montfort in the Battle of Lewes; 17 Protestants were burned at the stake, near the present town hall, between 1555 and 1557; Anne of Cleves's house (1599) is here; the timbered Barbican house, now a museum, has stood here since 1334; John Evelyn, the diarist, went to grammar school here; Tom Paine ("These are the times that try men's souls") lived in Bull House opposite Shelley's Hotel; John Harvard, founder of Harvard University, was married at South Malling Church, one mile to the north; Rudyard Kipling lived in nearby Burwash; and the discovery, in 1605, of the despicable conspirator, Guy Fawkes, in a cache of gunpowder kegs below the House of Lords is still celebrated here every November 5 with great enthusiasm. A short distance away are Firle Place (a handsome Georgian mansion with fine paintings and furniture and a splendid collection of Meissen china) and Glynde Place (a beautiful flint and brick Tudor house with interesting portraits and pottery).

PULBOROUGH   (London terminals: London Bridge, Victoria)

Pulborough, a charming village of 2800 inhabitants in the Arun River valley of West Sussex, is convenient both to London and to the coast. It is noted for its fine golf course. Interesting landmarks include a large Early English and perpendicular church and, three miles to the east at West Chiltington, a twelfth-century church, stocks, and a whipping post.

PETWORTH: Narrow streets, picturesque houses.

SHOREHAM-BY-SEA   (London terminals: London Bridge, Victoria)

Shoreham-by-Sea is on the Sussex coast, a few miles to the west of Brighton. Although it is still important as a port, it is better known today as a resort town. New homes, detached and semidetached, are available at moderate prices. It was from here that Charles II made his escape to France in 1651.

Surrey

ASHTEAD   (London terminals: London Bridge, Victoria, Waterloo)

Ashtead is not far from London and is near the Epsom Downs, where horse-racing enthusiasts can enjoy the Derby and the Oaks in May or June. There is a church with a stained-glass window made in Belgium c. 1500; and it was here that George MacDonald, author of many novels and poems dealing with Scotland and Scottish people, died in 1905.

BAGSHOT   (London terminal: Waterloo)

Bagshot is a rural district comprising about 16,000 acres in northwest Surrey adjacent to Berkshire. Many of the acres are designated as common land, and many are used for golf courses and for the propagation of trees and shrubs. Bagshot is convenient for commuters because of the excellent trains that pass through the district; and there are new modern housing developments with centrally heated homes.

BYFLEET   (London terminal: Waterloo)

Byfleet is in northwest Surrey and is a popular residential area because of its fast trains (34 minutes) to London. The combined facilities of Byfleet and its neighbors (Woking, Weybridge, Chertsey, and Esher) make for excellent educational and recreational opportunities and for shopping convenience. Modern housing is available.

CAMBERLEY   (London terminal: Waterloo)

Camberley, home of the Royal Military Academy, Sandhurst, is situated in the northwest corner of Surrey near the Hampshire and Berkshire borders. The surrounding country is rolling heathland and pine woodland. New homes are available but are, on the whole, rather luxurious "executive-type" homes and priced accordingly. The town has a new library, a civic center for entertainments, modern shops, and an outdoor swimming pool.

CHERTSEY   (London terminal: Waterloo)

Chertsey, one of the Thames River towns in northwest Surrey, stands on the site of a famous Benedictine abbey built in the seventh century and rebuilt in 1110. The abbey is almost totally gone now, but its highly prized floor tiles have found their way into a number of other English churches. There is a Chertsey Bridge built between 1780 and 1785, and a Chertsey Lock.

CHESSINGTON   (London terminal: Waterloo)

Chessington is a London suburb, located on the edge of the metropolis. Its amusement park and zoo provide popular weekend activities for Londoners.

CHILWORTH   (London terminal: Waterloo)

Chilworth is a very old settlement thought to have been the scene of religious rites many years before Christianity was introduced into England. In the early Middle Ages, the Pilgrims built a chapel on the hilltop, and in the nineteenth century the chapel was replaced by the church of St. Martha-on-the-Hill, which still dominates this charming village.

*ALBURY: A beauty spot near lovely Newlands Corner and the Silent Pool.

CHIPSTEAD   (London terminal: London Bridge)

Although Chipstead is on the edge of London, it has managed to retain its rural character, thus providing, within a few minutes' travel, a rather startling change of atmosphere from bustling metropolis to quiet country calm. There is a church dating from the twelfth century.

CLANDON, EAST *and* **WEST**

EFFINGHAM

HORSLEY, EAST *and* **WEST**   (London terminal: Waterloo)

Commuters have begun to discover the antiquated charm of a group of ancient settlements, all with interesting churches, in the vicinity of Guildford. The Clandons, the Horsleys, and Effingham are among these. Clandon Park boasts a splendid manor built by Giacomo Leoni c. 1733, redecorated by John Fowler in 1970, and containing the magnificent Gubbay collection of china and furniture. West Horsley is interesting historically because of its association with the Raleigh family—though the probability that Sir Walter's head is buried here is a rather questionable asset.

OCKHAM: Home of Richard ("Stone walls do not a prison make") Lovelace. RIPLEY: Where two historic coaching inns added color to a lively past.

CROYDON   (London terminals: London Bridge and Victoria)

Croydon is sometimes referred to as being in Surrey but is actually a London borough, only 15 minutes from the heart of the city. It is a peculiar mixture of ancient and modern, and has for the commuter every advantage in the way of shopping facilities, modern amenities, educational establishments (including the well-known Whitgift School and a modern technical college), theatre, and sports.

DORKING   (London terminals: London Bridge, Victoria, Waterloo)

Dorking is a fine old market town of about 23,000 people in central Surrey. It is a favorite spot for walking tours because of the wealth of historic and beautiful sites nearby: Polesden Lacey, a great mansion, once the home of Sheridan, the dramatist, and honeymoon place of George VI and the now Queen Mother, Elizabeth, set in 900 acres of beautiful grounds; Leith Hill, the highest point in southeast England (965 feet), from which—on a clear day—one can see St. Paul's in London; Ranmore Common, with extraordinary views; and 750 acres of National Trust Woodlands famed for its rhododendrons and bluebells.

ABINGER: Old stocks on the green; manor house with Jacobean porch.

EFFINGHAM   (See **CLANDON**)

EGHAM   (London terminal: Waterloo)

Egham is at the Berkshire border, just south of Windsor. Near here is the Savill Garden, where many delightful hours can be spent on the woodland walks among magnificent displays of camellias and rhododendrons and on the banks of the streams and ponds where lilies and daffodils grow in profusion. It was on an island in the Thames, near Egham, that King John in 1215 signed Magna Carta. There is a nineteenth-century church that contains some unusual monuments of Sir John Denham—poet, born in Ireland, educated in England, self-exiled in France because of his connection with the secret service of Charles I, died in London—and of his two wives.

EPSOM   (London terminals: London Bridge, Victoria, Waterloo)

The city of Epsom (72,000 inhabitants) is just a mile and a half from Epsom Downs (see Ashtead). It was at Epsom's mineral springs that Epsom salts—now, fortunately, out of fashion—originated in 1618. Epsom has an interesting parish church; a fine mansion (Durdans) once occupied by the fifth Earl of Rosebery, a former Prime Minister; and a beautiful park.

ESHER   (London terminal: Waterloo)

Esher is in north-central Surrey, within easy reach of London. It is a pleasant town with parks and an attractive and broad High Street, and is the site of Esher Place (a home built in 1477 and occupied by Cardinal Wolsey), of which only the gatehouse, known as Wolsey's Tower, remains standing. Nearby is Claremont, a girls' school housed in a mansion built in 1768–72 by the famous architect, Capability Brown, and occupied at various times by Princess Charlotte and Leopold I of Belgium (her husband), Louis-Phillippe, and the Duchess of Albany.

FARNHAM   (London terminal: Waterloo)

Farnham, on the River Wey, is Surrey's westernmost town, just a few miles from the Hampshire border. It has about 32,000 inhabitants and is surrounded by a number of pleasant small villages. Although Farnham is now an important shopping center, it is still a town of great historic interest with splendid Georgian homes and a castle that has belonged to the Bishops of Winchester since 688. In Vernon House, now occupied by the library, Charles I spent an unhappy night on his way from the Isle of Wight to the scaffold in London. The ruins of the earliest Cistercian house in England, Waverly Abbey (from which Sir Walter Scott probably took the title of his first novel), lie on the Godalming Road two miles to the southeast of Farnham.

SEALE: A pleasant village, through which runs the Pilgrims' Way of Chaucer's *Canterbury Tales*.

TILFORD: A pretty town on the upper Wey.

GODALMING   (London terminal: Waterloo)

Godalming, a very old and beautiful town with a population of about 19,000, is in southwest Surrey. It was at one time the center of Surrey's wool industry, and although some of the old buildings have been replaced by new shops and supermarkets, the town retains its ancient character with narrow streets, a museum that was the Town Hall in the eighteenth century, a Norman and thirteenth-century church (Sts. Peter and Paul), and many half-timbered and decorated brick houses dating from the seventeenth century. Godalming was the birthplace of Aldous Huxley and the home of General Oglethorpe, who founded the State of Georgia. Just north of Godalming is Charterhouse School, among whose alumni are Steele, Addison, Wesley, Thackeray, Vaughn Williams, Roger Williams of Rhode Island, and many other eminent men.

BRAMLEY and WONERSH: Ancient settlements, now modern residential centers popular with commuters.
HASCOMBE: Panoramic views of the South Downs.
PUTTENHAM: Excellent golf course.
*WITLEY: Site of King Edward's School (1553).

GOMSHALL and SHERE   (London terminal: Waterloo)

Gomshall and Shere lie to the southeast of Guildford (below) in the Tillingbourne Valley. Shere, especially, is renowned for the beauty of its cottages, its narrow streets, and its riverbanks lined with willow trees. One cottage (Tillingbourne Cottage) has an unusual garden designed in curved patterns, open by appointment in June and July. Shoppers will enjoy visiting the Gomshall Potteries, open weekdays from 10:00 to 6:00.

GUILDFORD   (London terminal: Waterloo)

Guildford is ideally situated in the center of the most beautiful part of Surrey and is the perfect place in which to set up headquarters while exploring the rest of the county. It is a town of sufficient size (55,000 people) to provide good hotel accommodations and excellent train and bus service into the capital, and its shopping facilities are second only to London's; yet the blending of new buildings with old has been so skillfully carried out that the town retains its historic quaintness. The granite-paved High Street, beginning at the Town Bridge over the River Wey and climbing upward past the seventeenth-century Guildhall with its great protruding clock, is justly acclaimed as one of England's most beautiful thoroughfares. It has been said that Guildford's main "industry" is education: There are schools of all levels, including a technical college; a College of Law; a school of art; the Royal Grammar School (for boys), which was founded in the early sixteenth century; and the University of Surrey. Guildford has a fine professional symphony orchestra (the Guildford Philharmonic), which has recorded the works of Arnold Bax, Chopin, Liszt, and Weber; a Repertory Theatre Company; a Philharmonic Choir; and a young people's choir (The Proteus) which has concertized in Holland and Germany. Guildford's Civic Hall is noted for its acoustics; its Cathedral of the Holy Spirit, the only entirely new Anglican cathedral to be built since the Reformation, is already famous for its skillful blend of twentieth-century architecture with traditional Gothic lines; and its new indoor Sports Centre, which houses three swimming pools, four squash courts, and a comparable number of other recreational facilities, is acclaimed as the finest in England. There are many excellent old Georgian houses and other buildings of historic interest, including St. Nicholas Church; the remains of Guildford Castle; the Guildhall; and, nearby, the Elizabethan Losely House, which is occupied by the family whose ancestors built it in 1562.

COMPTON: Double-chanceled Norman church (St. Nicholas); home town of G. F. Watts, the artist.
SHAMLEY GREEN: Cricket green in a typically English village.
WISLEY: Royal Horticultural Society gardens.

HASLEMERE   (London terminal: Waterloo)

Haslemere is an old and pleasant town situated in the southwest corner of Surrey, very near the Sussex and Hampshire borders. The surrounding area, owned by the National Trust, is often referred to as the "English Switzerland" because of the beauty of its hills and valleys and pine woods. Its population, already more than 13,000, is growing; and new housing developments are in evidence. Shops, schools, churches, transportation to and from London, and recreational facilities are all excellent.

ALFOLD and DUNSFOLD: Half-timbered dwellings of charm and antiquity.
CHIDDINGFOLD: A famous glass-making town from the thirteenth to sixteenth centuries; now the place where the beautiful English walking canes are made. Site of Le Crowne, oldest licensed inn in Surrey (1542).

HORSLEY   (See **CLANDON**)

KINGSTON-UPON-THAMES   (London terminal: Waterloo)

Kingston, a very ancient market town, is the starting point for the popular steamer journey northwest to Oxford (a trip that takes 2½ days). Its principal landmark is Hampton Court, three miles upstream, the Royal Palace that Cardinal Wolsey "gave" to Henry VIII. Rowing regattas are held at Kingston in July and August.

LEATHERHEAD   (London terminals: London Bridge, Victoria, Waterloo)

Leatherhead, on the Mole River, is a town of approximately 40,000 inhabitants in north-central Surrey, about midway between Epsom and Dorking. The surrounding countryside is magnificent, and there are several very old bridges crossing the river and a number of quaint houses and inns. Leatherhead is one of several towns that claim to be the "Highbury" in Jane Austen's *Emma;* but there is no question about its being the site of the old Kingston House, where John Wesley preached his last sermon. There are excellent shops and schools (including St. John's, a well-known boys' school), and excellent bus service into the town center for those who choose to live in the surrounding villages.

LINGFIELD   (London terminals: London Bridge and Victoria)

Lingfield is in the eastern part of Surrey, near the Kent border. Its church was rebuilt in the fifteenth century and contains fine brasses, carved stalls and misericords designed for use by monks who, because of having been bled for reasons of health, required special dispensations of food and drink.

MILFORD   (London terminal: Waterloo)

Milford is situated in southwest Surrey, about equidistant from the Hampshire and Sussex borders. It has some interesting restorations, notably a convent refectory and dovecot. The Milford and Witley commons comprise approximately 375 acres of National Trust property.

CHURT: Small settlement set among mounds known as "Devil's Jumps."
DOCKENFIELD: Near ancient royal hunting grounds.
ELSTEAD: Fifteenth-century stone bridge across the River Wey.
FRENSHAM: Noted for its rolling commons and its church with (according to legend) a witches' cauldron.
HAMBLEDON: Heavily wooded countryside, much of which is owned by the National Trust.
PEPERHAROW: A very ancient and tiny village; 600-year-old yew trees in the church grounds.
SHACKLEFORD: Old stone walls and charming cottages.
THURSLEY: A long main street lined with attractive houses.

OCKLEY   (London terminals: London Bridge and Waterloo)

Ockley is a small village in south-central Surrey, about midway between London's Victoria Station and the Sussex coast. It was at Ockley that Ethelwulf of Wessex, who succeeded his father to the throne of England in 858 and whose youngest son was Alfred the Great, slaughtered the Danes after they burned Canterbury and London.

CRANLEIGH: Fossilized winkle shells tell the story of a prehistoric fresh-water lake—now the site of Cranleigh's famous cricket grounds.

REDHILL and **REIGATE**   (London terminals: London Bridge, Victoria)

Redhill and Reigate are only two miles apart and have a combined population of almost 60,000. Redhill is an important railroad junction and is noted for its Royal Earlswood Hospital Museum. Reigate is important historically for its Reigate Priory, built on the site of a thirteenth-century Augustinian foundation, and its Mary Magdalen parish church with nave pillars dating back to c. 1200 and chancel under which Lord Howard of Effingham, conqueror of the Spanish Armada, is buried. The two towns are situated at the foot of the chalk downs amid some of the best scenery in Surrey and offer easy access to London (20 miles north) and Brighton (30 miles south). There are new housing developments with centrally heated homes, and excellent day schools and evening institutes.

*CATERHAM: Modern housing developments.

SHALFORD   (London terminal: Waterloo)

To the south of Guildford, on the River Tillingbourne, lies Shalford, an ancient and lovely hamlet with a church, a village green, old cottages, an eighteenth-century water mill, and stocks. Shalford claims to have been John Bunyan's home town.

SHEPPERTON   (London terminal: Waterloo)

Cruising on the Thames, past meadows and woodlands, lawns and gardens sloping to the water's edge, fine country estates and tiny bungalows, is a favorite pastime in England. There are 31 locks between Kingston and Oxford; and Shepperton Lock, at the northern edge of Surrey, is one of them. Nine miles from the Lock, and situated on a channel where the river flows quietly and pleasantly, is the attractive village center of Shepperton, dating from the seventeenth century.

SHERE   (See **GOMSHALL**)

SURBITON   (London terminal: Waterloo)

Surbiton is a London "dormitory," 16 miles from Waterloo Station. It is close to the market town of Kingston-upon-Thames and within easy reach of Hampton Court. There are new, attractive (and expensive) town houses in Georgian style, with three storeys, four or five bedrooms, and the most up-to-date conveniences.

VIRGINIA WATER   (London terminal: Waterloo)

Virginia Water lies just within the northwest border of Surrey. Its artificial lake, designed by Paul Sandby for the Duke of Cumberland in 1746, is the southern boundary of Windsor Great Park. Its Valley Garden, open to the public at all times, is famed for the beauty of its rhododendrons and azaleas. Ascot, where the royal family (attended by master and huntsmen of the Royal Buckhounds) go each June to enjoy the fashionable Gold Cup race, is only 3½ miles away.

WANBOROUGH (London terminal: Waterloo)

On the northern slope of the Hog's Back, a chalk ridge 350–500 feet high, lies Wanborough, a tiny village with just a few cottages huddled around an ancient manor house and a fourteenth-century church. The Hog's Back is a favorite place for field trips and provides enchanting views.

WEYBRIDGE (London terminal: Waterloo)

Weybridge, in north-central Surrey, is at the mouth of the River Wey. It is an ancient town, mentioned in the Domesday Book (1085–1086), and one of its hotels stands on the site of Oatlands, a royal palace built by Henry VIII for Ann of Cleves (but used by him for his marriage to Catherine Howard) and destroyed in 1650 at Oliver Cromwell's command. New houses, apartment buildings, shops, and schools are replacing the old properties. The favorite sports of Weybridge's inhabitants are those to which the River Wey lends itself so admirably—rowing, punting, and fishing.

WORPLESDON (London terminal: Waterloo)

Worplesdon, a town with a very old church and some interesting cottages, lies a little to the northwest of Guildford and just south of Pirbright—territory that belonged in the fourteenth century to the Black Prince (Edward, Prince of Wales and father of King Richard II, remembered as the "Black Prince" because of the color of his armor). Worplesdon is now a popular residential area.

NORMANDY: Home of William Cobbett.
PIRBRIGHT: Ancient moated manor house.

WOKING (London terminal: Waterloo)

Woking is one of the London "dormitory" towns with frequent and fast trains into the capital, just 27 minutes away. It is a busy and thriving town (76,000 people). Quieter and more interesting historically (because of its quaint church) is Old Woking, four miles away. Pyrford Court, near Woking, is famed for its gardens with magnificent rhododendrons and wisteria.

SEND: On the River Wey and near Sutton Place, built by Sir Richard Weston and visited by Henry VIII and Elizabeth I, now the home of J. Paul Getty.

Hampshire

ALDERSHOT   (London terminal: Waterloo)

Aldershot is a military base with a population of about 33,000 (including the troops). Its main attractions are the Airborne Forces Museum, with its photographs, maps, documents, and aircraft models illustrating the history of the British Airborne Forces, and its proximity (three miles) to the more attractive town of Farnham in Surrey.

ALRESFORD   (London terminal: Waterloo)

Despite its name, "New" Alresford dates from the eighteenth century. Its main thoroughfare (Broad Street) runs from the small lake to the church tower and is one of the most picturesque streets in all of Hampshire. This was the home of Mary R. Mitford (1787–1855), who wrote *Our Village*. One mile north lies "Old" Alresford, where Admiral Rodney, renowned for his victory over the French fleet in 1782, is buried.

ALTON   (London terminal: Waterloo)

Alton is an attractive market town with a population of about 12,000. The chalk and greenstone hills provide spectacular scenery in the surrounding countryside, and the town has many new homes, good shops, and excellent educational facilities. There is an interesting church (St. Laurence) dating from the thirteenth to fifteenth centuries and a museum (Curtis) with an unusual collection of old farm implements and craftsmen's tools.

CHAWTON: House occupied by Jane Austen.
SELBORNE: Timber houses, thatched roofs.

BASINGSTOKE   (London terminal: Waterloo)

Basingstoke, in the chalk Hampshire Downs, already has a population of over 50,000 and is one of the most rapidly expanding towns in England. It is the industrial center of Northern Hampshire, and its schools, hospital, library, shopping facilities, and Sports Centre are among the most up-to-date in England. New centrally heated homes are being built at the rate of 1000 a year, and the new housing developments are skillfully planned to provide safe pedestrian traffic among houses, churches, schools, and shops. Basingstoke is the home of the Haymarket Theatre (the only "live" theatre in northern Hampshire), which presents many forms of entertainment, including plays, jazz concerts, ballets, debates, and variety shows. There are a number of choral groups, an operatic society, a band, and a symphony orchestra. Although Basingstoke's history dates back to the days of the Saxons, it is now a thoroughly modern town. There are a few vestiges of the past (*e.g.*, St. Michael's Parish Church, the Holy Ghost Chapel, Church Cottage, and the James Deane Almshouses), but there is little resemblance to the Basingstoke of 1464—a village with well water and poorly lighted roads, inhabited by the brazier, the tanner, the currier, the chandler, the joiner, the hosier, the cooper, the miller, and a few other craftsmen and traders.

BASING (Old Basing): On the River Loddon; ruins of Basing House (Elizabeth I).

DEANE: Serene and picturesque, surrounded by woodlands.

DUMMER WITH KEMPSHOTT: Restful and extremely attractive, nestled on the side of Farleigh Hill.

ELLISFIELD: Hidden away near the crest of a wooded hill and reached by winding roads.

HERRIARD: Site of Herriard House (a Queen Anne mansion) and of beautiful Herriard Park.

MONK SHERBORNE: Peaceful, picturesque, seventeenth-century cottages.

PRESTON CANDOVER: Typically rural, cottages of many colors and shapes.

SHERFIELD ON LODDON: Houses overlooking village green; typical "Old England."

SILCHESTER: Ancient Roman town, site of many interesting archaeological expeditions.

STEVENTON: Brick and flint cottages; Jane Austen's birthplace.

STRATFIELDSAYE: Mansion of the first Duke of Wellington.

UPTON GREY: Pond, willow trees, houses of different periods.

BRAMLEY   (London terminals: Paddington, Waterloo)

Bramley lies in a predominantly agricultural area, although there is an abundance of woodland, mostly oak. It has a fine Norman church (St. James) with fifteenth-century altar rails and wall paintings dating from the twelfth and thirteenth centuries. There are many interesting houses.

FARNBOROUGH   (London terminal: Waterloo)

Farnborough is a pleasant residential town of about 42,000 inhabitants and is on the Hampshire border adjoining both Surrey and Berkshire. It is the site of the Royal Aircraft Establishment and is within easy access of London, both by rail and by motor. Near the railway station is a memorial church, built by the Empress Eugenie in 1887, where Napoleon III, the Empress, and the Prince Imperial are buried; and across the track is Farnborough Hill (now a convent) where Eugenie spent her last days.

FLEET (London terminal: Waterloo)

Fleet, a picturesque, wooded residential town of about 20,000 people, is in the northeast corner of Hampshire. There is a large pond (130 acres) that was once a favorite fishing haunt for the monks of Winchester. Educational facilities are excellent, with a number of well-known private schools (notably, the St. Nicholas and Eriva Dene preparatory schools) as well as county primary and secondary schools.

PETERSFIELD (London terminal: Waterloo)

Petersfield is a market town of about 9000 people in eastern Hampshire midway between the Hampshire Downs and the South Downs, in an area characterized by chalk and greenstone hills. Until the advent of the railway, it was an important sheep-raising center. It has a heath and a boating lake and an annual fair, and has had music festivals almost every year since their founding in 1900.

WINCHESTER (London terminal: Waterloo)

Winchester, now the county seat of Hampshire, was the capital of England from the reign of Alfred the Great (871–899) until Norman times. An Iron Age rampart and ditch dating from the third century B.C. may still be seen at the edge of town, and there are many relics of Roman occupation. Winchester lies in a valley on the banks of the River Itchen, where Izaak Walton fished, and adjoins the New Forest—the first royal hunting ground. Winchester Castle's Great Hall, dating from 1235 and still in use as a court, was the place where Sir Walter Raleigh was tried and sentenced to death. The cathedral, begun in 1079, is the second largest and one of the most famous in Europe: It was the scene of Queen Mary's marriage to Philip of Spain; the burial place of William II, Izaak Walton, and Jane Austen; and the second burial place of King Alfred's tutor, St. Swithun, who was so unhappy about being moved inside after lying in a courtyard for several centuries that he made it rain for 40 days and nights. Winchester College, founded in 1382, is one of the oldest public schools in England. Hyde Abbey is the reputed burial place of King Alfred; and the Abbey Gardens, on the site of a Benedictine nunnery founded by Alfred's Queen, is still a quiet and lovely retreat. The Hospital of St. Cross, a medieval almshouse where the inmates wear picturesque costumes and the Wayfarer's Dole of bread and ale is still given, was founded in 1136. Today Winchester is a thriving market town with fine hotels and modern shops scattered among the mellow stone buildings in its ancient streets.

Chapter VI

YOUR NEW HOME

RENTING VS. BUYING

Obviously, there is nothing about the act of renting that demands (of the tenant) a great deal of study. One finds a suitable vacancy and signs a lease.

The pros and cons of renting are much the same in England as they are in any country. If you've decided to live in the heart of a big city, it's probably easier to find an apartment than a house. It's possible to rent furnished and thus avoid the cost of shipping your own furniture to England or buying new furniture. Your apartment is likely to be on one level—a feature that becomes more desirable as you grow older. As a tenant, you are not responsible for building maintenance or for upkeep of the yard. If it turns out that you don't like your neighbors, you can move when your lease expires. You won't need as much cash to begin with; and even if you have enough money to pay for a house you may find that you can get a better return by renting a place to live and investing your capital in some other manner.

On the other hand, when you rent you forfeit the pleasures of home ownership. Your rent money goes out each month, and you may possibly watch your savings dwindle while you are not acquiring an asset that you can leave to your heirs. You're not as free to build cabinets or change your color scheme as you would be in your own house. If you found you just couldn't bear to part with your household furnishings and brought them with you, you're less likely to find a place to put them because, at least in London, it's much easier to locate a furnished apartment than an unfurnished one. You won't have a garden to putter in, and you may not be able to keep your dog. Neighbors will change more frequently, and long-lasting friendships are less likely to develop. You probably won't establish as close relationships with your business acquaintances or acquire for yourself as active a role in community affairs. And if you have to scrub a bathtub it's more fun to scrub your own than someone else's.

If, after considering all the angles, however, you decide to rent, there are the usual ways of finding a place: estate agents, notices posted in neighborhood shops, classified ads. There are rental firms who advertise in the subway trains and tube stations. There's a newspaper called *The London Weekly Advertiser* that you can buy at any newsstand. Make it a point to buy your paper as soon as possible after it comes off the press; desirable tenancies are always in demand and it pays to be early.

A word of caution: Do not offer the landlord a premium, such as a bonus payment or an extra month's rent—"key money," as it's called in New York. Rents in England are very rigidly controlled by the government, and premium payments (except in certain unfurnished tenancies where rents have never been fixed by the Rent Tribunal) are illegal. A landlord who demands an unlawful premium payment from you is committing an offense for which he can be fined and imprisoned.

Remember, too, that once you're lawfully settled in your rented premises you are entitled to protection against eviction. If your *unfurnished* house or apartment has a ratable value[1] of not more than £400 in London or £200 elsewhere, the Rent Acts provide that you can be forced to move out only by court order; and the court will not issue such an order except in certain circumstances, *e.g.*, if you haven't paid the rent or if you have failed to keep the place in good condition. If you are occupying a *furnished* house or apartment with a ratable value not exceeding £400 in London or £200 elsewhere, your landlord must give you four weeks' warning in his "notice to quit," and during that four-week period you may apply to a Rent Tribunal for a postponement.

If your landlord resorts to acts of harassment in order to force you to quit the premises—for instance, if he cuts off the water or the electricity or threatens you in any way—you can report him to your local council, which has the power to prosecute.

There is a Rent Officer to whom you can always go for assistance. If you feel that you're having to pay too much for *unfurnished* premises, you can ask him to "fix" a fair rent. If you are unhappy with the cost of your *furnished* premises, he will refer you to a Rent Tribunal, which has the power (but only in certain circumstances and at certain times) to alter the rent. To get the address of your local council or of the Rent Officer for your neighborhood, you can ring the nearest

[1]See pp. 114 and 159 for an explanation of rates and ratable values.

Citizens' Advice Bureau—it's listed in your telephone directory.

Keep in mind that the protection afforded you as a tenant can work to your detriment if you assume the role of landlord. For instance, if you should buy a house in England and then decide to rent it for a while (unfurnished) because circumstances arise that cause you to postpone your own occupancy, you could have trouble evicting your tenant when the time comes. Even if you and your tenant have agreed in advance on a fixed term of tenancy, it will take a court order (based on proof that you gave appropriate written notice at the time of renting) to get him out if he should decide not to stick to his end of the bargain.

It would be impossible to quote rental figures here. In London they range anywhere from £6 to £8 a week for a "bed-sitter" in a not-so-nice area to very high prices for luxury apartments. Rents in other areas of England are generally lower than in London, but the day is gone forever when a fishmonger can rent a room near London Bridge for an annual payment of 13s. 4d. (about $1.73) plus three lampreys, and promise in return only that he will protect the premises against wind, rain, and waste, except for other men's fires and sudden storms ("other mennes fuyer and soden and horrible tempest aloonly excepted"). The City of London, however, still renders to the Crown each year quitrent for two pieces of land. The quitrent consists of a hatchet and billhook, 6 horseshoes, and 61 nails. No one can remember exactly where the two pieces of land are located.

CHOOSING A HOME TO BUY

In Chapter V we noted that the cost of real estate in England has skyrocketed in recent years. The rise is attributable not only to inflation in general—a condition that is certainly not peculiar to Britain—but to the fact that Britain does not have an abundance of land on which to house its growing population. When prices first began to climb, various ways (95 percent mortgages, long-term mortgages, deferred interest, and so forth) were devised to help young British couples—whose salaries have not kept up with rising costs—acquire homes of their own. Such devices served only to increase demand, and prices rose still more. New housing developments began to spring up all over England;[2] but as the developers had to pay more and more for the land on which to build, they passed on their increased costs to the house purchasers.

The builders' need to obtain higher prices—and it was a legitimate

[2]There are at present 1675 new developments in England, Scotland, and Wales. The Housing Enquiry Service, Duke Street House, 415–417 Oxford Street, London W1R 2BD, will send you (at no charge) a listing showing their locations with the types and approximate costs of houses at each location.

need—led to an unfortunate practice that, although not illegal, was nevertheless morally suspect: the practice of "gazumping." Mr. Brown is "gazumped" when he agrees to pay a certain price and then is told that the vendor has found a prospective purchaser, Mr. Smith, who is willing to pay a higher price. Sometimes Mr. Brown is given an opportunity to match Mr. Smith's offer; sometimes he is not. The vendor has done nothing illegal because Mr. Brown's deposit was paid "subject to contract," and until contracts are actually exchanged between the two parties, either party may call off the deal. Parliament became pretty concerned about the ethics of gazumping and determined to "have a go" at banning it. And then, the supply of houses began to catch up with the demand, sales became a little more difficult, and prices began to stabilize (though, of course, at a much higher level than before all this began); and now the practice of gazumping has virtually died out. Parliament was never required to have its go at banning it.

A prospective purchaser cannot hope to find many detached houses within commuting distance of London for less than £15,000. Within the £10,000–£15,000 bracket, however, he has a number of options: He can choose between a semidetached house and a terraced house; between an old place that requires renovation and a new one in a modern development; between a leasehold and a freehold. He can buy an apartment or a maisonette. He might even find a detached bungalow for less than £15,000 if he looks along the Kent coast and if he can find one that doesn't have much land with it. Building a house from scratch is simply not feasible; a plot of unimproved land costs almost as much as a plot with a house already on it.

We are not concerned here with advising someone to whom money is of little concern. It seems unfair, but *he* is the one who gets a real break on British real estate: He can buy a fine manor house at a relatively low price because most Britishers can no longer afford to maintain and staff large estates. The options open to the rest of us are discussed below.

Leasehold vs. Freehold

There are parcels of land in residential areas throughout England that the owners have chosen to rent instead of sell. Generally, the leases on these properties were entered into initially for periods of 99 or 999 years.[3] Lessees have built houses on these lands and pay ground rent to the owners or their heirs, but the houses themselves are the prop-

[3]Nobody knows nowadays exactly why leases are so often made for 99 years or 999 years, though some people theorize that these figures are used because the early Anglo-Saxons thought 9 was a good number to have around when an evil spirit (the landlord, perhaps?) needed exorcising.

erty of the lessees. These houses are known as "leasehold" houses.

If the owner of the house also owns the land on which it stands, the house is referred to as a "freehold" even though the owner may have a mortgage.

The disadvantages of acquiring a leasehold are several: (1) ground rent must be paid to the landowner; (2) the house will decline in value with each passing year, since the property will revert to the owner at expiration of the lease unless the lessee chooses to buy the freehold or extend the lease—rights that were granted him, subject to certain provisions,[4] by the Leasehold Reform Act of 1967; (3) if the landlord renews the lease, he will very likely increase the ground rent; (4) building societies will not lend money on leasehold houses unless the term of the loan is such that the final payment can be made at least 30 years before the lease expires.

Flats and Maisonettes

The terms "flat" and "maisonette" are often used carelessly and interchangeably, but there is a difference between these two types of housing: a flat is all on one level; a maisonette is on two floors. Frequently one finds three-storey buildings that contain both—flats on the ground floor, maisonettes (with stairways leading to ground-floor entrances) on the upper two floors. Except in large cities and coastal areas, flats and maisonettes are not as popular as houses, probably because most of them are sold on a leasehold basis. The initial cost is less than the cost of a house, but there is an annual ground rent and, generally, there are covenants for such things as periodic painting of the exterior, maintenance of stairs and entrances, window washing, garbage disposal, and even insurance.

Most leases contain restrictions about such things as practicing musical instruments during certain hours, keeping dogs, and hanging out the wash; and, as a rule, the more expensive the flat or maisonette, the more numerous are the restrictions. The families who most welcome low initial outlay, *i.e.*, young families with children, often find the restricting covenants too limiting; to older people, flats and maisonettes can be a real boon.

---

[4] A leaseholder has the right to purchase the freehold or to have his lease extended for an additional 50 years if he meets the following tests: (1) his lease was originally entered into for a period of more than 21 years; (2) his lease covers the entire house; (3) his annual rent is less than two-thirds the ratable value as of 23 March 1965, and the ratable value is not more than £400 in Greater London or £200 elsewhere; (4) the property leased has been his principal place of residence for five years. Notwithstanding a leaseholder's rights to purchase the freehold or to extend his lease, the landlord may dispute these rights on the grounds of hardship to himself or his family. Such disputes are generally settled by a County Court.

If you consider buying a flat or maisonette, don't choose one that is nearing the end of its leasehold term. You can be held responsible for putting it in good repair when the leasehold expires, and after 999 years (or even 99) that may be rather a chore. The right to buy the freehold when the leasehold expires does not extend to flats.

Bungalows

You are the only one who knows exactly what your dream house looks like, and you will save yourself and others a great deal of time if you will describe it as accurately as possible to your estate agent and your mortgage broker. These gentlemen will be able to assist you much more effectively if you will tell them in advance whether you like bungalows or town houses and whether you prefer a shiny new home with modern conveniences to a "character house" (which is a British euphemism for a leaky roof and inadequate plumbing).

Each type of house has something to recommend it, and it is up to you, of course, to decide which type best suits your needs. A bungalow, for instance, has the advantage of being on one level. If you enjoy rearranging your furniture from time to time, you'll find it much easier to do so in a bungalow than in a multistorey house. You won't need to carry the vacuum up and down stairs on cleaning day. If one of you is sick in bed, it will be easier for the other to perform nursing chores. You lessen the hazard of falls. There will be no stairs between your bedroom and your WC (water closet)—which, in the older English houses, is seldom a part of the bathroom. These may seem like trivial matters now, but they will acquire more importance as you grow older.

A detached bungalow, however, is not likely to be conveniently located. You may not find one that is within walking distance of the post office and the grocery store. There may be no gas main or sewer; the road may be unlighted; there may not be a nearby bus stop; you may find that your yard is too big for you to keep trim; fire insurance rates may be high. Worst of all, you run the risk of isolation—and, especially to older people, isolation can mean loneliness and fear, and sometimes tragedy.

It's a good idea to buy a house with a spare bedroom. Your relatives and friends will be coming over for visits and you'll need a place for them to sleep. Also, if you have brought your own furniture to England, the quantity and type will help to determine the sort of house you should buy. You won't want to cram massive wardrobes and china presses into a tiny bungalow, and you will need rooms of the proper size to accommodate your rugs. As a general rule, however, it's better to pick a house that's on the small side. Remember that economy of maintenance will be important to you when your earning years are over and that the older you become the more you will appreciate a house that requires a minimum of physical effort. Small detached houses are not as easy to find in England, however, as in the United States, and since it isn't likely that you will luck into one in the center of town, you may have to make a compromise of one sort or another—a bungalow in a remote area, or a larger house in a more convenient location.

Town Houses

Many town houses in England are what the British call "terraced" houses. These are houses that are joined to each other on both sides.[5] The terraced houses now being erected are not particularly appealing because, generally, they tend to look alike; but the older ones, even though they have common walls, have individual features that set them apart from each other. Many of the older terraced houses have charm and dignity, and most of them have established yards. Often, purchase of furnishings already in the house can be arranged at a very reasonable price. A terraced house of the older variety may well be your best buy, particularly if you like living in town and enjoy puttering.

Terraced houses have two, three, or four storeys, but there are ways of cutting down on the physical burden of maintaining such a home. For one thing, you might consider occupying only the ground floor yourself and converting the upper floors into apartments. (Before you decide on this solution, however, be sure to ask your solicitor whether there are any restrictions in the "deeds" that will prevent you from making such alterations.) If you decide against renting out a portion of your house, try to put in improvements that will make things easier for you: Furnish one of the ground-floor rooms as a bedroom so that if someone is ill you won't have to carry trays upstairs; if there is not already a water closet on each floor, have one installed; make certain there is adequate lighting on the stairways, particularly at the top and bottom steps; and, in addition to the banisters already there, have handrails attached to the wall side of the stairways.

The older terraced houses generally have minuscule front yards. You can avoid entirely the need to mow the front by paving this area or putting the whole thing in ivy. As for backyards—they, too, are on the small side but they are usually large enough to be made into attractive gardens. The lawn area should be kept to a minimum: It's easier to putter in a flower bed than to cut grass.

If you decide to buy one of the older homes, you may be lucky enough to find one that already has a garage or at least a backyard shed where you can store garden tools. (You will have to get permission

[5]A "semidetached" house is one that shares only one wall with an adjacent house.

from the local authorities to make such improvements yourself.)

Road charges—which in some locations can be quite substantial—will have already been paid on the older variety of town house and therefore need not concern you. On the other hand, there may be renovating costs. For instance, plumbing may be inadequate, or the kitchen may require a new sink and wall cabinets. If the house is heated by coal, you should figure on converting to gas, electric, or oil-fired central heating; shoveling coal and carrying scuttles are chores that are a nuisance to people of any age and a hazard to the older ones.

New Houses

There are two house magazines[6] will give you a good idea of the types of new homes being built in England, and their cost. Building standards in general are higher now than ever before; in fact, we are told that there is no truth to the statement "They don't build houses like they used to." However, you may find the new English houses disappointing in some respects. The split-level houses to which we have grown so accustomed in the United States are rare in England, and most of the new houses are rather stark in appearance with severe, unbroken lines. During the past ten years central heating has become fairly common, but many of the little added frills and niceties that are so much a part of the American home are missing. A house with more than one bathroom is likely to be expensive, and you will probably find that your hot-water tank, instead of being concealed, is occupying, quite prominently, one corner of your kitchen. Certain features that are taken for granted in American homes—such as formica cabinet tops, colored bathroom fixtures, chrome-plated towel racks, and toilets with low-level tanks instead of ceiling-height tanks that one flushes by yanking on a chain—are advertised as luxuries by English builders. Remember, too, that if you buy a new house you will have to start your yard from scratch, and cultivating a beautiful lawn is a long, tiring process.

It is, however, much easier to get a mortgage on a new house than on an old one. Whereas mortgages in general average 75 percent to 80 percent of the purchase price, many mortgage companies will lend 90 percent on new houses, and there are instances in which developers of subdivisions make arrangements with a building society, in advance of sales, to offer 95 percent mortgages to acceptable customers. Although you may not be in the market for a long-term mortgage yourself, you would probably do well to remember that a readily mortgageable house

[6] *Home Finder,* published by Homefinders (1915) Limited, 199 Strand, London WC2R 1DN, or 10 East Road, London N.1; and *House Buyer,* published by Haymarket Publishing, Ltd., Gillow House, 5 Winsley Street, Oxford Circus, London W1A 2HG.

will facilitate a quick sale if you decide to leave England or a quick settlement when your estate is liquidated.

Most of the new houses in England are erected by builders who are registered with the National House-Builders Registration Council (NHBRC), an organization established in 1936 for the protection of house purchasers. In order to become registered with the Council, a builder must first prove that he is technically capable and financially responsible. Be certain, if you purchase a new house, that the builder is NHBRC-registered and that he furnishes you with a "House Purchaser's Agreement"—a legal document that assures you the house will be inspected by Council experts and the builder will be required to remedy defects that may become apparent during the two-year period immediately following completion.[7] Protection against *major* structural defects (dry rot, collapse of roof, warping of joists, and the like) is extended by the Council for a longer period of time—occasionally as long as ten years, but with a deductible of £15 after six years and with a limit of £5000 per dwelling. The Council also provides the purchaser a certain amount of protection in the event the builder takes bankruptcy or goes out of business.

BUYING THE HOUSE

The Estate Agent

After you have chosen your location and have decided which type of house suits you best, you are ready to put the purchasing machinery in action. You may hear of a house for sale through one of your new acquaintances, or you may spot an advertisement in the newspapers or house magazines for an attractive-sounding place. There are two weekly papers[8] that may be particularly helpful. A lot of English real estate—the finer homes and country cottages, especially—are sold by auction, and the house magazines and newspapers all carry notices of forthcoming auction sales.[9] Probably, though, you will find your house through an estate agent.

Most estate agents have display windows in which you can examine

[7]Normal wear and tear are excluded, and so are hazards covered by the owner's insurance policy, such as windstorm and hail damage. Central heating systems are covered for only one year.

[8]*Daltons Weekly*, Daltons House, Windsor Avenue, London S.W. 19; and *The Property Advertiser*, Gillow House, 5 Winsley Street, London, W.1.

[9]Be cautious about the auction sales. The auctioneer—believe it or not—actually is empowered by law to append the purchaser's name to the contract, even though the purchaser may regret his haste in bidding and refuse to sign. Once the hammer has fallen, it is too late for surveys, consultations with solicitors, or mortgage arrangements, and the deposit must be paid on the spot.

pictures of houses for sale and get some idea of prices. Many agents also have "flyers" for each house, with pictures and detailed descriptions. When you examine the flyers, you will notice that most agents' names are followed by some letters, like MNAEA or FRICS or ARICS. These letters indicate that the agent is a member of a professional organization that has required him to pass rigid examinations, that has an established code of ethics, and that guarantees the safety of the buyer's deposit, even if the agent should take bankruptcy. It is unlikely that you will encounter an agent who is not a member of one of these protective societies; but if you do, you should take your business elsewhere, because it is customary for the agent to act in the capacity of "stakeholder" when you make your deposit. There is no reason why you should not visit as many estate agents as you like, but you should tell them in detail what you are looking for and you should be frank about what you can afford to pay.

Perhaps the most important thing to remember in your dealings with the estate agent is that his first responsibility is to the seller, not to you. It is from the seller that he will get his commission, and it therefore behooves him to move the house quickly and to get as big a price for it as he can. The seller is not legally bound to volunteer any information about the house, and therefore, although he will take care not to be guilty of gross misrepresentation, there is no redress if he and his agent simply forget to mention that the fireplace doesn't have a damper or that water runs from the patio into the basement during heavy rainstorms. The safest thing to do is to ask questions. The agent is obligated to answer your questions truthfully and to get the answers for you if he doesn't already know them. Two of the most important questions are: (1) Is the house occupied by anyone other than the owner and his family? (2) Is the property registered? The first of these questions is important because of the legal difficulties involved in removing a "sitting tenant" (see p. 98). The matter of property registration is dealt with later in this chapter (see p. 108).

Once you have selected your house, tell all the other estate agents you visited that you are no longer looking. This is the courteous thing to do because they can then remove your name from their mailing lists and needn't spend any more time house hunting in your behalf. But *do not sign anything* until you have consulted a solicitor.

The Solicitor

Engaging the services of a solicitor is important to every prospective house buyer, and it is a must for the immigrant to whom British house-buying procedures are totally unfamiliar. Selecting your solicitor and informing him of your plans is one of the first moves you should make;

in fact, you would be wise to do this even before you visit any estate agents. (If you don't know how to find a solicitor, ask a local bank manager to recommend one.) The solicitor will probably not charge you for the initial consultation if he hopes to serve you in the actual transaction, and his help will be invaluable. He is the most important of the men you will consult.

There are often as many as three solicitors involved in the sale of one house—your own, the seller's, and the mortgage company's. If possible, avoid sharing a solicitor with the seller. Remember that you are already sharing an estate agent and that since the agent's first duty is to the seller it will be to your advantage to have a solicitor whose first concern is *you*. Furthermore, neither you nor the seller can save money by sharing a solicitor. The solicitor has a fixed scale of fees for services to buyers and services to sellers; you will each have to pay the full scale.[10]

On the other hand, you will benefit by sharing a solicitor with the mortgage company. There is not likely to be a conflict of interest in these two areas, and the use of only one solicitor for mortgage services will save time and red tape and, consequently, money.

The importance of the solicitor lies in the fact that he assumes all responsibility for the legal adequacy of the transaction. It may appear to the uninitiated that the purchase of a house is a simple, cut-and-dried process from which legal complications cannot possibly arise. But suppose the seller dies or takes bankruptcy between the signing of the sales contract and the delivery of the deed of conveyance? Or suppose you've committed yourself to the purchase of too expensive a house, expecting to ease your financial strain by renting out an upper apartment or by using a room or two for a moneymaking hobby such as portrait photography or dressmaking—not knowing that there are restrictions in the deeds against such ventures?[11] The money you pay your solicitor for keeping you out of hot water is the best-spent money in the entire transaction.

By making formal inquiries to various sources of information, your solicitor will find out all there is to know about the property. From the seller's solicitor he will get all the data about water mains, electric and gas lines, boundaries, easements, and the like. He will also have the seller's solicitor furnish him with an exact accounting of rates, including water rates, and the pro-rata shares of buyer and seller. From the local

---

[10]Solicitors' fees and all other expenses incidental to the purchase of a house are set forth in the "Closing Costs" section of this chapter.
[11]In addition to restrictive covenants in the deeds, there may be other reasons why you cannot turn a portion of your house to these uses. Your mortgage company may object to occupancy of the house by anyone other than the owner. And you will have to obtain the consent of the Immigration and Nationality Department before you can set up a business.

authorities, he will find out about long-range plans for your area such as road widening, public libraries, construction of factories, designation of certain buildings or parcels of land as places of historical interest. (These long-range plans can include plans for "compulsory purchase" —the acquisition of property by the local authorities with or without the consent of the owner.)[12]

Your solicitor will carry out the title search. He will find out whether there are any undischarged liabilities on the property, that is, whether there are monetary claims against it, such as unpaid road charges or mortgages. He will find out what, if any, restrictive covenants are in the deeds—agreements that may prevent you from doing such things as erecting a fence or an outbuilding, renting out an apartment, or opening a business.

If you require a mortgage, all the information obtained by your solicitor must be passed on by him to the mortgage company's solicitor, and that gentleman then prepares a deed for the mortgage company which is submitted to your solicitor for approval. (The solicitor who prepares the mortgage company deed is entitled to a fee, and your own solicitor is entitled to a fee for examining the work of the mortgage company's solicitor. That's why you come out ahead if your solicitor and the mortgage company's solicitor are one and the same.)

Your solicitor can recommend a chartered surveyor. He will also probably suggest things to you that you may not think of yourself—such as the advisability of demanding detailed construction specifications if you are buying a new house. He can help you determine how much money you should spend, how much you can reasonably expect in the way of mortgage money, and where mortgage loans are most likely to be available. He can also advise you about insurance.

Your solicitor will examine the draft of the contract of sale that the vendor's solicitor has prepared and will advise you to sign it only when he is satisfied that it contains nothing that will act to your detriment. Later, he will examine the final document—the actual deed of conveyance[13]—to make certain that it is in exact accord with the contract of sale and that your interests have been fully protected.

The sale is called a "conveyance" if the property is an unregistered freehold, a "transfer" if it's a registered freehold, and an "assignment" if it's a leasehold. There is not a great deal of difference in the mechanics

---

[12]Long-range city plans are something that you may want to find out for yourself before you consult with either an estate agent or a solicitor, so that you can know in advance what section of town you want to buy in. You can do this by visiting the clerk's office or the surveyor's office in the town hall. Here you will probably find on display a map with shaded areas depicting projected changes. Office personnel will explain the map to you in detail.

[13]Commonly referred to in England as "the deeds."

of the three types of transaction, though the purchase of registered property is less costly than the purchase of unregistered property because the title search is not extensive.

Registered Property vs. Unregistered

England has a system of land registration that greatly facilitates the transfer of property. Because of the vast amount of work required to change over to this system, however, its implementation is being spread over many years, with the result that certain areas of England have had compulsory registration for a long time[14], while in other areas the system has not yet been introduced.

Once an area is designated by the government as a compulsory registration area, every property within that area must be registered at the next transfer of ownership. It follows, then, that the longer an area has been under compulsory registration the greater the likelihood that a property within it is registered.

The three-part registers (property register, proprietorship register, and changes register) are maintained by a government department called the Land Registry, with head offices in London and district offices throughout the country.

The property register contains a plat on which the property is clearly outlined and there is a written description—boundaries or street address. If the property is a leasehold, this register will also contain details such as the date the lease was entered into, its duration, names and addresses of lessor and lessee, and amount of ground rent.

The proprietorship register contains the name and address of the owner and the price paid. When the property changes hands, the Land Registry simply strikes through the old information and adds the name of the new owner and the price he paid.

The charges register lists all encumbrances against the property, such as mortgages and restrictive covenants.

The fact that a property is registered means that the title has been searched up to the last entry on the register and that the owner's right to sell has been established and is guaranteed by the state.

Thus your solicitor's task of title searching is greatly simplified, if you are buying registered property, since he need go back only as far as the last entry on the register; whereas if you are buying unregistered property, he must dig through all the deeds that have been drawn up within the last fifteen years or longer.

---

[14]Parts of Greater London, for example, have had compulsory registration since 1899. See Appendix E for a list of compulsory registration areas and dates of implementation.

The Surveyor

Just as it will pay you to share the mortgage company's solicitor, it will also pay you to share the mortgage company's surveyor.[15] Both you and the lender will require a surveyor—you to make certain that you are spending your money wisely, and the mortgage company to make certain that it is lending its money wisely. Both fees will be charged to you, and if the same surveyor serves you both the fee should be somewhat less than if you and the mortgage company engage different surveyors. Ask your solicitor to work out a surveyor-sharing arrangement between you and the mortgage company.

The mortgage company does not require as detailed a survey as you require; it needs only to find out whether the house is adequate security for the loan. You, however, want to know specifically what defects you are going to be confronted with—what condition the roof and gutters are in; whether the house is afflicted with dry rot or wet rot or, as the British call it, "rising damp"; whether the drain pipes and brick work are going to last for a reasonable length of time; whether the wiring is safe or hazardous;[16] whether the gates, fences, and driveway are in satisfactory condition.

The mortgage company is not going to let you see its report of survey (although, if there are major defects, it may tell you what those defects are and set a deadline by which you must remedy them). Your own report of survey, however, will be a detailed written report, and in addition to an enumeration of the defects it will include an estimate of the cost of repairs and an opinion about whether the house is fairly priced.

Even if a mortgage is not required, you should never consider buying without first getting a survey unless, perhaps, you are buying a brand-new house with an NHBRC guarantee. Ask your solicitor to recommend a surveyor—preferably a local one familiar with the types of housing available in your district—and then check on his qualifications by looking for the letters FRICS, ARICS, FSVA, or ASVA after his name.

Don't be too alarmed if the surveyor's report has all the rosy appeal of a chronicle of Job's sufferings. Remember that it is the surveyor's business to find fault. He won't feel that he has proved his importance unless he shows you that he is capable of detecting the slightest flaw. No house is without defects. Besides, the surveyor's report may

[15]In the United States, the surveyor is often thought of as the man who takes linear and angular measurements, applies the principles of geometry and trigonometry, and comes up with the form, extent, and position of a tract of land. In British house-buying procedure, the surveyor is a structural engineer whose business it is to examine and ascertain the condition of the property.
[16]To determine this, the surveyor may have to call in an electrician. This will cost you an additional sum of money.

give you some ammunition with which to negotiate a lower price.

It is always advisable to get an estimate from the surveyor before you actually engage him, because he does not have fixed fees for his services. His price to the mortgage company is based on the cost of the house; his price to you depends on many factors—for example, the size of the house, the number of storeys, and whether or not the house is furnished at the time of the survey. (It is much easier for him to survey an unfurnished house because he is not required to shift furniture about and look under carpets.)

Two points to remember: You will have to pay the surveyor for his services to you even if you don't buy the house; and you will have to pay for his services to the mortgage company even if his report is negative and the loan denied.

The proper time for the survey is the period between the offer and the exchange of contracts.

The Mortgage

Probably the toughest problem that will confront you is one of timing: the sale of your house in the United States and the purchase of your house in England. Which comes first? You can tie yourself in a double bowknot just thinking about this one.

The ideal way to handle this double transaction is first to buy the house in England, then come back and dispose of the one in the United States. This is the only way you can know for sure whether you'll have a place to put that third bedroom suite after going to the expense of shipping it across the Atlantic. It's also the only way you can know what electric conversions are required to make your appliances operate in your new house and whether it will be worth your while to have those conversions made.

If you have enough money to buy a new house while you still own the old one, fine and good; but most of us are not in such happy circumstances. The average person has his capital tied up in his house and he can't buy a new house until he gets the money from the sale of the old one. This means that he must first sell out in the United States. Immediately, problems begin to crop up: How long will it take to find a buyer? How long will it take to find the right house in England? And, meanwhile, what should he do with his furniture?

No matter what puzzling situations develop, remember this golden rule: Don't commit yourself to buying anything until you have the money in hand.

There are a couple of *undesirable* ways to get the money before you sell. This book is going to mention them only to point out the dangers involved:

An equity loan (or, as it's called in England, a bridging loan). Such a loan is made by a bank, not a building society. In the United States, this is always a short-term loan—usually 60 days, at most 90—secured by your equity in your U.S. house and to be repaid in full when the house is sold. If your bank should agree to such a loan—and it's not very likely that it will, since you'll be moving to a country where it has no jurisdiction—you can get in real trouble. The loan period may expire before your sale is completed, and if you have already used the money for the new house your only hope is to borrow from a British bank to pay off the American bank. This, too, is going to be difficult because the British bank has no knowledge of you, though in recent months there has been some easing of loan requirements in British banking facilities. You may now be able to get a longer-term loan from a British bank, but your interest rate will probably be around 12 percent.

A mortgage loan on the U.S. house. A loan of this type will be more expensive than a bank loan because in addition to interest you must pay for a survey, a title search, and the like. If you already have a mortgage on the property do not, under any circumstances, consider raising money with a second mortgage. This is the most expensive money of all and, furthermore, you will run into difficulties (and penalties) if you try to pay off a second mortgage ahead of time. Companies who take second mortgages are in business only to invest at the highest possible rate of interest. They expect, when they make you the loan, that their money will be invested for a certain period of time; it is not to their advantage for you to pay off the loan quickly.

If you don't have the capital to buy a second house outright, the safest way to handle its purchase before the sale of your U.S. home is with a mortgage on the English house. Here, too, all will not be smooth sailing because you are not a British citizen; and, if you are a retiree, your age and the fact that you are not gainfully employed will work against you. But this is the most sensible way to get the money you need, and although it will require considerable "shopping around," it *can* be done. The attitude of English lending institutions toward older persons seems to be somewhat more lenient than the attitude of their American counterparts: although the age of the borrower is taken into consideration, the main emphasis is upon the amount of provable income that is to be directed to the borrower in England. Income per week must equal the monthly repayment figure on the mortgage.

There are four types of mortgage loans in general use in England. Probably the only one of these for which you may hope to qualify is a building society mortgage. However, a few facts about each type are given here so that you can discuss the matter more knowledgeably with your broker and solicitor:

Building society mortgage.   This is the most common type of mortgage and can be set up over varying periods of time. The interest rate currently being charged by British building societies is 9½ percent.[17] Over a period of 20 years, the monthly repayment figure would be about £ 9.46 per thousand pounds; over a period of 25 years, £ 8.83. Although mortgages are generally set up for periods of 20 to 30 years, you can, and should, negotiate the type of mortgage that can be paid off within a shorter time. The maximum loan which you are likely to get if you are at or near retirement age is 75 percent; therefore, even if you are fortunate enough to obtain a building society mortgage, you must have a fourth of the purchase price readily available. All building societies have the same interest rate at any given time, but that rate can, and does, vary during the term of the mortgage, depending on the current money market. Generally, if the building societies raise the interest rate they will offer the mortgagees the option of increasing their monthly payments or extending the terms of their loans. You can rest assured that British building societies are ethical in their handling of interest rates. Their margin of profit is governed by law. Building societies do differ to some extent in the amounts they will lend on various types of property and to various types of customers. Some of them won't lend money on houses with more than two storeys; others don't care how many storeys there are but won't advance loans on houses built before, say, 1914, or 1930, or some other particular year. Some will take into consideration the wife's income, others will not.

Local authority loan.   Some local councils (but not all) will lend money on property, and those that do are generally more lenient than building societies about advancing loans on older properties. Most local councils establish a fixed rate of interest for the entire life of the mortgage; thus, while the borrower cannot benefit from a declining money market, neither will he be penalized in a rising market. The principal difficulty in obtaining a local authority loan is scarcity of money. The council's funds come from the Exchequer and are allocated at the beginning of each fiscal year; in a few weeks, the money has all been disbursed. And those borrowers who are fortunate enough to get there in time will seldom be allowed more than £4,000.

Endowment mortgage.   This type of mortgage is designed for young people. The borrower takes out a life insurance policy that covers the amount and period of the mortgage. The building society (or other lender) is the beneficiary. The borrower pays the premiums on the insurance policy and the interest on the mortgage. Thus the amount of the loan is not reduced during the term; but when the policy matures

[17]This is a constantly fluctuating figure.

(or if the borrower dies before the policy matures), the lender is paid in full by the insurance company. This type of loan is generally very expensive—unless the borrower is in such a high tax bracket that his allowable deductions (interest to the lender and two-fifths of the insurance premiums) will reduce his tax to the point where he gains more in tax savings than he pays out in the added costs of an endowment mortgage.

Government Option Mortgage Scheme. This plan is designed for a borrower with very low income. The borrower pays a low rate of interest,[18] and the government subsidizes the difference between the amount of interest the borrower pays and the amount the lender requires. You are not going to be eligible for a loan of this type.

There are two other mortgage plans that are not generally advertised but that are available through solicitors, trust funds, and some building societies to the customer who expects to come into a substantial sum of money with which he can repay the mortgage in full. Since you expect to receive the proceeds from the sale of your U.S. house in the not-too-distant future, you should know about these plans and inquire about them before you make any definite commitment to some other scheme. One of these is called the *half-repayment mortgage.* In this type of mortgage, your monthly payment covers principal and interest on half the amount of the loan; on the other half you pay interest only during the term of the mortgage, and pay off the principal in a lump sum at the time of final settlement. The second type is called a *standing mortgage.* Here you pay interest only, for the full term of the mortgage; the entire principal is repaid in full when you receive your money. The amount advanced on these two types of mortgage is normally two-thirds of the purchase price or two-thirds of the lender's valuation of the property, whichever is lower.

Now that you have familiarized yourself to some extent with the various types of mortgages, you may find it advisable to engage the services of a mortgage broker in arranging your loan. It is possible that your solicitor serves as a member of the board of some building society; nevertheless, if he is unable to arrange a satisfactory mortgage for you through his own connections he can recommend a reputable broker. (Make certain in advance that the mortgage broker you select is not planning to charge you a fee; he is compensated for his services through commissions paid by the lenders.)

A competent mortgage broker can be extremely valuable to you

[18]At present, 8 percent.

because he has access to many lending facilities and knows which ones are most likely to approve your qualifications. He can help in the actual negotiation of the loan, and he can advise you on income tax deductions related to your mortgage.

The mortgage is usually negotiated after the house has been selected. However, a preliminary consultation with a mortgage broker right at the outset of your house hunting will help you in determining whether a mortgage will indeed be available to you when the time comes and, if so, what size and type of loan you may hope for.

Rates and Ratable Value

England does not have property taxes, as such, on real estate. Instead, it has a "ratable value" system. It works this way:

The Inland Revenue Department (British counterpart of the U.S. Internal Revenue Service) assesses two values on each property: (1) the "gross" value, which is the amount of annual rent that the property could be expected to bring in; and (2) the "ratable" value, which is a fraction of the gross value. The owner or occupier pays "rates" that are assessed against the ratable value at a percentage determined by the local authorities.

Rate percentages vary widely from area to area, depending on the local government's needs. In rural areas the rates may be only a few pence in the pound; in heavily populated areas, they may be close to a full pound (100 pence); and there are some instances, though rare, where the rates exceed 100 percent of the ratable value. "Rates" cover upkeep of streets and sidewalks, street lighting, gas and electric mains, drainage, fire and police protection, education, libraries, parks, welfare benefits, and a multitude of other public services. (The cost of water is sometimes included in the rates that are quoted to the prospective buyer; you will have to ask about this.)

Even in high-rate areas, there is no comparison between "rates" in England and property taxes in the United States. To check out the actual savings over the American property-tax system, we inquired about rates on a specific $23,000 house situated one mile from the center of a town of 40,000 population in the western part of Kent—a desirable area. The annual rates (including water) on this house were $147.30, and this could be paid in ten installments of $14.73 each with no interest added for the installment privilege. On another house, valued at $34,375 in an equally desirable but more rural area, annual rates (*excluding* water) amounted to $73.60.[19]

[19]You will find more about rates in the chapter on taxes, Chapter IX.

The Offer

Think back now to the early days of your house hunting. When you were looking at the pictures displayed in the estate agents' windows, you probably noticed that some of them were stamped "UNDER OFFER." This means that a prospective buyer has indicated that he would like to have the house and has made an offer for it but no contracts have yet been signed.

You, also, can make an offer whenever you feel certain that you have found the house you want. The fact that the house has a price tag on it does not necessarily mean that you must pay that exact amount. Perhaps, after comparing it with similar houses, you have concluded that the house you want is overpriced; offer an amount that you think is reasonable. There is no guarantee, of course, that your offer will be accepted, but the agent will submit your offer to the vendor.

Although you may make your offer yourself to the estate agent, it is wisest first to discuss the matter with your solicitor and get his opinion on the figure you have decided to offer. When you and he are in agreement on this point, let him be the one to make the offer to the agent for you. In no case should you make the offer direct to the vendor.

If your offer is acceptable to the vendor, the estate agent will ask you for a deposit (probably £50) as evidence of good faith. Have your solicitor make this deposit for you; he will accompany it with a written stipulation that the offer is "subject to contract" and that the deposit is refundable if the deal falls through. (It's not a bad idea to have your solicitor stipulate further that the offer is "subject to survey." You may want to revise the figure if the surveyor finds that you'll soon need a new roof.)

At this point, you are not legally committed to the purchase.

The Exchange of Contracts

When all the preliminaries have been completed and you and your solicitor are both satisfied that the survey, the purchase price, and the financial arrangements are acceptable, it is time to begin closing the deal. At this point you hand over (through your solicitor) a deposit that usually, added to the "earnest" money you paid earlier, totals 10 percent of the purchase price.

The vendor's solicitor has by now drafted a contract of sale. He submits this to your solicitor, who makes certain it is in order before he permits you to sign. Your solicitor then delivers the signed contract to the seller's solicitor and in turn obtains a copy signed by the vendor. This ritual is known as the "exchange of contracts." You are now committed to the purchase, although the house is not legally yours until, a few weeks later, the deed of conveyance is "signed, sealed, and delivered."

Insurance

From the moment you sign the contract of sale, you are responsible for hazard insurance on the property (even though the deed of conveyance has not yet been drawn up and signed). You should not waste a minute in placing a binder with an insurance agent. If you have arranged a mortgage, your lender will require insurance in an amount adequate to cover the loan, and if your mortgagor is a building society, it may very likely suggest that the insurance be placed with its own agent. There is no reason why you should not go along with this; but you must take care to cover the full value of the house and not just the lender's interest. There could be few mishaps more disheartening than to have committed oneself to the purchase of a house that has burned to the ground.

If no mortgage is involved and you are free to choose your own insurance company, go to an insurance *broker*. A broker's services are free, and, unlike an agent (who represents only a few companies), a broker has access to many companies and can give you reliable and unbiased guidance. Try to find one who is a member of the Corporation of Insurance Brokers, 15 St. Helen's Place, London EC3A 6DS.

Hazard insurance rates in England are very low. The average cost of fire insurance on a dwelling is 31¢ per $250 of insurance per annum; thus insurance on a $17,500 house would cost you about $21.70 each year. Average cost of insurance on contents is $.625 per $250, so add another $12.50 per year for a $5,000 policy on contents. (Keep in mind that these are *average* figures. Rates vary according to the location and construction of the house.)

There are, of course, many different types of insurance, and it is impossible to explore them all here. The important thing to remember is that you must arrange for adequate fire insurance immediately. Later, after you've had a chance to read specimen policies and discuss the various possibilities with your solicitor or some other knowledgeable person, you may wish to adjust the amount of coverage or convert to a more comprehensive type of policy.

Closing Costs

The down payment on your house will, of course, be the biggest cash outlay you will have to make. There are, however, a number of other expenses incidental to house purchase that you must be prepared to cover. The tables below will give you some idea of what this additional cash outlay will amount to:[20]

Your Solicitor's Fee

Price of House	Registered Property	Unregistered Property
£ 5,000	£ 43.75	£ 67.50
6,000	47.50	75.00
7,000	51.25	82.50
8,000	55.00	90.00
9,000	58.75	97.50
10,000	62.50	105.00
11,000	66.25	110.00
12,000	70.00	115.00
13,000	73.75	120.00
14,000	76.25	125.00
15,000	78.75	130.00
18,000	85.75	145.00

Note that the gap between fees on registered and unregistered property widens as the purchase price increases.

The Mortgage Company Solicitor's Fee

Amount of Loan	Registered Property	Unregistered Property
£ 2,000	£ 14.00	£ 14.00
2,500	16.25	16.50
3,000	17.50	19.00
3,500	18.75	21.50
4,000	20.00	24.00
4,500	20.93½	26.50
5,000	21.87½	29.00
5,500	22.34	31.50
6,000	22.81	34.00
6,500	23.28	36.50
7,000	23.75	37.50
8,000	24.68½	39.37½
9,000	25.62½	41.25
10,000	26.56	43.12½
11,000	27.50	44.37½
12,000	28.43½	45.62½
15,000	30.62½	49.37½

[20]These figures are certain to fluctuate with changes in economic conditions. They are intended only as a guide.

If you and the mortgage company share a solicitor, the registered property scale applies. If you have different solicitors, the unregistered scale
applies.

Land Registry Fee on Transfer

Price of House	Fee
£ 5,000	£ 13.00
6,000	15.20
7,000	17.40
8,000	19.60
9,000	21.80
10,000	24.00
11,000	26.20
12,000	28.40
13,000	30.60
14,000	32.80
15,000	35.00
18,000	41.60

*Land Registry Fee on Mortgage
(If Property Is Already Registered)*

Amount of Loan	Fee
£ 2,000	£ 2.60
2,500	3.25
3,000	3.90
3,500	4.55
4,000	5.20
4,500	5.85
5,000	6.50
6,000	7.60
7,000	8.70
8,000	9.80
9,000	10.90
10,000	12.00
11,000	13.10
12,000	14.20
15,000	17.50

NOTE: If property is not already registered, you will have to pay the same
fee that is shown in the preceeding table unless mortgage and purchase are
simultaneous.

*Your Mortgage Company
Surveyor's Fee*

Amount of Mortgage	Fee
£ 2,000	£ 9.00
2,500	10.00
3,000	11.00
3,500	12.00
4,000	13.00
4,500	14.00
5,000	15.00
6,000	17.00
7,000	19.00
8,000	21.00
9,000	23.00
10,000	25.00

Stamp Duty on Transfer

Price of House	Duty
£ 10,000	Nil
10,001	£ 50.00
11,000	55.00
12,000	60.00
13,000	65.00
14,000	70.00
15,000	75.00
16,000	160.00
17,000	170.00
18,000	180.00

Your Surveyor's Fee

There is no set scale, but count on about £60 for a £10,000 house and about £85 for a £15,000 house. Get an estimate in advance.

Remember that you may require a survey on more than one house and that each one must be paid for in full. You can't get a "package deal" on multiple surveys.

Miscellaneous Costs

Ask whether you will be required to pay road charges. You probably won't, unless you are buying a house in a private road—but it won't hurt to ask.

Have enough cash available to pay for connection of gas and electrical appliances and telephone, the initial fire insurance premium, and your pro-rata share of the rates.

Listed below are a few points that you should keep in mind throughout the entire transaction. They may save you a little money:

1. Make sure that the purchase is made in the names of both you and your wife as *joint tenants.* When one of the partners of a joint tenancy dies, the property passes automatically to the survivor and there is no need to inquire into the will of the deceased partner if the survivor wishes to sell.[21] Joint tenancy can simplify the matter of title registration; it can also result in a saving on estate duties, since when one partner dies the death duty would be payable only on half the value of the house rather than on the full value.

2. There is a difference between "fixtures" and "fittings," and your contract should leave no room for doubt about which is which. You are entitled to assume that anything actually affixed to the property—a bathtub, lavatory, radiator, or kitchen sink—is a "fixture" and is included in the purchase price. The things you must be careful about are the marginal items, such as fitted cupboards, kitchen stoves, garden sheds, television aerials, and even shrubs. It is advisable to have a definite understanding about these marginal items and to make certain that your contract specifies whether or not they are included in the sale price of the house. "Fittings" are items that are easily removable— curtain rods, stair carpet, wall mirrors, and the like. Be sure you know whether or not the vendor plans to leave these in the house and whether he has included them in the sale price; you may not want to buy them.

3. Although stamp duty on mortgages was abolished in August, 1971, there is still a stamp duty on the property transfer itself if the price of the house is *more* than £10,000. It is quite legitimate, in figuring stamp duty, to separate the cost of fittings from the cost of the house and permanent fixtures. For instance, if the total purchase price is £10,200, but the fittings included in that total are valued at £200, you can

---

[21]Don't confuse "joint tenancy" with "tenancy in common." When husband and wife are tenants in common, the share of one may pass to the other only if the deceased has *willed* his share to the other. Such an arrangement complicates settlement of the deceased's estate because the value of the deceased's share must be determined before probate is granted; and even if the two partners' shares were equal to begin with, the death of one partner lowers the value of his portion simply by enabling the other party to continue living in the house. Estate valuation is based on current market values, and a partially occupied house has a very low market value.

subtract the cost of the fittings and avoid the stamp duty altogether. Also, you will note from the Stamp Duty on Transfer table earlier in this chapter that the stamp duty jumps from .5 percent to 1 percent *past* the £15,000 mark. Here again, you may be able to save on stamp duty. If the total purchase price is, say, £15,200, but the fittings are valued at £200, you can keep your stamp duty in the .5 percent bracket.

4. Pay for your English house with U.S. dollars (see p. 17).

RENOVATION

One effect of the housing shortage has been to spur interest in the renovation of old houses that are solidly constructed but short on modern amenities. Such houses are frequently advertised in the newspapers, but the buyer must generally have sufficient cash to cover the full purchase price. Usually, however, the asking price of such a house is relatively low to begin with; and there is a very real possibility that a still lower price can be negotiated, particularly after your surveyor has provided you with a list of defects.

Improvement Grants

Old houses in need of renovation are generally not mortgageable. It is often possible, however, to obtain financial help with the renovation. In 1949 the British government introduced a grant system, the purpose of which is to assist homeowners in converting nonresidential structures such as garages and stables to residential use, or in modernizing dwellings built before 1961, bringing them up to present-day standards of sanitation, safety, and convenience. Improvement grants are available not only to freeholders, but also to leaseholders—either landlords or owner-occupiers—whose leases have a minimum of five more years to run. Approval and administration of the grants—and to a large extent, the amounts—are functions of the local authorities in the areas in which the properties are located.

There are several types of improvements grants, but only two that concern us here—standard grants and discretionary grants.

STANDARD GRANTS cover only the most basic improvements. Half the cost must be paid by the owner; and the other half, subject to the maximums set forth below, is covered by the grant.[22] Standard grants

---

[22]The maximum grant applies only if the improvement is being made for the first time; smaller amounts apply in other instances.

	Maximum Grant Available
Bath or shower	£ 30
Lavatory	£ 10
Sink	£ 15
Hot and cold water in:	
(a) bath or shower	£ 45
(b) lavatory	£ 20
(c) sink	£ 30
Water closet	£ 50
Total	£ 200

covering the above improvements are mandatory; that is, if the authorities determine that the house is habitable and will remain so for at least ten years, they have no alternative but to allow the grant. There are a few circumstances in which the applicant for a standard grant may be allowed money in excess of the normal £200 maximum: For example, if water must be piped into the house or a cesspool installed before the improvements can be carried out, the authorities may allow 50 percent of the cost of this additional work.

DISCRETIONARY GRANTS cover a wider range of improvements and a larger amount of money: £1000 maximum per single house, or £1,200 maximum per apartment, if the applicant proposes to convert the upper floors of a three- or four-storey house to apartments. Grants of this type are not mandatory, and because of the money involved the local council will take a much closer look at the applicant's plans for using the grant. After work is completed, the council must be satisfied that the house now has a life expectancy of at least 30 years and that it meets certain standards in respect to plumbing, lighting, ventilation, electric and/or gas connections, and heating.

There are some restrictions against resale of the property within a short time after renovation. Improvement grants are not intended to subsidize profit-making ventures.

Applications for improvement grants of any type are submitted to the local council, and work must not be begun until approval has been obtained. The money is generally payable at completion of the work but may, at the council's discretion, be supplied in installments as work progresses.

In the first six months of 1972, 164,000 improvement grants were allowed.

Central Heating

Some of my American acquaintances seem astonished to find that central heating is available in England. Why, I don't know—because all the heating methods known to Americans are known to the British, and England is short neither on engineering know-how nor on the materials for putting this knowledge to use. It's true that, a few years back, central heating was available only to the wealthier British; but now it has lost its "luxury" status and is fast taking on the status of "necessity." Almost all new homes in England have central-heating systems, and many of the older ones are being converted. If you buy one of the older homes, you should certainly install central heating to increase your own enjoyment of the house as well as its resale value.

As to which kind of heating system is preferable—this is a choice that you will have to make (hopefully in conjunction with a qualified heating engineer)[23] after you have decided where to live. No recommendations can be made in advance because too much depends on fuel costs and availability in different areas of England, on layout and type of house, and on personal preferences. Neither can installation costs be accurately forecast—although a common rule of thumb is to allow $25p$ for every square foot of living space, plus £70 to install a hot-water supply.

Don't forget to tell the engineer that you are accustomed to American indoor temperatures and want your house heated accordingly. If you don't, you will find that your living and dining rooms are heated to 65° and your bath, kitchen, and hall to 60°; your bedrooms will be an icy 55°. Your British friends will suffocate at your American temperatures, but you can throw open a window or two when they come to call.

Remember, too, that it's wasteful to install a heating system in an uninsulated house. Lack of adequate insulation can add between 25 percent and 50 percent to your fuel bills. A reasonably competent do-it-yourselfer with a pair of scissors should be able to lay a 2-inch fiberglass insulation in the attic of his 1000-square-foot house for about £30.

Wiring

If the house you buy has not been rewired within the past 15 years, you can safely assume that the job needs doing; insulation of domestic cables begins to fail after this length of time. Of all the things that need to be done to an old house, wiring is the most important. Modern appliances can place too great a stress on old circuits that were designed to supply

[23]The National Heating Centre, 34 Mortimer St., London W.1, (phone 580–3238) maintains a register of heating engineers with whom they have signed an agreement that legally binds the engineers to a two-year guarantee on workmanship and materials.

electricity only for lighting and a few small gadgets: Breakdowns, loss of time, and costly repairs are the results, and fire is a very real hazard. The only sensible approach to the problem is to make a list of the appliances you expect to install, decide where they will be placed in your house, mark the spots at which you may need additional points (outlets), and then call a qualified electrical contractor[24] to design a system that fits your requirements.

Costs vary from area to area and are difficult to estimate, but you should not hope to get the job done for less than, say, £ 7 for each point. Whatever you do, don't fiddle around with the wiring yourself. Even if you consider yourself to be a good electrician, you will not be familiar with English building codes.

Alterations and Additions

You will undoubtedly want to add closets[25] (the old houses generally don't have them) and modernize your bathroom and kitchen. You may want to remove a front porch, add a bay window, or block up a doorway. Your best approach to any such changes will be to consult an architect.[26] At the very least, you will need an engineer to advise you which structural changes the house can tolerate and which it cannot. By all means, check with the local authorities to make certain that your plans will not violate any zoning ordinances or that a bulldozer will not be coming down your street to widen it, collecting your new lamppost in the process.

The prices of building materials in England are comparable to those in the United States. Labor, on the other hand, costs far less. One contractor has provided me with the following estimates (materials and labor included):

To lay a good-quality floor tile	£ 4.50/sq. yd.
To install bathroom wall tile	£ 4.50/sq. yd.
To paper the walls of an average room (one requiring eight rolls of paper)	£ 32.00
To paint the same size room, including ceiling	£ 45.00

The Department of Employment has furnished the following average hourly earnings taken from its April, 1972 survey:

[24]If you are in doubt about how to find a qualified electrical contractor, ask the Electricity Council, Trafalgar Bldgs., Charing Cross, London SW1A 2DS (phone 930–6757).
[25]Better refer to them as "cupboards" or "wardrobes" in England.
[26]Tell the Royal Institute of British Architects, 66 Portland Place, London W1N 4AD (phone 580–5533) what type of work you want done. They will send you a list of members willing to undertake the job.

Carpenter and joiner	66.5p
Bricklayer	66.1p
Electrician (building and wiring)	74.6p
Plumber, pipe fitter	69.7p

These average figures are taken from a 1 percent sampling over the whole of Great Britain. The rates within commuting distance of London are at the top of the scale.

LANDSCAPING

England's gardens are so lovely that you will want one of your own. Even a small, narrow backyard—the kind that goes with the older town houses—can be made into a charming garden spot by erecting a fence and bordering it with ornamental shrubs and a small tree or two, building a patio of flagstone or paving blocks, and putting the center in grass.

A nurseryman in Tunbridge Wells wrote that he has in his possession a 1961 catalog from an Ohio nursery and that prices in England today are less than they were in Ohio 12 years ago. He specifically noted that a pot-grown hydrangea from Ohio cost $1.75 in 1961; in England, 12 years later, the same size hydrangea sold for 60p ($1.50). Rhododendrons in England cost £1.75; clematis costs 60p; standard ornamental trees cost £1.50 to £2.00. That beautiful English turf is advertised in today's papers at £4.00 to £4.50 per 100 turves (each 1 ft. by 3 ft.); thus enough sod to cover an area 40 ft. by 75 ft. would cost between £40.00 and £45.00.

To have a new garden built for you from scratch—including fence, patio, plants, trees, turf, and labor—you should allow, another nurseryman advised, 5 percent of the cost of the house. His estimate was made before house prices went up so spectacularly; the cost of garden building has not risen at so rapid a rate. The Department of Labor states that in April, 1972, the average wage of gardeners was 52.8p per hour.

FURNISHINGS

Shopping for furniture and appliances in England is very much like shopping for furniture and appliances in the United States: You have to learn where to look for the best buys. My advice to anyone who moves to England is to subscribe to *Which?*, and don't wait until you get to England to enter your subscription. Write to Consumers' Association, Freepost, Hertford, as soon as you decide to move, and ask the Association to start sending your monthly issues to your U.S. address at once. They will bill you,[27] and they will send you a list of past issues with instructions about how to obtain them. *Which?* is chock-full of valuable information about products, services, and prices. It is especially useful in selecting appliances from among brands with which you are not familiar. Keep all your *Which?* copies in a binder and take them to England with you.

Below, converted to American dollars, are recommended 1973 retail prices for some appliances. The brands listed here are the best available; there are cheaper ones on the market. By shopping carefully you can often obtain discounts; but, as a rule, your English appliances will cost you more than you paid for your American ones.

Refrigerator-freezer (11.2 cu. ft. capacity)	$343.95
Spin dryer	88.00
Tumble dryer	150.00
Automatic washing machine	250.00
Zigzag semiautomatic sewing machine	125.00
Console stereo	137.00
Color TV (22 in.)	675.00
Black-and-white TV (24 in.)	195.00
Dishwasher	250.00
Cylinder vacuum cleaner	110.00
Cooker (double oven)	235.00
Steam iron	25.00
Blender	25.00
Hand mixer	18.50
Shaver	16.85

The cost of your other furnishings will depend entirely on your own taste and pocketbook. Some of the most beautiful antique furniture in the world is in London (try Harrod's), and you'll pay a pretty price for it. Moderately priced furniture is available at discount houses, at some department stores, and through mail-order firms. But if you're interested in some really great bargains, try the classified ads. Nice effects can be achieved by slip-covering used sofas and chairs and by painting or antiquing wooden pieces. Here are a few samples taken from a recent *Kent Messenger:*

"Brand-new teak dining room suite, 6-ft. sideboard, table, four chairs, £69 delivered."

"Dining room suite, walnut, £20; oak bureau, £10."

---

[27] £2.50 per year.

"Two fireside chairs, £8."
"Grandfather clock, early nineteenth century, nice condition, £75."
"Gateleg table, six matching chairs, £49."
"Loungette convertible, two matching fireside wing chairs, £22.50."
"Three-seater bed-settee, nearly new, £25. One carver and three straight-backed dining chairs £10."
"Three-piece golden oak bedroom suite, £15."
"9 ft. by 12 ft. Axminster carpet with matching rug, £12."
"Studio couch with arms, converts to double bed, seats four, good condition, £15. o.n.o."

Incidentally, you will frequently encounter the abbreviation "o.n.o." in English advertisements. It means "or nearest offer."

DOMESTIC HELP

The average hourly wage of cleaning women in April, 1972, was $39p$; the average hourly wage of cooks was $43.1p$.

You must make an "employer's contribution" to the National Insurance Scheme for every domestic servant over the age of 18 who works for you as much as eight hours in any one week or to whom you pay as much as £4 (including the value of food and lodging) in any one week. Your employee will already have a National Insurance card; you, the employer, must buy a National Insurance stamp in the appropriate denomination, affix it to the card in the appropriate weekly space, and cancel it by writing across it, in ink, the date on which it was affixed. The amount of the contribution is governed by the age, sex, and retirement status of the employee, and, of course, by the amount of remuneration for services performed. From the Department of Health and Social Security, Alexander Fleming House, Elephant and Castle, London SE1 6BY, you can request Leaflets N1–20 and N1–11, which explain fully your liability for National Insurance contributions.

Chapter VII
EMPLOYMENT

Most Americans realize that Britain's first duty is to its own citizens, although we may be disappointed at the obstacles placed in our way when we try to earn our livelihoods in England. There is no point in looking for ways to circumvent these obstacles; they are there, and they should be. The best we can do, if we have our hearts set on working in England, is to familiarize ourselves with Britain's requirements and try to find legitimate ways to conform. If we attempt to find work in England by any other means, we are in for trouble.

GENERAL RULES

With few exceptions, an American who wants to work in England must be in possession of a work permit issued by the British Department of Employment before he enters Britain for purposes of employment. Since it is the employer—not the employee—who applies for the permit, and since most employers will not hire people whom they have not personally interviewed, the American encounters his first obstacle almost immediately. He will have to locate a prospective employer before he enters Britain. Then, if he is successful in this, he *may* be permitted to go in for an interview. He will have to show the immigration officer that an interview has been arranged and that he can provide not only for himself while he is there but also pay his fare back to await the arrival of his work permit if the employer wants to hire him and succeeds in getting permission to do so. When he enters Britain for the interview, he will be on "visitor" status and his passport will be stamped for a short-term stay. Not until he has the actual work permit in hand will he be allowed to enter as an employee, and then only for one year initially. His permit will entitle him to hold only the specific job for which he has been hired, and a change of job will have to be approved by the Department of Employment. After four years in approved employment, the job holder can be accepted as a permanent resident, and from that point on he will be free to take any job he wishes. (Part-time employment during one's student years does not count toward the residency requirement.)

In general, the only permits issued to Americans are to: (1) people with professional qualifications; (2) skilled craftsmen and technicians; (3) highly skilled workers in the hotel and catering fields (and unskilled workers in these fields for seasonal work only); (4) resident domestic employees in private households, educational institutions, hospitals, and nursing establishments (if they do not have children); (5) administrative and executive workers, and specialized clerical and secretarial staff; (6) people with specialized qualifications for posts in commerce or retail distribution.

To qualify for a job in any of the above categories, the prospective employee should be between the ages of 18 and 54.

The employer will have to convince the Department of Employment that the job is "reasonable and necessary in the circumstances" and that he has been unable, despite diligent efforts, to find a citizen or a long-term resident of Britain who can satisfactorily fill the vacancy. In addition, he must agree to provide the foreigner with wages and working conditions that are not inferior to those he would offer a British employee.

An American fortunate enough to obtain a work permit must contribute to the National Insurance Scheme and will be entitled to share in its benefits. (As soon as he begins work, he should visit the nearest Social Security office and ask for a National Insurance card and instructions about its use.) His wages will also be subject to P.A.Y.E. (Pay-As-You-Earn withholding tax). He is encouraged to apply for membership in the appropriate labor union.

STUDENT JOBS

Foreign students, like other foreign job applicants, must obtain work permits. Generally, however, they are not permitted to work in regular full-time jobs, but only in supernumerary jobs for which they do not receive full pay. Their permits are seldom issued for periods in excess of 12 months, and they are expected to return to their own countries when the permits expire. They may not transfer to full-time jobs.

(There are no restrictions on employment of students' wives and children during the students' stay in England.)

One way to get a student job is to take advantage of the plan operated by BUNAC (British Universities North America Club), whereby students from one country may work during summer vacations in the other country without work permits. To qualify for one of these jobs, the U.S. student must be an American citizen between the ages of 18 and 30, resident in the United States, and enrolled (part-time or full-time) as a degree candidate in an accredited college or university. He must also have previous work experience, proof of round-trip transportation, and a minimum of $200 to live on until his salary begins. If you think you can qualify for BUNAC employment, your first move should be to obtain an "Application for Summer Jobs in Britain" by writing to the CIEE (Council on International Educational Exchange), 777 United Nations Plaza, New York 10017, or 607 South Park View, Los Angeles, Cal. 90057. The application form is in two parts: One is to be completed by the applicant and returned to CIEE with a $10 fee and two passport-size photos; the other (a reference form) is to be completed and returned to CIEE by a previous employer.

The CIEE also publishes a 336-page paperback called *Whole World Handbook: A Student Guide to Work, Study, and Travel Abroad,* which lists many work opportunities, including teaching jobs, in various countries. The book may be ordered from the New York address of CIEE (above). Enclose a check for $2.95 payable to CIEE.

You can't expect to make much money with a student job, but you should be able to earn enough to take care of yourself while you are in England.

JOBS WITH BRITISH SUBSIDIARIES OF U.S. FIRMS

Many large American corporations have British subsidiaries or affiliates. To apply for a job with one of these companies, begin by submitting a letter of inquiry to the U.S. office of the firm's international division. You may be able to obtain an introduction to an official of the British company.

U.S. firms having British subsidiaries or affiliates are listed in a volume called *The Anglo-American Trade Dictionary,* published by the American Chamber of Commerce in London, 75 Brook Street, London W1Y 2EB. This is an expensive book; see if your public library has a copy before you invest the $12.50 required for its purchase.

Another book, *Who Owns Whom,* gives essentially the same type of information but costs even more. It is published by O. W. Roskill & Co., Ltd., and is distributed by International Publications Service, 114 East

32nd Street, New York 10016. The volume that deals with the United Kingdom costs $60, and there are four supplements that add another $6.50. If you happen to be in New York, you may examine *Who Owns Whom* at the British Information Services, 845 Third Avenue.

JOBS WITH BRITISH FIRMS

There are a number of ways to find out about openings with British firms:

1. One way, of course, is to subscribe to a London newspaper (*e.g.*, the *Times*, Printing House Square, E.C. 4; *The Guardian*, 192 Grays Inn Road, W.C. 1; the *Daily Telegraph*, 135 Fleet Street, E.C. 4); or you may examine these papers at the British Information Services in New York or at your nearest Consulate. There are also professional journals that advertise vacancies; the reference desk at your local public library should be able to provide you with the names and addresses.

2. Management Selection, Ltd., 17 Stratton Street, London W1X 6DB (a management consultant firm), has a "Career International" operation that publishes a list of qualified engineers, technologists, and managers, and distributes it to British companies. In theory, the operation is a placement service for senior international career men of any nationality; in practice, it centers mainly on United Kingdom nationals who are returning to Britain from overseas. If you want to try getting on MSL's list, send them a résumé and state whether you are prepared to pay your own expenses if you are invited to England for an interview.

3. An American woman who wants to work in England but who does not require a permit (*e.g.*, the wife of a student or of a man already accepted for settlement) may be able to get some assistance from Judy Farquharson, Ltd., a firm established for the express purpose of introducing well-educated women to executive jobs available within its clientele of British companies (and of introducing its clientele to the vast, untapped wealth of talent within this group of women). Judy Farquharson, Ltd., is an associate of Management Selection, Ltd. (above) and is located at the same address. Most of the women placed by Judy Farquharson have been editors, librarians, market researchers, and systems analysts; but the field is beginning to broaden, and demand for women statisticians, investment analysts, and managers is increasing.

4. Massachusetts Institute of Technology operates a Job Information Exchange that circulates résumés of job applicants among employers seeking research assistants, junior faculty members, and postdoctoral fellows. The service is concerned primarily with placement of recent

graduates in science and public policy. Details may be obtained from the Science and Public Policy Studies Group, Inc., Room E53–449, Massachusetts Institute of Technology, Cambridge, Mass. 02139.

5. From the Government Bookshop, P.O. Box 569, London SE1 9NH, you can order three volumes (revised annually) that will give you details on active research topics at British universities and other British institutions. From these, you can learn where research in various fields is being carried on, and you may be able to obtain some useful addresses from which you can gain details about teaching fellowships and other job opportunities. Volume I, *Physical Sciences,* costs £6.74; Volume II, *Biological Sciences,* costs £6.24; Volume III, *Social Sciences,* costs £5.74.

6. Secretarial work as "relief help" during the holiday season (March 1 through October 31) is sometimes available through employment agencies. Your agency will introduce you to your prospective employer; then it is up to *him* to apply for your work permit. Such permits are issued for a maximum duration of six months and are for jobs only in London—nowhere else in England. Some of the best secretarial agencies are:

Brook St. Bureau of Mayfair, Ltd., Brook Street House, 47 Davies Street, London, W. 1;

Alfred Marks Bureau, Ltd., 8 Frith Street, London, W. 1;

Conduit Bureau, Ltd., 4 Conduit Street, London, W. 1.

7. People who don't require permits (*e.g.*, wives of students or of men already accepted as residents, or people who have completed four years in approved jobs and have thus acquired the privilege of accepting jobs of their choice without referral to the Department of Employment) may obtain from the Federation of Personnel Services of Great Britain, Ltd., 133–135 Oxford Street, London W1E 5EZ, a "List of Registered Members." The list—in alphabetical order, first by county, then by city within the county—includes most of the employment agencies in England and tells what categories of placement are undertaken by each agency.

TEACHING JOBS

Primary and Secondary Levels

Publicly Maintained Schools. Although the hiring of teachers in publicly maintained primary and secondary schools is the responsibility of the local education authorities, no full-time teacher can be selected whose qualifications have not been approved by the Department of

Education and Science, Mowden Hall, Staindrop Road, Darlington, County Durham DL3 9BG. The applicant should first write to that Department for instructions on how to apply for qualification and for the necessary forms. If his qualifications are approved (a process that may take several months), he can then apply for a teaching position to the Local Education Authority in the area or areas of his choice. Addresses are published in a volume called *The Education Authorities Directory and Annual,* available from Pendragon House, Inc., 220 University Avenue, Palo Alto, Cal. 94301, for $10.50. Sending out "blind" letters of inquiry to a number of Local Education Authorities at the same time is probably the best way to turn up an opening. Vacancies are advertised in the local papers and in the *Times Educational Supplement,* but may well be filled before the U.S. applicant has access to the papers. The Appointment Board, Hamilton House, Mabledon Place, London WC1H 9BB, will assist a teacher who cannot find a suitable post on his own. Salaries range from £1,179 to £3,672.

Independent Schools.   Schools not financed by local or central government funds are permitted to choose their faculties without official approval of teachers' qualifications (although they *will* be required to obtain work permits), and application may therefore be made direct to the school. Names and addresses of independent schools are available from Pendragon House for $3.60. Ask for "List 70." Help in locating vacancies is available from Truman and Knightley Educational Trust, 76–78 Notting Hill Gate, London W11 3LJ.

College and University Level

Applications for teaching positions at publicly maintained colleges may be submitted to the Local Education Authorities. For a post at one of the independently run universities, the applicant should address the appropriate department of the university. British universities are listed in Appendix G, and details are available in *Commonwealth Universities Yearbook,* which you will probably find at your local library. Salaries range from about £1,500 for an assistant lecturer to about £5,600 for a full professor.

A few lecturing appointments are made through the Fulbright-Hays program. A candidate for one of these appointments must be a U.S. citizen and must have college or university teaching experience at the level of lectureship for which he is applying. Announcements of openings are available from Suzanne McLaughlin, Committee on International Exchange of Persons, Conference Board of Associated Research Councils, 2101 Constitution Avenue, N.W., Washington, D.C. 20418.

Depending on experience and academic rank in a U.S. college or university, the stipend ranges from £3,114 to £3,663 for a single person; from £4,005 to £4,554 for a grantee with one dependent; and from £4,302 to £4,851 for a grantee with two dependents.

Britain and the United States have a regular program of teacher exchange, designed primarily for (but not limited to) teachers in schools below university level. The applicant should be below the age of 50 and in good health and should have at least five years of teaching experience. His salary is paid by his "home" school, but he is required to finance his own transportation. Details are available from Teacher Exchange Section, Division of International Exchange and Training, Institute of International Studies, U.S. Office of Education, Washington, D.C. 20202.

OTHER PROFESSIONS

Certain professional people, if they plan to follow their own professions in England, are exempt from the requirement to obtain work permits: doctors, dentists, clergymen, free-lance writers and artists, and journalists who represent overseas newspapers. These people should not assume, however, that they may enter England and begin work there whenever the fancy strikes them. They must first consult an overseas British Consulate or Embassy about entry requirements.

SETTING UP A BUSINESS

Anyone wishing to set up his own business or join a partnership in England should do a little groundwork in the United States before he attempts to embark on his new venture. He should consult a British Consulate about obtaining Home Office permission for residence, and he should seek advice from a large U.S. bank about obtaining Treasury permission through the Bank of England for the formation of a new company. The company will have to be registered with the Companies Registration Office, Companies House, 55–71 City Road, London EC1 133; and if the owner of the new firm hopes to employ any nonresident aliens he will require strong justification in order to obtain work permits for them from the Department of Employment. He may also, because of the recent rather spectacular increase in the cost of land and building space, encounter some difficulty in finding a suitable location at a reasonable price.

The undertaking is not a simple one, and it is further complicated by the necessity for learning all about the effect of Exchange Control regulations on the owner's investment and about capital gains and corporation taxes.[1]

VOLUNTEER WORK

A work permit is not required for volunteer work for which no pay is received.

Opportunities for volunteer work are discussed in Chapter XII.

Anyone who seeks employment in England should remember that there are many factors that make one's earning capacity abroad differ from his earning capacity in the United States: fringe benefits differ; taxes differ; differing levels of importance are attached to similar job titles; an occupational category that is well paid in one country may be poorly compensated in the other; living standards and commodity prices differ. There is far more to consider than a simple conversion of dollars into pounds.

[1]The tax rate on corporation profits for the fiscal year ending 31 March 1973 was 40 percent, but a substantial increase (perhaps to as much as 42 percent for small corporations and 52 percent for larger ones) is expected when the Finance Act 1974 becomes law.

Chapter VIII
HEALTH

The average cost of a day in a U.S. hospital is $80, and the figure is rising. An American entitled to Medicare may be able to recover 60 percent of this; the remaining $32 must come out of his pocket or from private insurance plans for which he pays substantial premiums.[1] And what of the person who is not yet eligible for Medicare? If he's fortunate, he is partially covered by group insurance through his employer; if he's self-employed or works for a firm that does not offer such a fringe benefit, he's out of luck. Experts predict that the average hospital bill for a heart attack will soon reach $16,000; a leukemia patient may require as many as 250 treatments over a three-year period at an approximate cost of $15,000. There is no surer way to wipe out a family's savings than by an extended illness.

Most Western countries have some form of national health plan, but Britain's is the most comprehensive and probably the most efficiently administered. (West Germany's plan is so cumbersome that 40 percent of its own officials subscribe to private insurance.) Only 6 percent of Britain's national income is spent on the National Health Service; yet this pays for 750,000 employees, 450,000 hospital beds, and 20,000 family doctors; and though the tax money that makes up this 6 percent comes from British citizens, the services provided are for the benefit of

---

[1]It is interesting to note that the average family's annual out-of-pocket medical expenses now total more than they did in the year before Medicare was introduced. This is, of course, attributable largely to inflated hospital charges and to the tendency of more and more physicians to make extensive use of hospital facilities; but no matter what the reason, the facts are not comforting to retired people on fixed incomes.

noncontributors as well as citizens. The casual tourist, the foreign student, the retired American living in England, the rich, the poor—all are protected to some degree by the NHS.

The stated objectives of the National Health Service are to make accessible to everyone, regardless of age or financial status, the most up-to-date and comprehensive medical care covering everything from treatment of minor ailments to major surgery; to provide all general services (family doctor, dentist, nursing care, health education) and all necessary drugs, medicines, and most prosthetic devices; and to encourage the promotion of mental and physical well-being by enabling people to seek early advice without fear of incurring debt.

At the same time, Britain has made participation in its health services noncompulsory. Everyone is free to use the facilities available to him or to decline them if he prefers to make private arrangements at his own expense. Doctors paid by the NHS may use their own judgment in treating their patients, without fear of bureaucratic interference. Patients are free to choose their own family doctors; and doctors are free to decide which patients they will accept. The plan is designed to foster the doctor-patient relationship, with the doctor always serving as the link between the patient and the hospital or whatever other health service the patient may require.

Perhaps because of his willingness to see the doctor (he isn't afraid of the bill), the British male lives, on the average, two years longer than the American male.

It stands to reason, of course, that you are not expected to move to England for the sole purpose of obtaining free medical care; this is not what British citizens have been paying taxes for. You will be expected to pay, as a private patient, for treatment of pre-existing conditions. So buy your new spectacles, have your bunions removed, and get your cavities filled before you go, and try to arrive in mint condition. Once a resident [2] of Britain—if you have acted honestly and in good faith—your worries are over.

The health services provided by the NHS that will be available to you as a resident of Britain fall into three broad categories: (1) hospital and specialist services; (2) general practitioner services; and (3) local health authority (LHA) services.

[2]"Residency"—a tricky area—is discussed in more detail in the chapter on taxes. For the purpose of determining whether or not the National Health Service will consider you a bona fide resident, eligible for full benefits, it is enough at this point to keep in mind that short-term visitors are *not* residents and are expected to make, at their own expense, private arrangements for any treatment or prescriptions that they require while in Britain. However, a short-term visitor will not be denied help if he falls ill or has an accident while he is in England; the NHS operates on a "Good Samaritan" principle that makes emergency treatment available to everyone.

HOSPITAL AND SPECIALIST SERVICES

Hospital and specialist services are usually arranged by the family doctor and administered through regional hospital boards. These services include all types of hospital care and treatment for both in-patients and out-patients, as well as specialist advice and treatment in hospitals, clinics, maternity homes, rehabilitation centers, and even in patients' homes. Blood transfusions, pathological laboratory services, X rays, diagnostic services, Pap smears, occupational therapy, and confidential treatment of venereal disease are a few of the free services available.

The nonpaying NHS patient is cared for in a general ward unless, as sometimes happens, a single room or small ward, usually reserved for a patient who requires privacy for medical reasons, becomes available. The NHS patient who requests private accommodation and is fortunate enough to find it is charged a fee of approximately $6 a day for a single room or $3 a day for a bed in a small ward. No time limitation in hospital is imposed by NHS; the patient remains hospitalized until the medical staff determines that he may be discharged or until he discharges himself. (The non-NHS patient may ask for accommodations in a hospital with "pay beds"; he, of course, pays the full cost of the accommodations provided and the fees of the staff physician attending him.)

Children's hospitals and children's wards in general hospitals are available to NHS families. Here, special attention is given to the need for organized play and continuing education if the child is to be confined for an extended period.

Mental disorders are handled in much the same way as physical disorders: Family doctors arrange specialist treatment at out-patient clinics or in hospitals. (The NHS is authorized to detain a mental patient in hospital when detention is necessary for the safety of the patient himself or of those around him, but this authority is exercised only as a last resort—and when it *is* exercised, there are procedures by which the patient himself or his family can appeal to an independent tribunal for his release.)

Many hospitals serve as distribution centers where, on the recommendation of a specialist, free hearing aids may be supplied and fitted. These free appliances are not the daintiest; if you want a smaller one than is available through the NHS, you will have to pay for it.[3]

Treatment and supervision of drug addiction—England's medical approach to the problems of drug abuse and crime arising from drug abuse—is another of the British hospitals' major responsibilities. Drug addicts willing to undergo the withdrawal and rehabilitation process

---

[3]The Royal National Institute for the Deaf, 105 Gower Street, London WCIE 6AH, will send you a list of commercial hearing aids with their approximate costs.

are accepted as in-patients; those who reject the idea of withdrawal may receive medically supervised drug maintenance at out-patient clinics.

GENERAL PRACTITIONER SERVICES

General practitioner services cover four major areas: Family Doctor Service, Dental Service, Ophthalmic Service, and Pharmaceutical Service.

The Family Doctor Service

In addition to treating fee-paying patients, every doctor in England may participate in the NHS if he so elects—and he usually does. The NHS doctor generally has his own "surgery" (office and examining rooms)—though often in conjunction with a group of other doctors—and he expects his patients to visit him during office hours. He *will*, however, make house calls if his patient is too ill to leave home. Because he regularly treats the same patients—those on his register—he becomes well acquainted with their family backgrounds and circumstances, and a personal relationship develops between doctor and patient that is of immense importance in diagnosis and treatment and in prevention of ill health. It is the family doctor who arranges hospitalization when necessary (the patient does not admit himself to the hospital, except in emergency situations), refers the patient to a specialist if circumstances require specialized knowledge, and helps his patient apply for local health authority services.

Lists of NHS doctors are available at all general post offices. One of the first things you should do after you're settled is decide which doctor you want for your personal physician (inquiries to your new neighbors will help) and then ask that doctor to put you on his list. He will give you an application form (EC1) to complete and return to him. He will then submit the form to the local NHS Executive Council, who will send you a card bearing your NHS number. (Keep the card in your wallet.)

Of course, the doctor you select may already have his full quota of patients, and you may have to make another choice. If you're totally unlucky in finding a doctor, you may apply to the Executive Council for help. Make your choice as wisely as possible: Once on a list, you are expected to stay on it, unless you move—or the doctor moves. If you wish to change doctors for some other reason you may do so, but you will first have to obtain your present doctor's consent, or apply to the Executive Council for a transfer—a process that will take several weeks.

If, for a period of not more than three months, you are a visitor in some area of England other than the one in which you normally reside, you may apply to an NHS doctor for treatment as a "temporary resident." And in case of emergency, any NHS doctor will treat you immediately if you cannot reach your own doctor.

There is no charge for doctor services performed under the NHS.

The Dental Service

Most British dentists accept NHS patients in addition to private patients but, unlike the doctors, they do not have lists of registered patients. Each time you need dental treatment or a course of dental treatments you must first ask a dentist to accept you. (You will find him, like your doctor, on a list in the post office.) If he agrees, his acceptance is only for that one treatment or course of treatments; the next time you need dental care, you will have to apply all over again.

The most important thing to remember when you seek treatment is that you must inform the dentist, *at the time you set up an appointment,* that you wish to be an NHS patient. Remind him again of this when you make your first visit, and show him your NHS card. (If you fail to do these things, you may find yourself paying the full cost.) He will give you an application form, and, if treatment is required immediately, he may ask you to pay a statutory charge in advance. Don't be offended by this; pay the charge.

Remember, too, to keep your appointment; you will probably be charged for wasted time if you fail to show up.

The initial checkup itself is free and will enable the dentist to determine what specific treatment is going to be needed. If it turns out that something other than the usual filling or scaling is required—for instance, if you must have crowns or oral surgery or prolonged orthodontic treatment—the dentist must obtain the approval of the Dental Estimates Board before he agrees to NHS treatment.

Free dental services include, in addition to checkups, arrest of bleeding, denture repairs, and cost of travel (up to five miles) if the dentist has to come to your home. For other services, including dentures, you will be charged half the cost—up to a maximum of £10—for any one course[4] of treatments.

Certain people are exempt from all dental fees, including dentures:

[4] A "course" of treatments is a schedule of services (the need for which is determined as a result of the initial consultation) performed within a relatively short period of time. At the end of the course, you will be asked to sign a form stating that, to the best of your knowledge, the work has been completed. If additional work is required at a later date —for instance, if dentures must be adjusted after gums have shrunk—a "new" treatment or course of treatments is begun, and, consequently, a new set of charges.

All children under the age of 16;
Young people over 16 who are still full-time school[5] students;
Expectant mothers;
Mothers who have borne a child within the previous 12 months.

Remember that what the NHS strives to achieve in its dental program is oral *fitness*, and the services offered are adequate for that purpose. If you demand a service that is not clinically necessary—for instance, gold inlays where plastic ones will suffice—you will have to pay the extra cost.

Remember, also, to schedule regular six-month checkups; they're free, and you will be doing yourself—*and* the NHS—a favor by taking advantage of them.

The Ophthalmic Service

The purpose of the NHS Ophthalmic Service is twofold: to test sight, and to provide spectacles. Anything falling outside the realm of this twofold service—for example, diagnosis and treatment of eye diseases and other abnormal eye conditions, and the furnishing of unusual or special lenses (including contact lenses)[6]—is the responsibility of the Hospital and Specialist Service.

The services of three classes of professionals are available under the NHS Ophthalmic Service—the ophthalmic medical practitioner (a GP who is qualified, by virtue of special ophthalmic training, to determine whether any treatment other than glasses is required), the ophthalmic optician (who can test sight and prescribe lenses and also supply lenses), and the dispensing optician (whose sole function is to supply lenses prescribed by the ophthalmic medical practitioner or ophthalmic optician).

Whether you need special eye treatment or just a new pair of glasses, your first stop must always be at the offices of the family doctor. The doctor will give you a form (OSC1) authorizing you to seek the services of either an ophthalmic medical practitioner or an ophthalmic optician. (The list is available at the post office, and the choice is up to you.) Your eyes will be tested free of charge (show your NHS card) and then you may proceed to any dispensing optician for spectacles.

Lenses and frames are not free, but they are supplied at cost. The usual charge is from £1.20 to £2.10 for each single-vision lens and from

[5]The NHS definition of "school" does not include institutions of higher education, such as universities and technical colleges.
[6]Contact lenses are available under NHS only when they are determined to be clinically necessary; they are not furnished for cosmetic purposes.

£2.45 to £3.50 for each bifocal lens, plus 70p to £1.74 for frames. If you want special frames, outside the standard range of fifteen styles provided by NHS, you will have to pay extra for them.

Once you've made use of the NHS Ophthalmic Service, you need not go through the family doctor again; you may go directly for your free checkups and for your prescriptions and spectacles. Whether or not you must pay the full cost of replacement when you break or lose your spectacles depends on whether the breakage is due to your own negligence, and it probably is; the optician will advise you on this if you wish to pursue it.

Children under ten are provided with lenses and NHS frames at no cost. Children between the ages of 10 and 16, and those over 16 still in school, [7] may have free lenses but must pay for the frames.

A person who requires ophthalmic service but is unable to leave home may request the ophthalmologist to visit him at his home. He will be charged a reasonable fee for the house call.

The Pharmaceutical Service

Private patients must pay the full cost of drugs and medicines, but anyone who is a registered participant in the NHS Family Doctor Service is entitled to prescriptions at a cost of 20p each. The word "prescription" covers not only medicines, but also minor appliances such as trusses and hypodermic syringes.[8] The only exception to the 20p price is the charge for elastic hosiery, which costs 25p for each anklet, legging, kneecap or thigh piece, and 50p for each full stocking.

Almost all druggists ("chemists" in England) handle NHS prescriptions, but if you are uncertain about whether the one you wish to patronize takes part in the service look for a notice posted in his shop window or check the list at the post office. If he's closed when you need him, look in his window for the addresses of other chemists in the area who are open at that hour. Chemists usually arrange their hours so that at least one shop is accessible in an emergency.

Certain categories of NHS patients are *totally* exempt from prescription charges: people over 65; children under 15; expectant mothers and mothers with children under one year of age; people who suffer from diabetes, epilepsy, and certain other specified medical conditions requiring continuous and extended medication. If you do not qualify for total exemption, however, you can still save by purchasing a prepayment certificate that will exempt you from paying prescription charges

[7]See footnote 5 in this chapter.
[8]Major appliances are the responsibility of the hospitals and are supplied upon the recommendation of specialists.

for a specified period of time. A six-month certificate will cost you £ 2.00; a 12-month certificate, £3.50. Prepayment certificates are available to everyone, and it will pay you to take advantage of them if you anticipate the need for more than 10 prescription items in a six-month period or 17 in a year.

People who are exempt from prescription charges because of age need only sign (or, if under 15, have a parent sign) the declaration on the back of the prescription; other eligibles must have exemption certificates. Leaflets EC91 (explaining in detail how to claim exemptions and refunds) and EC95 (explaining prepayment certificates) are available at—guess where?—the post office.

LOCAL HEALTH AUTHORITY SERVICES

Local health authority services are perhaps best described as *supporting* services, supplementing and complementing the work of the hospitals and specialists and the general practitioners. LHA services include: family planning advice; midwifery, and prenatal and postnatal maternity care (including care of unwed mothers and their babies); skilled home nursing; health visiting (for the purpose of giving advice on such matters as hygiene, diet, and spread of infection); domestic help; child welfare; vaccination, immunization, and services for prevention of and recuperation from illness; ambulance service;[9] special services for the elderly, such as meals-on-wheels and chiropody services; and the establishment and maintenance of health centers where various NHS services in the area can be concentrated for easy accessibility.

Because—as the name implies—these services are administered by local governing bodies (some of whom have more money at their disposal than others), they vary greatly from county to county. LHA day nurseries, for example, are available in some localities, not in others; the same is true of child-guidance clinics and of such nursing aids as laundry services and night sitters who go to private homes to relieve people burdened with round-the-clock care of relatives.

Some of the services are free, others are provided at cost, and still others are charged for according to income. The free services include home midwifery, health visiting, home nursing, vaccination and immunization, ambulance service, and medical and dental services for expectant and nursing mothers.

A person who decides to live in England should visit the health center nearest his new home to familiarize himself with the services available

[9]Usually arranged by your doctor, but in an emergency dial 999 and ask the operator for "Ambulance."

to him. It is particularly important that a foreigner who has never earned a salary in England learn to distinguish between benefits for which he is eligible (*i.e.*, the National Health Service) and those for which he cannnot qualify because he has never been a contributor to the National Insurance (Social Security) Scheme.

OTHER HEALTH SERVICES

Many other government organizations share with NHS the responsibility for public health: the Department of Education and Science (for school health programs); the Department of Employment (for occupational health programs); the Ministry of Agriculture, Fisheries and Food (for food and drug administration); the Ministry of Defence (for medical services in the armed forces); the Home Office (for immunization and vaccination of immigrants); the Medical Research Council—to name a few.

In addition, services in specialized areas are provided by many voluntary and self-help organizations such as Alcoholics Anonymous; the Cancer Information Association and the Marie Curie Memorial Foundation; the Family Planning Association; the National Institutes for the Blind and for the Deaf; the British Diabetic Association; the National Association for Mental Health; the Multiple Sclerosis Society of Great Britain; the Muscular Dystrophy Group of Great Britain; the Association of Psychotherapists; the British Red Cross; and many more.

There is considerable overlapping of services, not only among the many non-NHS organizations, but within the NHS itself. A person who requires help is likely to become utterly bewildered if he takes it upon himself to find the service that most nearly meets his needs. He should always turn first to his NHS family doctor; and then, if he has need of further assistance, he can consult the nearest Citizens' Advice Bureau, which he will find listed in his telephone directory.

If, when you prepare to leave the United States, you entertain any doubts as to the advisability of your move or the permanency of your stay in England, hang onto your U.S. hospitalization policy for a few months. The protection offered by most large insurance companies is worldwide, except in a few poor-risk countries and except for coverage under the Medicare program.[10] There is time enough to cancel after you are settled in England and are certain that you wish to stay.

---

[10]Medicare does not, as a rule, pay for services obtained outside the United States. More information about Medicare as it relates to overseas residents and about NHS benefits of special interest to retirees is given in Chapter XII.

Chapter IX
THE TWO INEVITABLES

The British Empire made up a large part of "this world" when Benjamin Franklin wrote to his friend, M. Leroy, that "in this world nothing is more certain than death and taxes." The Empire has altered considerably since that letter was written in 1789: Its colonies have forsaken it, its power has waned, the divine right of its monarchs has been challenged by popular vote; only death and taxes remain as certain as ever. We must try to content ourselves with the realization that the methods of collection, if not the assessments, have taken a turn for the better: Our profits may be wrenched from us against our wills but a late tax remittance is more likely to be punishable by fines and added interest than by an hour on the rack, and death is more likely to find our heads on our pillows than on the block.

To soften the impact of a chapter concerned only with two unsavory topics, I shall devote the first part to what I feel (though there are some who may dispute me) is the lesser of the two evils.

Part 1 / TAXES

Most of the literature published about the tax liability of United States citizens living in England is so general and sweeping in content that the reader doesn't know much more after he's finished reading it than he did before. The reasons are understandable: Tax laws are complex, and there is so wide a variance in the circumstances of Americans living abroad (marital status, age brackets, amounts and sources of income) that each case must be considered on its own.

To get the complete picture, the American planning to move to England must turn to the tax regulations themselves, and here he is likely to run into such an overabundance of detail and bog down in such a morass of ifs, ands, and buts, that he will throw up his hands in horror. A number of publications are available from the Superintendent of Documents, U.S. Government Printing Office, Washington, D.C. 20402,[1] but although these documents are not too difficult to understand they are lengthy and tedious and they are intended for U.S. citizens living abroad in any country and not specifically in England. Furthermore, they tell you all about the taxes you must pay to the United States government but not about the taxes you must pay to the British government.

Britain, I am happy to say, has as one of its avowed purposes the simplification of its tax laws and is constantly revising them to make them easy to administer and easy to understand. For example, in April, 1973, it put into operation a new "unified tax" system that did away with the separate computation and administration of income tax and income surtax and (except for a surcharge in the higher brackets of investment income) with the differentiation between earned income and investment income. But the British Inland Revenue Service cannot be of much help in your dealings with the U.S. Internal Revenue Service.

This chapter will attempt to give you a little better understanding of what will be expected of you than you will get from the bulk of the general literature. It will *not* attempt to go into the detail that characterizes the publications of the Internal Revenue Service. The emphasis here will be on your liability (or exemption from liability) to the British government, since that is the information that is not so readily accessible to you. Even so, you will need professional assistance in preparing your returns.

There is, apparently, a widespread belief among Americans that taxes in Britain are much higher than in the United States. This is true for the wealthy person; but the American in average circumstances will not be severely, if at all, penalized by the British system of taxation.

Britain and the United States have a reciprocal taxation agreement whereby, broadly speaking, income taxed by one country is not taxed by the other, thus precluding the possibility of double taxation. In addition, whereas the income tax levied on a U.S. citizen by the British government may be at a higher rate than that at which his U.S. federal

---

[1]Publication #54, *Tax Guide for U.S. Citizens Abroad;* #569, *Questions Asked by U.S. Taxpayers Abroad;* #516, *Tax Information for U.S. Government Civilian Employees Stationed Abroad;* #563, *Tax Return Filing Requirements for U.S. Citizens Abroad.*

tax is computed, the aggregate of all U.S. taxes (federal and local) versus the aggregate of all British taxes may well work out in favor of the British resident. For example, in the United States one generally pays, in addition to his federal income tax, a state income tax and, not infrequently, a county or city income tax as well; in England there are no local taxes other than the "rates" (see pp. 114, 159) and a few miscellaneous license fees. In the United States, one must usually pay a property tax on his home and taxes on his utilities; in England, there are no property taxes other than the rates, and no utility taxes except that in some localities water rates are charged for separately and apart from the other rates. In the United States, sales taxes are imposed on almost every item purchased; in England, the value added tax, though heavy (10 percent), is designed to cover, in the main, luxury items.

Taxes in Britain may be grouped into four broad categories: (1) taxes on income; (2) taxes on capital (capital gains and estate duty); (3) taxes on expenditure (customs and excise duties, value added tax [VAT], stamp duties, license duties, and special tax on new and imported cars); (4) local taxes (rates).

TAXES ON INCOME

Income tax in Britain is administered by the Board of Inland Revenue. It is an annual tax covering the period between April 6 of each year and April 5 of the following year and, in general, is payable on all income accruing to British residents, regardless of its source.

The word "residence" has different definitions in Britain, depending on where and by whom it is defined. You will discover, for instance, that you may be considered a resident by the National Health Service before you are considered one by the Board of Inland Revenue, or that Inland Revenue may consider you a resident before the Treasury Department and the Bank of England consider you a resident for "exchange control" (see p. 16) purposes. It is necessary at the outset of this section, therefore, to explain "residence" as it is defined for income tax purposes.

Stated as simply as possible, the Board of Inland Revenue considers you a resident if: (a) you spend six months, consecutive or piecemeal, of the tax year (April 6 through April 5) in the United Kingdom; *or* (b) you are a *habitual* visitor to the United Kingdom for substantial periods of time (annual visits of three months' duration in four successive years are enough to make Inland Revenue consider your visits "habitual"); *or* (c) you establish and maintain a place of abode in the United Kingdom for your own use and visit it during the tax year, no matter how short the visit.

If, when you enter Britain, you do so *with the intent of becoming a permanent resident,* you are regarded as a resident for income tax purposes from the date of your arrival.

Another word, "domicile," requires defining, because it becomes relevant when one attempts to ascertain the extent of his tax liability to the United Kingdom on certain investment income. "Domicile" does not have quite the same meaning as "residence." A person can be a resident of more than one country at any given time, but he is domiciled in only one—the one in which he has his permanent home. At birth, he acquires his *domicile of origin* (generally, his father's domicile, which may or may not be his place of birth). He acquires a *domicile of choice* if he settles in a different country and establishes a clear intent to remain there permanently. A *domicile of dependency* is acquired by the wife and minor children of a man who has a different domicile of origin or who has acquired a new domicile of choice.[2]

The Double Taxation Conventions

The general rule that income tax is payable by all residents is, like all rules, subject to certain exceptions. For example, disability pensions from the British Armed Services and supplemental benefits paid under the British National Insurance Scheme to the sick, the elderly, and the unemployed are not normally taxable; and remuneration of foreign diplomatic representatives is totally exempt.

The exceptions that will interest the readers of this book, however, are those that fall under the reciprocal taxation agreement between the United States and Britain.[3] The agreement has two basic aims: (a) to insure that the sum of the taxes paid to both countries does not exceed the amount that would have been payable to whichever country has the higher rate of tax; and (b) by providing for exchange of information between the two countries, to "avoid unnecessary administrative complications"—which is probably a polite way of saying "to preclude the possibility of tax evasion."

Under the terms of the reciprocal taxation agreement, relief from double taxation may be achieved in two ways: (1) by one country's exempting, or charging at a reduced rate, certain categories of income; or (2) if the income is in a category not wholly or partially exempted by either country, by allowing the tax charged by one country to apply as a credit against the tax charged by the other country.

[2]The domicile of dependency remains unchanged after death or divorce of the husband/father, until the dependents acquire for themselves new domiciles of choice.
[3]You may examine the complete agreement at the library of the British Information Services, 845 Third Avenue, New York; or you may purchase a copy for 60¢ from Pendragon House, Inc., 220 University Avenue, Palo Alto, California 94301. Ask for "The Double Taxation Conventions between the United Kingdom and the United States."

The exemption or reduced-rate method is generally applied to dividends, interest, patent and copyright royalties, pensions, purchased annuities, government salaries, earnings of temporary business visitors, and trading profits not arising through a "permanent establishment."

The relief-by-credit method is generally applied to income accruing to a person resident in one country from real property owned in the other country; to trading profits realized by a person resident in one country but emanating from a permanent establishment in the other country; and to dividends, interest, or royalties earned by a person resident in one country but paid by someone in the other country, provided partial or total exemption is not granted by the other country. The general principle is that the United Kingdom allows a credit against United Kingdom tax to persons resident in the United Kingdom with income emanating from the other country; the other country allows a credit against *its* tax to *its* residents against income emanating from the United Kingdom.

Because the provisions of the Double Taxation Conventions are so broad, and because no two cases are exactly alike, it is impossible accurately to forecast what percentage of your income will be liable to United Kingdom tax. A few specifics have been extracted from the Conventions, however, which may apply to the readers of this book:

1. If you are a visiting professor or instructor, being paid by a British college or university or other British educational institution for your teaching services, and if you are not to remain in England for more than two years, the money paid to you by the British institution will not be taxed by the United Kingdom.

2. If you are a full-time student at a British institution, money that is remitted to you by U.S. sources for your tuition and maintenance will not be taxed by the United Kingdom.

3. If you are drawing a salary paid by the U.S. government, that salary will not be taxed by the United Kingdom.

4. If you are drawing a pension from the U.S. government paid to you for services rendered to the United States in discharge of governmental duties, that pension will not be taxed by the United Kingdom.

5. Pensions other than the type described in 4 above, *including Social Security*, are subject to United Kingdom tax, *but only insofar as they are remitted to Britain or in any way received in Britain*. (However, see footnote 4, next page.)

6. Your investment income (dividends, interest, etc.) will be liable to United Kingdom tax whether or not it is remitted to Britain *if* you are domiciled in Britain. If you are resident but not domiciled, only that portion which is remitted to Britain is subject to tax by Britain. (Here is where the difference between "residence" and "domicile" becomes relevant. Suppose, for example, that you are on temporary duty assign-

ment, perhaps for a year, at the British affiliate of your American firm:
You are a *resident* of Britain during that year, but you are not *domiciled*
in Britain because it is not your permanent home; your investment
income emanating from the United States is not taxable by the United
Kingdom unless the money is remitted to the United Kingdom. If,
however, you are both resident *and* domiciled in the United Kingdom
—as you would be if you retired in England and made it your permanent home—your U.S. investment income, whether it stays in the U.S.
or is remitted to Britain, is liable to tax by the United Kingdom.)

By now, you will have reached the obvious conclusion that, in general, the less money you take into Britain the better. All income arising
from British sources (unless you qualify for exemption under the Double Taxation Conventions as a short-term visiting professor) will, of
course, be subject to United Kingdom income tax.[4]

Allowances and Reliefs

Certain allowances and reliefs may be deducted from total income
before the tax rate is applied. (If husband and wife are living together,
the wife's income is declared on her husband's return and all allowances
are claimed by the husband against their joint incomes.)

Personal allowances are as follows (and U.S. citizens residing in England are entitled to them):

Single person	£ 595
Wife's earned income	595 (maximum)
Married man	775 (maximum)
Child	
Under 11	200
11 to 16	235
Over 16 (if full-time student)	265
Dependent relative	
Single woman	145
Other	100
Housekeeper	100
Daughter's services	55
Blind person	130

[4]The tax regulations and rates cited in this section are those established for the tax year
1973–1974. A new budget has since been proposed which will effect certain changes, but
these changes will not become law until Parliament acts on them. It is probable that the
government will take steps to tax pension money of foreign residents even though it is
not remitted to Britain, but the percentage of unremitted money that will be liable to
U.K. tax has not yet been decided. See Appendix F for a chart illustrating the current basis
of liability to the United Kingdom for tax on *earned* income.

Depending on your circumstances, you may be able to claim, either by deduction or by reduced-rate tax, certain additional reliefs, *e.g.*, fees to professional organizations; special tools and clothing required for your job; contributions toward death and old age benefits paid to a trade union; license fees required in your profession; certain business losses; premiums on life insurance policies; interest on mortgage loans (except option mortgages); interest paid to banks and finance companies; alimony and support payments.

Income Tax Rates

The standard rate of tax on the first £5,000 of earned income is 30 percent, *after* allowable deductions. The rate increases as the income goes into higher brackets:

The next £1,000 (*i.e.,* income between £5,001 and £6,000) is taxed at	40 percent
The next £1,000 (£6,001–£7,000)	45 percent
The next £1,000 (£7,001–£8,000)	50 percent
The next £2,000 (£8,001–£10,000)	55 percent
The next £2,000 (£10,001–£12,000)	60 percent
The next £3,000 (£12,001–£15,000)	65 percent
The next £5,000 (£15,001–£20,000)	70 percent
All income over £20,000	75 percent

When the Finance Act 1974 becomes law, the standard tax rate on the first £5000 of earned income will probably jump to 33 percent, and there will be increases all along the scale to a maximum of 83 percent in the top-income bracket. (Restructuring of personal allowances and reliefs may, however, offset the increased rate for low-income families.) The press has made much of Britain's proposed tax increases; what the press has *not* told you is that the standard rate in 1972 was 38.75 percent—5.75 percent more than it will be under the Finance Act 1974.

Investment income (dividends, interest, rents, and so forth) is taxed at the same rate as earned income, up to £2,000. Investment income in excess of £2,000, however, is subject to a surcharge of 15 percent.

Despite all the foregoing provisions, the calculation of United Kingdom income tax is not too complex for the American citizen residing in Britain if his entire income emanates from the United States. If he has income emanating from both countries, however, it's a different story. In any case, it is advisable to seek assistance from professionals knowledgeable in the Double Taxation Conventions. (Any doubt about the wisdom of obtaining professional assistance should be dissolved when you review the definition of "residence" and realize that the same person can be a resident of both countries in the same tax year, and when you realize, further, that the dates of the tax year differ in the two countries, thus requiring apportionment of taxes and of credits allowed.)

During the tax season (January–April), the Internal Revenue Service has agents stationed at the United States Embassy in London who will help you prepare your U.S. return. Assistance with your British return will be available at your local tax office (listed in your telephone directory under "Inland Revenue"), or you may write to the Chief Inspector of Taxes, Magdalen House, Stanley Precinct, Bootle, Lancashire L69 9BB. If you feel that your financial circumstances are too complex for you to handle your own tax returns, even with the assistance of these offices, engage a solicitor.

Perhaps the most important thing to remember is that you should not rely on either country to volunteer credits and exemptions and claims and "reliefs": You will have to ask for them. When the time comes to seek out your professional assistance, therefore, review this chapter, fix in your mind the items on which you think you may be entitled to relief in one form or another, and arm yourself with the appropriate evidence.

TAXES ON CAPITAL

Capital Gains Tax

Disposal of U.S. Assets

Your first concern about capital gains tax in England will probably relate to the disposal of your U.S. assets. To which country will you be liable for capital gains tax?

If you are not a resident of the United Kingdom at the time the property is sold and the profits realized, and if you have not been a resident during the preceding 36 months, you will not be liable to the United Kingdom for capital gains tax unless the assets on which the gains were realized derived from an agency or company branch or other permanent establishment through which you have been carrying on a trade in the United Kingdom.

If you are a resident of the United Kingdom but are not domiciled in the United Kingdom,[5] you will be liable to the United Kingdom for capital gains tax only on that portion of your gains that is actually received in the United Kingdom. (It follows, therefore, that you cannot claim relief from United Kingdom tax if your sale results in a loss instead of a gain.)

[5]See pp. 147–148 for the distinction between "residence" and "domicile."

If you are both resident and domiciled in the United Kingdom when the U.S. property is sold and the profits realized, you will be liable to the United Kingdom for capital gains tax.

Under the provisions of the Double Taxation Conventions, you will not be charged capital gains tax by both countries on disposal of the same assets.

Disposal of British Assets

For purposes of the capital gains tax, "disposal" occurs whenever and however ownership of an asset is transferred from one party to another, except upon death.[6] Although the general principle is that liability for tax arises at disposal of assets, there are certain exceptions. There is no capital gains tax, for example, on profits totaling less than £500 during the year of assessment; nor is there a capital gains tax on profits accruing from the disposal of:

A business, if the owner is retiring and if he's over 60 years old
A principal private residence and one additional residence occupied by a dependent relative (plus a proportionately suitable amount of land to go along with the houses)
Tangible chattels worth £1000 or less
Tangible chattels with a life expectancy of less than 50 years
Life insurance policies on maturity or surrender
Savings certificates and premium bonds
Private automobiles
Gifts to charities and certain organizations concerned with the national heritage
Gifts to individuals not exceeding £100 in the tax year
Betting winnings
Objects of artistic, historic, national, or scientific value—provided they stay in the United Kingdom and are not sold except to a university, a national institution, or a local authority. (If they are sold to anyone else at a later date or removed from the United Kingdom, the capital gains tax becomes due and payable.)

The "tax year" for purposes of computing capital gains runs from April 6 through April 5, and the rate is 30 percent. Losses are offset against gains during the same period.

There are alternative ways of computing an individual's capital gains

---

[6]Prior to 1971 a person's assets were considered to have been disposed of at the time of his death, and his estate became liable for capital gains tax on net gains resulting from their disposal. This is no longer true. When a person dies, however, his personal representatives (*i.e.*, the administrators of his estate) are considered to have acquired the assets of the estate at market value on the date of the death and are liable for capital gains tax if they dispose of those assets at a profit; but if the administrators transfer the assets to a legatee or legatees in the ordinary course of administering the estate, they are not considered to have disposed of the assets at a profit even if the values have increased during the period between death of the testator and transfer to the legatee(s). Instead, the assets are considered to have retained the market value they had at the testator's death, and the legatees are considered to have acquired the assets at the same value.

tax that may or may not be to the taxpayer's advantage. It is always advisable to retain professional assistance.

Gains realized by *companies* are charged to corporation tax.

Estate Duty

When anyone of British domicile dies, the net value of his estate, wherever the property may be located, becomes subject to estate duty by the British government.[7] The duty is chargeable in accordance with a graduated scale of progressively higher percentages levied against each succeeding "slice" of net capital value. The rates are set forth below:

Net Capital			Cumulative Duty at the Top of Each Slice
Exceeding	Not exceeding	% of Duty	
(A)	(B)	(C)	(D)
£ 15,000	£ 20,000	25	£ 1,250
20,000	30,000	30	4,250
30,000	40,000	35	7,750
40,000	50,000	40	11,750
50,000	60,000	45	16,250
60,000	80,000	50	26,250
80,000	100,000	55	37,250
100,000	150,000	60	67,250
150,000	200,000	65	99,750
200,000	500,000	70	309,750
500,000	———	75	

No duty is chargeable on an estate with a net value of less than £15,000, nor does the rate of duty ever exceed 75 percent.

To calculate the duty on an amount falling between these slices, follow these steps: (1) find in Column B the figure that comes closest to, *but does not exceed,* the net capital value of the estate; (2) pick up from Column D the cumulative duty on that amount; (3) subtract the figure you used in Column B from the value of the estate and multiply the difference times the applicable percentage *for the next slice up the scale;* (4) add the amount you arrived at in Step 3 to the amount you arrived at in Step 2. Example:

---

[7]Even if the owner was not of British domicile, any portion of his estate that is situated in Great Britain is subject to duty at the owner's death.

Net capital value of estate	£48,560
Step 1 (from Column B)	£40,000
Step 2 (duty on £40,000—Column D)	£7,750
Step 3 (£48,560 − £40,000 = £8,560 × 40 percent)	£3,424
Step 4 (Step 2 plus Step 3)	£11,174
	(duty chargeable)

The net capital value of an estate is its current market value after certain deductions and reliefs. Any unpaid capital gains tax chargeable against the estate for disposal of assets prior to death is an allowable deduction. Funeral expenses and debts incurred by the deceased for his personal use and benefit are also deductible. Legitimate "reliefs" include:

£15,000 to a surviving spouse
£50,000 to charity
No limit on bequests to the National Gallery, the British Museum, the Royal Scottish Museum, the National Museum of Wales; or to other *national* institutions devoted to the preservation, for the public benefit, of items of scientific, historic, or artistic interest.

These reliefs and deductions are applied to the amount of the gross estate, and the assessment (*i.e.*, the applicable percentage shown in the above table) is then applied to the remainder.

Payment of estate duty is required before probate can be granted, except that payment of the duty on a freehold may be deferred for as long as eight years.

Farm property (*e.g.*, farmland, farm machinery, barns) is subject to estate tax at a reduced rate. The value of the total estate, including the farm property, is used in determining the appropriate tax bracket; but that portion of the estate that is categorized as "agricultural" is taxed at 55 percent of the rate applicable to that bracket.

To circumvent the tax dodge that so many people use to avoid estate duties (*i.e.*, giving away assets prior to death), British law allows such tax avoidance only if the donor continues to live for seven years after making the gift(s). If he dies between four and seven years after making the gift(s), the estate duty is reduced[8] but not eliminated; if he dies *within* four years of the gift(s), estate duty is chargeable on the full value. This is accomplished by treating the gift(s) as having been disposed of and then reacquired at time of death at current market value (but although current market value is applicable in determining the

[8]15 percent in the fifth year; 30 percent in the sixth year; 60 percent in the seventh year.

gross value of the estate for purposes of *estate duty,* no gain or loss upon reacquisition of assets at death is chargeable or allowable to *capital gains* tax.)

Under the provisions of the Double Taxation Conventions between the United States and the United Kingdom, you will be protected from payment of estate duty to both countries on the same capital.

TAXES ON EXPENDITURE

Customs and Excise Duties

All articles brought into England must be declared, whether or not you accompany them. Any agent who handles your shipment of household effects and other unaccompanied baggage will ask you to complete a written declaration (Customs Form C3), and the customs officer at the port of entry has legal authority to open your packages.

Normally, no duty will be assessed on household effects or personal professional effects brought into England only for your continued personal use (or that of your dependents) *if* these articles have already been in your possession and use for at least a year. In addition, if you have owned and used them for as long as three months, you may bring in, duty free, your watch and other jewelry up to a total value of £100 (if you carry them in personally); your clothing and textile articles (excluding rugs and carpets); and any *thing* or *set of things* valued at not more than £5. New or little-used goods are subject to payment of the appropriate duty[9] plus value added tax at the standard rate of 10 percent of duty-inclusive value.

Antiques (*i.e.,* articles over 100 years old) are not liable to duty or value added tax except for pearls and loose gem stones (which are liable only to VAT) and spirits and wine in excess of the duty-free allowance (which are liable only to duty). To take advantage of this exception, you will have to produce documentary evidence of the article's age.

You may also take into England, without payment of duty, 2 cartons of cigarettes, 100 cigars, 1 liter of spirits exceeding 38.8 percent U.K. proof or 2 liters not exceeding 38.8 percent proof, 2 liters of table wine, 2 fluid ounces of perfume, 8½ fluid ounces of toilet water, and 1 cigarette lighter.

For the duty on automobiles, see Chapter III, page 32.

[9]It is impossible to reproduce here a schedule of the current duties: There are 500 pages of them. You can examine a copy at a British Embassy or order one for £2.25 from Pendragon House, 220 University Ave., Palo Alto, Cal. 94301. Ask for "Customs & Excise Tariff."

Value Added Tax

On 1 April 1973 Britain abolished the Purchase Tax (a sales tax on commodities at varying rates depending on the type of commodity) and the Selective Employment Tax (a tax levied against employers on certain categories of services employed by them), and substituted a Value Added Tax (VAT) covering on both goods and services. (VAT is already well established in France, West Germany, Belgium, The Netherlands, Luxembourg, and the Scandinavian countries. It will soon be introduced into Ireland and Italy, and, as you probably already know, is being considered by the United States.)

The principle behind VAT is that each producer or trader along the way, from the initial production or importation of raw material to the final distribution of the end product, becomes liable for a tax on the value added by him to the goods or services at the time he contributes the added value.

Suppose, for example, that a producer imports raw material for which he pays $50p$:

1. He pays a $5p$ tax to the government and converts the raw material into fabric worth £1. He has then added to the value and he becomes liable for a $10p$ tax. He sells the fabric to a shirt manufacturer, bills the shirt manufacturer for £1 plus $10p$ tax, takes credit for the $5p$ tax he paid at importation, and turns the remaining $5p$ over to the government.

2. The shirt manufacturer makes a shirt worth £2.50. He has then added further to the value and becomes liable for a $25p$ tax. He sells the shirt to a retailer, invoices the retailer for £2.50 plus $25p$ tax, takes credit for the $10p$ tax for which he was invoiced by the fabric manufacturer, and turns the remaining $15p$ over to the government.

3. The retailer prices the shirt at £4, and becomes liable for $40p$ tax. He charges the customer £4.40, takes credit for the $25p$ tax for which he was invoiced by the manufacturer, and turns the remaining $15p$ over to the government.

Thus, although the government collects a tax at each step of the way, the ultimate effect is a tax on the consumer amounting to 10 percent of the sales price of the finished product and representing the sum of all the VAT paid before the consumer takes possession.

Certain commodities and services are "exempt" from VAT and others are "zero-rated." It doesn't make a lot of difference to the consumer, however, which goods and services fall into which category (exemption or zero-rating): all he cares is that he doesn't have to pay VAT on either.

Exempt commodities and services include education, insurance, health, burial, cremation, finance, postal services, betting and lotteries, and land. Zero-rated commodities and services include food, water, fuel and power, books, news services, newspaper advertisements, building construction, and transportation. You can be housed, fed, warmed, bathed, educated, informed, carried to and from work, medicated, and buried—all without paying VAT. Do your skimping on clothes and automobiles.

Stamp Duties

Many documents—for example, transfers and conveyances of property, leases, life insurance policies, stocks, shares and debentures—must be stamped to denote payment of duty.

Seeing to it that a document is stamped with the proper duty is the responsibility of the taxpayer. The government enforces payment of the duty by imposing penalties on taxpayers who fail in this responsibility and on persons whose duty it is to register the documents if they register them improperly stamped. A further assurance that the stamp duty is paid is the fact that documents not duly stamped cannot, except in criminal cases, be used as evidence or made available for any other purpose.

In some transactions there is a fixed duty; in others the amount of duty depends on the value of the property or the amount paid for it.[10]

License Duties

Motor Vehicles.   A license for a private car costs £25 per year but can be purchased for a four-month period at a cost of one-third the annual fee plus 10 percent or £9.15. Motorcycle licenses start at £2.50 and go up to £10, depending on the size of the cycle. No vehicle license that costs less than £8 can be purchased for a period of less than a year. County authorities issue the licenses (see p. 44).

Game Licenses.   Game licenses may be purchased at a post office on an annual or seasonal basis for the following fees:

August 1 through October 31	£4
November 1 through July 31	£4
Annual	£6
Occasional (any 14-day period)	£2

Firearms Licenses.   Firearms certificates are issued by the police. Their initial cost is £3.50 for each firearm owned, and they must be renewed every 24 months at a cost of £2.50. The only exception is

[10]A table showing stamp duty applicable to the transfer of real estate is on p. 119.

a shotgun certificate, which costs £1 and covers any number of shotguns.

Television Licenses.   Licenses to own television sets are obtainable at post offices. The cost is £7 for black-and-white sets and £12 for color. Only one license is required for each household, regardless of the number of receiving sets. License fees for radio receivers were abolished in April, 1971.

Special Car Tax

A 10 percent car tax is levied on all new cars (domestic and foreign) purchased in England, unless purchased by foreign visitors for export.

LOCAL TAXES ("RATES")[11]

With the exception of motor vehicle license fees (which are paid into the Exchequer), moneys from the miscellaneous license fees listed above are used to help defray the public service expenditures of the local governing authorities. Income from these sources is, however, small. Local governments are dependent on non-tax sources (central government grants, trading operations, rents) for a large percentage of their operating funds; most of the balance (about 40 percent) comes from local "rates."

Rates are based on a percentage of the net annual renting value of a property, after allowances for repairs and insurance. The percentage (or rate poundage) is determined by setting the total ratable value of properties in a given area against the local government's budget. If, for example, the total ratable value of all properties in a given town is £600,000, and the local government's expenses amount to £300,000, the rate will be:

$$\frac{£300,000}{£600,000} \;=\; \tfrac{1}{2}, \text{ or } 50p \text{ in the pound}$$

This rate is then applied to each property. Thus, if the ratable value of a particular house has been established as £100, the annual "rates" for that house will be £50.

Rates vary widely from area to area, depending on need, but the average figure in 1970–1971 was 72p in the pound. Ratable values are reassessed at ten-year intervals.

---

[11]Additional information about rates is given on p. 114.

Part 2 / DEATH

In Chapter VIII, "Health," it was noted that the British male lives, on the average, two years longer than the American male. Unfortunately, England does not guarantee immortality: Even the royal family has an occasional funeral—and there is no hope at all for us commoners. I was tempted to omit this section, lest some readers find it depressing, but the information in it is important. I shall make it as brief as possible. Meanwhile, laugh (as the British do) at the rather ludicrous image of the stern-faced, black-clothed undertaker. He has, of late, been striving earnestly to learn how to smile in public and thus divest himself of the familiar label with which his countrymen have so fondly endowed him —"The Dismal Trader."

PREPLANNING

There are just two ways to handle things when someone in your family dies—(a) sensibly, and (b) foolishly. It's easy to choose the latter: All you have to do is let your emotions get the better of you. Decide that nothing is too good for John or Mary, order up a blanket of orchids and a fancy casket with silver handles and velvet "eternity-rest" mattress, and hire the Royal Philharmonic to play the slow movement from the *Eroica*. John or Mary won't give a hang, but at least the neighbors will be able to recognize genuine grief when they see it and you will always have the satisfaction of knowing that you didn't let a mundane matter like a bank balance deter you from paying your last respects with adequate devotion.

Though few people would go to such extremes, almost all of them find it difficult to think clearly when they are faced with the loss of a loved one. They accept without question every frill and every special service that the funeral director recommends. They need to "buy" a funeral, and there is not time to shop around; they think it is not proper to quibble about extravagancies; their bargaining instincts go by the board. The Dismal Trader stands in wait with a crepe-hung countenance, but his insides are wreathed in smiles.

The sensible thing to do, of course, is to face up to the fact—right now, when you have full control of your emotions—that some day there will be a death in your family. Learn the facts and procedures while that death still seems improbable, or at least remote. Do your planning now. Visit a number of Dismal Traders (preferably ones who are members of the National Association of Funeral Directors), ask for *itemized* estimates, and do your bargaining as calmly and cool-headedly as if you were buying a sofa or a refrigerator. (Itemizing is particularly important, because many undertakers want to furnish only a lump-sum estimate that they refer to as "complete" but which is actually far from all-inclusive.) Write down what kind of funeral and which services you would choose for yourself and the approximate amount you would be willing to pay, and see to it that your spouse does the same. Bring to the purchase of a cemetery lot or mausoleum space as much business acumen as you would bring to the purchase of any other piece of real estate[12]—or if you want to be cremated, say so. (The British undertaker who assists you in your preplanning will enter you in his files as "NYD" —Not Yet Dead. Don't let *that* bother you: You may be still NYD long after he is D.)

Hopefully, you will have followed the suggestions in the Checklists in Chapter II. If so, you will already have relieved yourself of many of the onerous details that crop up suddenly when you do have a death in the family. You will have at hand the addresses and phone numbers of relatives and friends who should be notified; you will have accurate information for the obituary; insurance policies will be in order; there will be no question about how much money is available and where it's located or how much indebtedness has to be paid off from the estate. And if you and your spouse have preplanned your funerals, you will not be beset by fears that John or Mary would not have approved your choice of casket or tombstone or that some relative may think you were a little less—or a little more—extravagant than you should have been. The knowledge that decisions were made jointly at a time when you could approach the problems and discuss the alternatives in a level-headed and dispassionate manner will give you a feeling of self-assurance at a time when you need it most. And, above all, if the Dismal Trader should attempt to dissuade you from your original plans remember that the money he wants you to bury in the ground could go into a heart fund or a cancer-research foundation or help a young person through college.

WHAT TO DO WHEN DEATH OCCURS

Notify the Doctor

It is the doctor's business to issue a certificate of death in which he states what he believes to be the cause of death and enters the date on which he last attended the deceased. He may or may not view the body,

---

[12]Everyone in England, regardless of his religious beliefs, has the "right" to be buried in his own parish churchyard; the only thing wrong with this is that most of the churchyards are full. Ask your local vicar.

depending on his familiarity with the case and how recently he has seen his patient.

If cremation is desired, tell the doctor when you first tell him about the death; he is *required* to view the body if it is to be cremated, and to have a second doctor come in also.

If the death is sudden or unexpected or occurs during an operation or appears to have been caused by alcohol or drugs or abortion or suicide—or if he can't determine the cause at all—the doctor will notify the coroner, and the coroner will probably order a post-mortem examination. Your consent is not required for a coroner's post-mortem (as it is for a doctor's or hospital's post-mortem), but you should not object, because it is important that you know the cause of death: There could be legal proceedings; relatives may demand an explanation; you, too, will want a full understanding of the circumstances after you have gotten over the initial shock. If the coroner becomes involved, do not begin preparations for the funeral until you are given the go-ahead by the coroner's office.

If the death appears to have been the result of an accident or of intentional violence, call the police as well as the doctor—and don't touch anything.

The coroner determines whether or not there will be an inquest. He is *required* to hold one if the death appears to have been unnatural; and if there is reason to believe that death resulted from murder or manslaughter, a travel accident, industrial disease or certain occupational hazards, there will be a jury at the inquest whose majority opinion (provided there are not more than two dissenting votes) prevails. If you become involved in an inquest you may want to retain a solicitor (lawyer) in case there are insurance or compensation claims to be filed afterward.

Notify Relatives and Friends

After you have made the initial calls—to the doctor, and to the police if appropriate—you will want to notify family members and close friends.

Register the Death

As soon as the doctor's medical certificate is available (and the coroner's determination if a coroner is involved), the death must be registered. The doctor may send the medical certificate to the registrar by mail, but since you have to attend to the registering in person, anyway, he will more likely give it to you and tell you to take it along. (If the coroner has become involved, you must wait until the registrar has received the coroner's determination. The registrar's office will let you know when this is, if they have your address; if not, you will have to ask each day.) Under no condition should more than five days elapse; burial or cremation cannot take place, except in unusual circumstances, until registration is completed.

On the back of the medical certificate is a notice telling you what information you should have at hand when you visit the registrar: full name and address of the deceased, his marital status at time of death, his date and place of birth, his occupation, his National Health Service number (take the card with you), and so forth. It is extremely important that the information you furnish to the registrar be accurate; an error could complicate probate and delay payment of pension and insurance claims. The name of the deceased on the register should be stated just as it appears on his birth certificate, his marriage license, his bank statements, and other important documents. (If the deceased was a married woman, the maiden name must be furnished.) Once the formal entry on the register is made and signed, it can be changed only by the Registrar General and that may involve considerable red tape.

When the deceased has died in hospital, the death must be registered in the district where the hospital is located. Except for this, the registration procedure is the same as it would be if the death occurred at home.

If you don't know where the registrar's office is, ask at the library, the doctor's office, the Citizens Advice Bureau, the Town Hall, the police station, or at that fount of all British information—the post office.

Obtain Death Certificate

The death certificate is issued by the Registrar's office at the time of registry. There is no charge for the original, but additional authenticated copies cost 25p each. Be sure to get a sufficient number of copies at the time of registration; they will be required for insurance claims, for Social Security and other lump-sum death benefits, for claiming widow's benefits under Social Security or other pension or annuity plans, for claims on bank accounts and savings bonds, for obtaining probate, and so on. If you find at a later date that you need additional certificates, you will have to pay 40p apiece for them if you go get them in person, 65p if they must be mailed to you. Within the year following the death, you may get additional certificates from your original registrar; after a year has passed, apply to the General Register Office, Somerset House, London W.C. 2. If, at the time of registration, you have taken care to jot down the location of the registrar's office and the date and number of the entry, you will be able to get additional certificates fairly quickly.

Since the death certificate is required before the body can be buried or cremated, it is often referred to as the "disposal" certificate. It can be issued only by the registrar or the coroner; and if the circumstances of death were such that the coroner did become involved, only he can authorize cremation.

The registrar will issue a disposal certificate prior to registration of the death only if illness or an equally valid reason prevents your prompt signing of the register and only if he has been furnished a medical certificate and all the information needed to complete his records.

Call the Funeral Director

Whether the death has occurred at home or in hospital, it is up to you to see that the remains are disposed of. Your next step, therefore, is to call the funeral director and arrange to have the body taken to the mortuary. At this point, it is customary to give the death (disposal) certificate to the funeral director. (You can, if you prefer, give it directly to the church, the cemetery, or the crematorium; but in no event can burial or cremation take place until the disposal certificate is in the appropriate hands, and it is best to let the funeral director attend to this.)

Now here is where your preplanning will stand you in good stead. There won't be a mad scramble through desk drawers for the will or for a letter that might contain burial instructions of which you are not aware. You will already have your itemized list of services and cost estimates and you need only to "book" the services and check over your list with the funeral director to make certain that every single item you want included has been included and that there will be no unexpected extras. (It is possible that the funeral director may have omitted from his original estimate such items as transportation of the body from home or hospital to the mortuary, the use of the chapel, cemetery and cremation fees, tips to gravediggers and bearers, newspaper notices, and so forth.) As you go through the list, have him confirm estimated costs and explain any increases over the original estimates. And tell him that when you pay him you will expect him to send you receipted bills for his own services and for money that he has paid out to others in your behalf.

You should, of course, let the funeral director know what the deceased's religious affiliations were so the appropriate ritual can be performed. If the deceased had expressed no denominational preference, he will probably get a Church of England service. There is, of course, no reason why there must be a religious ceremony at all if you have reason to think the deceased would have preferred it that way, but there will undoubtedly be one unless you make a specific request to the contrary.

Get Rid of Drugs

If the deceased left any drugs or medicines, get rid of them in such a way that no person or animal can ever be harmed by them. If you have any doubts about disposal, ask the doctor, the nurse, or the Local Health Authority officer.

PAYING FOR THE FUNERAL

As in the United States, the cost of the coffin is the basis for determining the cost of the entire funeral. It seems a little ridiculous that the rental of a limousine in which mourners follow a mahogany casket should cost more than the rental of that same limousine when it follows a casket made of elm—and I think you would have a hard time making a funeral director own up to this, but it nevertheless seems to be the way things work out. If the body is to be cremated, there is certainly no reason for considering an expensive coffin: It is customary and sensible to buy a simple, unfinished one; you may cover it with a pall if you are concerned about its appearance.

Funeral prices vary throughout England and are generally higher in the south. Nevertheless, if you have planned carefully, the total cost should not exceed £100. The funeral director is usually willing to wait for his money until the estate is settled.

One final word of caution: The tombstone or memorial plaque need not be purchased immediately; in fact, it is customary and proper to let the ground settle for several months before erecting a headstone. There are a few unsavory characters who watch the papers for death notices like carrion buzzards watch the cow pastures below them, and who feel no hesitancy in knocking on the door of a bereaved family immediately after the funeral to explain the urgency of contracting for a memorial and to accept a deposit toward its cost. *Never* enter into an agreement with one of these fellows. Before you make any commitment at all, get written advice from the appropriate authorities about restrictions governing shape, materials, lettering, and so on, of memorials to be placed in the churchyard or cemetery where the deceased is buried. (The least expensive memorial will cost about £20, and, of course, it is possible to spend a great deal more.)

SHIPPING A BODY OVERSEAS

If you want to ship the body of the deceased back to the United States, ask the registrar for a form 104 when you register the death. (A form

104 is a notice to the coroner that you intend to remove a body from England.) The registrar will give you the name and address of the coroner to whom the form should be sent.

The form 104 does away with the need for a disposal certificate. Therefore, if you have already obtained the disposal certificate before you decide to ship the body to the States, you will have to send the disposal certificate to the coroner along with the form 104.

Now you must wait four days for the coroner to release the body. The remains can stay at the mortuary. Inform the undertaker of your plans and ask him to arrange airline passage. You will also undoubtedly want to have him embalm the body. Seek the undertaker's help in completing the necessary freight documents and customs declarations. Visit or call the American Embassy in London (24 Grosvenor Square, W. 1, phone 490–9000) and ask if there are additional arrangements that should be made to insure acceptance of the body when it reaches the United States.

Be prepared to pay dearly for shipment of your cargo. Many airlines will not carry a body at all unless it has undergone a special type of embalming process and unless the coffin is enclosed in an airtight crate; and then, to top it all off, some of them double the freight rate.

There are no restrictions whatever on shipment of cremated remains out of England—no authorizations required, no notifications; but you should call the American Embassy and make sure there will be no trouble at destination.

WILLS AND ESTATE SETTLEMENT

To the question: "Should I have a will?" the answer in England, as in the United States, is most emphatically "Yes." There are two very good reasons:

1. The laws of succession were necessarily devised with the intent of making them suitable for all people who die intestate. Obviously, one set of laws is no more adaptable to the peculiarities of each and every estate than one size of shoe is adaptable to all feet. If your estate is to be divided among your heirs in the manner in which you *want* it divided, you will have to state your wishes in a will.

2. "Letters of administration" (legal authority to dispose of the estate of an intestate or of someone who left a will but failed to appoint executors) actually cost more and take longer to handle than probate of wills.

To the question "Is the will I had drawn up in the United States valid in England?" the answer again is "Yes"—but have a new one drawn up anyway. Again, there are two very good reasons:

1. Your circumstances have changed: You have probably disposed of property that you owned when you made your U.S. will, and you have acquired new and different property; values have changed, and inflation may have put an entirely different light on the amount you originally bequeathed for the support of your spouse; it may no longer be feasible to pass along certain property to heirs you originally designated —others may be better able to make use of it; death duties may take a bigger bite, depending on the size of your estate.

2. U.S. executors named in your present will are certain to encounter difficulties in obtaining a grant of probate from the probate registry of a British court. Not only is the sheer burden of trying to handle an estate in accordance with the laws of a different country too much to impose on your executors—they will incur considerable expense, all of which is properly chargeable to your estate. And, no matter how conscientious your U.S. executors are, the hardships placed on them by distance and time and their lack of knowledge about your current affairs will almost certainly cause something to go wrong: Collectible assets may be overlooked (and probably no one will volunteer their existence); or a debt may be overlooked and not called to the attention of the executors until the bequests have been distributed—in which case, if the executors have failed to advertise for creditors, they may find themselves paying the debt out of their own pockets.

The moral, then, is clear: Have a new will drawn up in England by a British solicitor. (If you are a married couple, both of you should have new wills.)

Keep these points in mind when you ask the solicitor to prepare the will:

1. *Have him include a statement that all previous wills are revoked.* (Issuance of a superseding will does not automatically cancel out the old will.)

2. After you have named your specific bequests (*e.g.,* your house, your library, your Strad, and monetary bequests for stated sums), *make provision for the "residue,"* so that there will be no assets left "unbequeathed." Normally, the residue is left to the spouse.

3. *Have bequests to your spouse made conditional upon the spouse's surviving you by a certain length of time*—say, 28 days. The reason for this is the avoidance of double imposition of estate duty if husband and wife die within a short period of each other, *e.g.,* as the result of an accident. Without this provision, the estate could be taxed as it passes from A to B and again as it passes from B to B's legatees (C) (although the burden is eased to some extent by a "quick succession relief" law). The theory behind this conditional provision is that if B survives A by as long as 28 days, there is a good chance that B may continue to survive

a sufficient length of time to enjoy and benefit from the inheritance; if, however, B dies within the 28-day period, the estate goes directly from A to C and estate duty is therefore imposed only once.

4. *If the estate is a large one, which will produce sufficient income for the subsistence of the surviving spouse without disposition of the capital, it may be advisable to word the will so that the spouse is bequeathed a life interest in the estate* rather than an absolute interest. When a life interest has been bequeathed, there is no further imposition of estate duty following the second death.

5. *Appoint two executors.* Normally, your spouse will be one of them; the other should be someone knowledgeable in matters of probate—preferably a bank or a solicitor. Deciding which you should designate—bank or solicitor—is difficult. Both will charge for their probate services, but the bank will probably charge more than the solicitor. The scale recommended by the Law Society for a solicitor's services in administering an estate is as follows:

No fixed fee on an estate under £2000 (but don't expect less than £75)
3 percent on estates between £2,000 and £10,000
2.5 percent on estates between £10,000 and £50,000
A bit less on estates over £50,000

If you choose a solicitor instead of a bank, name the one who prepares the will, and don't wince when he includes a clause that entitles him to collect a fee for settling the estate: If he didn't include this clause, he could not legally collect a fee, and he is entitled to be paid for his services. (And if he is to be an executor, he will probably charge you only a very small fee for preparing the will.) If you choose to appoint a bank as executor, you can expect to pay well for its services: It will probably demand a percentage of the estate's value, plus a percentage of annual income (if there is a trust fund), plus fees for the services of its own solicitors. You can be fairly certain, however, that the bank will be there when you need it, whereas you could outlive your solicitor. If you prefer a solicitor to a bank (and this is not said facetiously), retain a young, healthy one; and then, just in case, appoint an alternate to act in place of either of your executors if the need arises.

6. *Designate someone in the U.S.* (relative, friend, bank, lawyer) to assist your British solicitor with U.S. affairs that he cannot readily handle from overseas. It may be that your solicitor will have someone in mind. Ask his advice.

7. *Take your "journal"* (the one you keep in accordance with Checklist #4, Chapter II) when you visit your solicitor to begin preparation for drawing up the will; and when he has finished with it, get it back and keep it current.

Now let's see what happens when the time comes to settle your spouse's estate. We will assume that two executors have been named in the will (you and a solicitor) and it is time to request the grant of probate. What do you do?

First, give the journal back to the solicitor-executor. He will welcome all the information you can provide about the deceased's pensions, annuities, insurance, and death benefits; the value of his car, house, and furnishings; his stocks and bonds, bank accounts and cash; his mortgages, hire purchase agreements, and all other debts. The more such information you can hand over to him, the easier his job will be and the more quickly he can accomplish it.

The solicitor-executor will attend to the filing of various forms, and then both you and he must go to the probate registry to "swear the papers." At this point, you will have to pay the estate duty (or at least a part of it)[13] and a probate fee—both of which are based on the value of the estate. Separate checks are required for the two payments.

There's just one big problem: Bank accounts solely in the name of the deceased will be frozen as soon as the bank learns of the death,[14] and life insurance claims will not be honored until the estate is settled. You may not have the money to pay the estate tax until probate is granted; and probate can't be granted until the estate tax has been paid. There are two ways out of this dilemma, but one of them (*i.e.*, paying the estate tax with national savings certificates, premium bonds, or money in the Post Office Savings Bank—all of which can be made available for this purpose) will probably not be of any use to a U.S. citizen residing in England. You will therefore have to resort to the other way, which is to ask your banker for a short-term loan just big enough to cover the estate tax and the probate fee, the proceeds of the loan to go into a special joint account (an "executorship account") and to be used for no other purpose. There should be little difficulty in obtaining such a loan, since the insurance should serve as collateral.

While you are waiting for the grant of probate and final settlement of the estate, keep busy. There are a number of little loose ends you can tie up, and it's good to feel useful. Here are some suggestions:

Look through dresser drawers, pockets, and wallets for such items as

---

[13]The estate duty on a freehold may be deferred for as long as eight years. No interest is charged for the first year.

[14]In England, joint checking and savings accounts (the "either/or" variety) are *not* frozen upon the death of one of the parties; the survivor may continue to draw against the accounts. In addition, the survivor may continue to have access to a safe deposit box that was held jointly.

pension books,[15] British Rail or London Transport season tickets, passport, driver's license, club membership cards, charge plates, and U.S. Social Security card. Give the pension books, charge plates, and Social Security card to your solicitor-executor. Take unexpired British Rail tickets to the issuing station and unexpired London Transport tickets to the London Transport Board (55 Broadway, London S.W. 1) and ask for refunds. (Take along copies of the death certificate if some time has elapsed and you want the refunds backdated to the date of death.) Send the passport to Passport Office, Clive House, Petty France, London S.W. 1, with a covering letter of explanation. Mail the driver's license to the motor taxation office of the local authority. (If you can't find the address, call your nearest Citizens' Advice Bureau.) Return to the issuing organizations any cards evidencing membership in clubs or fraternal organizations and request cancellation of membership.

Gather together unwanted clothing to be sold or given away after grant of probate and *after* you have checked the pockets.

Return library books and records.

If you are living in a mortgaged house, either find a way to continue making the mortgage payments or ask your solicitor-executor to make some arrangement with the mortgage company. If you were sharing rented accommodations, don't vacate the premises for any length of time unless the rent is paid; and if you have any questions about your rights as a tenant, address them to the Citizens' Advice Bureau, not to the landlord. Whether you are renting *or* buying, don't take a lodger without first checking out the terms of your lease or of your agreement with the mortgage company.

After grant of probate, your solicitor-executor will proceed with the business of settling the estate. He will notify the U.S. Social Security Administration and the deceased's employers of the death and arrange for payment of death benefits and annuities. He will collect all other moneys owing to the estate and deposit them to the executorship bank account. Then he will pay the funeral costs and all other debts; attend to transfers of stocks, bonds, real estate, and so forth, and pay whatever stamp duties are required on the transfers; and he will take the logbook of the car (if you plan to keep the car) to the Motor Taxation Office to have the change of ownership recorded. He will then collect his own fee; distribute the property according to the will and obtain acknowledgments from the heirs and legatees; and, finally, close the account with a check for the "residue."

---

[15]A U.S. citizen residing in England will not normally have any pension books, except, perhaps, his "Over–80" book (see p. 203), unless he has been working for a British employer under the National Insurance Scheme. Noncontributors to the National Insurance Scheme are not entitled to British death grants, widows' benefits, guardians' allowances, and the like.

Legacies to Heirs Overseas

Although the amounts that may be sent out of England to nonresidents as gifts, loans, dependents' support, and so on, are limited by Exchange Control regulations (see p. 16), there are no restrictions on the transfer of legacies and inheritances *willed* to nonresident beneficiaries by persons who were residents of the United Kingdom at the time of death.

Chapter X
EDUCATION

Full-time education is compulsory in England for every child from his fifth to his sixteenth birthday, yet the manner in which the child acquires his education is not fixed by law. Most British children attend free schools operated by the local education authorities, but a parent who prefers to send his child to an independent school or a private tutor may do so if he can convince the authorities that such schooling is adequate, *i.e.*, suited to the age and learning capacity of the child and performed on a full-time basis.

INDEPENDENT SCHOOLS

Some of the terms used in the British educational system are confusing to Americans. A "public school," for instance, is not, by American criteria, a public school at all, *i.e.*, it is not financed by public funds. It is one type of independent private school—the kind that had its origin in Canterbury (King's School) in the sixth century and is exemplified today in such renowned institutions as Winchester and Eton. The public schools traditionally provide a classical education and concentrate on preparation of their students for entrance into universities such as Oxford and Cambridge and thence into the "learned" professions.[1] The adjective "public" was applied to these schools when they began to

---

[1]Originally, law and theology. Technical education had its beginnings in trade guilds and apprenticeships.

attract pupils from outside their local areas. There are 270 public schools—some for boys, some for girls, and a few coeducational ones. Many of them are boarding schools, and tuition and boarding fees are high: £500 to £800 a year.[2]

Preparatory schools, attended mostly by boys between the ages of eight and thirteen who plan to enter public school when they are older, are also independent schools.

The term "grammar school" derives from the importance attached by these independent schools to instruction in Latin grammar.

PUBLICLY MAINTAINED SCHOOLS

Government interest in education (as in other social improvements) was aroused by humanitarians who protested the indignities of child labor at the time of the Industrial Revolution. In 1833 Parliament budgeted £20,000 for education, and since that time education has occupied a position of steadily increasing importance in British national policy. In 1944 the Board of Education was elevated to the status of "Ministry," and a threefold system of education (primary, secondary, and further education) was established. The aim of the British educational system is stated rather nicely: "To secure for children a happier childhood and a better start in life; to ensure a fuller measure of educational opportunity for young people and to provide means for all of developing the various talents with which they are endowed and so enriching the inheritance of the country whose citizens they are."[3]

The publicly maintained schools are the responsibility of local authorities, who are free to hire teachers, determine curricula and choose textbooks, and otherwise administer their schools as they see fit—within a framework of rather general guidelines established by the central government. Because of these guidelines, certain elements are common to all publicly maintained primary and secondary schools:

1. Tuition and books are free.
2. All schools must meet certain minimum standards set by the Department of Education and Science, both in education provided and in teacher qualification, and are subject to review and evaluation by Her Majesty's Inspectors.

[2]A list of public schools that have been declared "efficient" may be obtained for $3.60 from Pendragon House, 220 University Ave., Palo Alto, California 94301. Ask for "List 70." (The fact that a school is not on the list does not necessarily mean that it is below standard; it may mean only that the school has never applied for recognition.)
[3]Quoted in *Education in Britain*, a publication of the Central Office of Information, London, November, 1971.

3. The school day begins with an "act of worship," and nondenominational religious instruction is given unless parents request that it be withheld.

4. Transportation to and from school is provided for children under eight years of age who live more than two miles from school and for older children who live at least three miles from school.

5. Physical education is mandatory, and all schools have playgrounds.

6. Midday meals, sufficiently nourishing to be "main" meals, are provided for a nominal fee.[4] Milk is free to children between the ages of two and seven, to older children who require it for medical reasons, and to all children in special schools.

7. Every child is given a medical and physical examination when he first enters school and periodically thereafter.

Nursery Schools

Although schooling is not mandatory until a child reaches the age of five, it is available from the age of two to those fortunate enough to live in localities with nursery schools, and from the age of three in areas where the local authority infant schools (ages five through seven) have affiliated nursery departments.

The steadily increasing number of children of compulsory school age has resulted in a shortage of building accommodations for preschool children. Most nursery schools are still privately owned and operated, but the picture is changing. There are about 500 local authority (publicly maintained) nursery schools in operation, and plans for expansion are under way.

Each local authority nursery school is staffed by a superintendent, and each class or group within the school is conducted by a qualified assistant teacher and a full-time nursery assistant. Although these schools are open from 9:00 A.M. to 3:00 P.M., half-day attendance (either morning or afternoon) is encouraged.

The local authority nursery schools are financed by national government grants and by local rates.

Primary Schools

Primary schools are attended by children between the ages of five and eleven, and are usually divided into two sections—infant schools (ages five to seven or eight) and junior schools (ages seven or eight to eleven).

Entrance into the infant school marks the child's introduction to reading, writing, and arithmetic. Imaginative play and creative paint-

[4]At present, about 30 cents. The meals are free to needy children.

ing and music engender an attitude of inquiry and experiment, and books and stories develop an awareness of the pleasures to be found in reading.

The basic skills introduced in the infant schools are further developed in the junior schools, and other courses are added. For the past few years, the junior schools have been a sort of proving ground for new subjects and new teaching methods on a rather large scale. The study of French has recently been added to the curriculum; mathematics and science are approached from a practical-usage viewpoint; and a new alphabet consisting of 44 characters (called "ITA"—Initial Teaching Alphabet) has been introduced as an aid in reading.[5]

Secondary Schools

It was the original intent of the publicly maintained educational system established as a result of the 1944 Education Act to offer "secondary" education (for pupils age 11 and over) in three types of schools: (1) *grammar schools*, specializing in academic subjects leading to higher education in a university; (2) *modern schools*, offering general education with a practical slant; and (3) *technical schools*. All three types are still in existence, but their original aims are becoming lost in a maze of broadened curricula. Many secondary modern and technical schools are now offering academic courses, and grammar schools are offering everything from engineering to economics. As a result, there has been a swing toward nonselective "comprehensive" schools, equipped to provide secondary education in all fields to children of all levels of intellectual ability.

Middle Schools

The growing number of comprehensive schools is bringing about still another change in the traditional system—the establishment of "middle" schools, which span the last few years of primary education and the first few years of secondary education. There are not many middle schools as yet, but more are planned.

Special Schools

Since it is felt that handicapped children benefit from opportunities to share in the activities of their more fortunate peers, they are placed in

---

[5]Whether or not the ITA is here to stay is a matter for conjecture. Test results have been, on the whole, favorable; but it is the function of the primary school to prepare its pupils for entrance into secondary schools, and when the transition occurs, the children will have to learn the use of standard symbols.

regular schools unless they require intensive specialized help. Many of the regular schools have special classes attached to provide the assistance required by these children.

More severely handicapped children, however (*e.g.*, the blind, the deaf, and the mentally subnormal), who have difficulty competing with their peers or even participating in school activities, are placed in specialized schools that the local authorities are required by law to provide. Children with the gravest handicaps, or with multiple handicaps, may be taught at home or in hospitals.

As with normal children, education up to the age of 16 is compulsory, and many handicapped children stay on beyond that age to receive additional education or vocational training.

Admission of Foreign Children

Children of parents of any nationality, residing in England temporarily or permanently, may attend the publicly maintained primary and secondary schools without charge. If you want to enroll your child, write for information to the Chief Education Officer, Local Education Authority, in the town or county where you reside.

The school year runs from September to late July. There are three terms, separated by three-week vacations at Christmas and Easter and a longer vacation in summer.

Examinations

When the student has completed his mandatory schooling at the age of 16, he may qualify, by taking examinations, for a Certificate of Secondary Education (CSE) or a General Certificate of Education (GCE). The number and choice of subjects on which he is examined is at the option of the student (and he knows that it is to his advantage to prove his abilities in several subjects since the information on his certificate may be used by prospective employers in determining his qualifications for a job or by an institution of further education in determining his qualifications for admission). To some extent, the GCE candidate has a third option—the degree of difficulty of the examinations. If he plans to leave school at the age of 16 with a GCE, he will probably take the "O" (Ordinary) level examinations; if he hopes to enter a university, he may elect to stay on for an additional two years and take the "A" (Advanced) level examinations in a few of his subjects. (Requirements for university admission vary, but the normal minimum is a GCE with five "passes," of which two are at the "A" level.)

FURTHER EDUCATION AND HIGHER EDUCATION

The term "school" is applied to education through the secondary stage, and all education beyond that stage is broadly categorized as "further" education. It is common practice, however, to exclude universities and colleges of education when speaking of "further" education, reserving the term "higher education" for these institutions.

What is commonly meant by "further" education, therefore, is education offered by the technical and agricultural colleges, the colleges of art and of commerce, the evening institutes, and the "polytechnics." The polytechnics (of which there are thirty) provide a flexible system with minimum entrance requirements and opportunities for making up deficiencies. Students may attend part-time or full-time, or may arrange (if their employers agree) alternate periods of work and study. The courses offered are of a practical nature, closely related to business and industry. Certificates and degrees are awarded, and tuition fees are nominal.

Great Britain has 42 universities (not counting the Open University) —34 in England and Wales and 8 in Scotland.[6] The universities are concerned mainly with the arts and sciences and social studies, and to a lesser extent with engineering, medicine, and dentistry. Bachelors', Masters', and Doctors' degrees are awarded, as well as diplomas and certificates for short courses in some subjects. More than half of the students are engaged in research.

In addition to the universities, the Cranfield Institute of Technology, Cranfield, Bedfordshire (postgraduate science); the Royal College of Art, Kensington Gore, London SW7 2EU (postgraduate art); and the Council for National Academic Awards (CNAA), 3 Devonshire Street, London W1N 2BA, have authority to confer degrees.

The Open University, for which there are no formal entry requirements, provides instruction through radio and television, correspondence courses, and short residential courses. It is financed by the Department of Education and Science and by fees, and degrees are awarded. Students who are residents of other countries cannot be accepted by the Open University.

Admission of Foreign Students

Although most British colleges and universities have no objection to accepting foreign students, space is limited and applicants far outnumber vacancies. Entry into a British institution is therefore highly com-

---

[6]The English universities and their addresses are listed in Appendix G.

petitive, and an American student who has had at least a year or two of college-level education in the United States will stand a much better chance of admission than one who is just out of high school.

Classes run from October to June, and tuition for a full-time course is usually £250 for the academic year; but the student should allow an additional £750 to cover the cost of books and living expenses (more if he hopes to travel during vacations).

Preliminary inquiries to Oxford, Cambridge, and the University of London should be made at least 18 months in advance and may be addressed to:

Oxford:
The Adviser to Overseas Students
Oxford Colleges Administration Office
58 Banbury Road
Oxford OX2 6PP

Cambridge:
The Adviser to Overseas Candidates for Admission
The University Registry
The Old Schools
Cambridge CB2 1TN

London: Send your inquiry to the appropriate college, but if you're not certain which one this is ask for "The General Information Pamphlet for Internal Students" from:
The Academic Registrar
Senate House
London WC1E 7HU

Preliminary inquiries to other universities should be made at least a year in advance and may be addressed to "The Registrar." Always enclose four international reply coupons with each inquiry to cover return postage; and if you want a full prospectus send an international money order for $3.

Undergraduate Study.   When you are ready to apply for admission for undergraduate study leading to a "first" degree, send along another International Money Order for $3—this one to UCCA (Universities Central Council on Admissions), P.O. Box 28, Cheltenham GL50 1HY, and ask for its handbook "How to Apply for Admission to a University." Give yourself plenty of time, because applications must be filed between September 1 and December 15 of the *year before* the academic year in which you wish to enter (if you are hoping for admission to Oxford or Cambridge the deadline is October 15 not December 15). Do not send transcripts, examination certificates, photographs, or copies of letters to UCCA. Normally, four years of study are required to obtain a "first" degree—although some universities offer diploma courses requiring a somewhat shorter time and some graduate students are admitted for two-year honors courses leading to a "first" degree. Dentistry, however, is a five-year course and a bachelor's degree in medicine takes five or six years. Dentistry is offered at the universities of Birmingham, Bristol, Cambridge, Leeds, Liverpool, London, Manchester, Newcastle, Nottingham, Oxford, Sheffield, and Southampton; applications are handled by the UCCA. There is not much point in applying for admission to a British university for a degree in medicine; there are too few vacancies. Undergraduate courses of one or two years' duration, intended for American students who plan to return to the United States and take their degrees at their "home" colleges, are offered by 26 British universities.[7] The British institutions will generally provide certificates attesting to attendance and satisfactory performance; but "credits," as such, are not given unless the home college works out a way to grant them. Students in the "Junior Year Abroad" programs are accepted by the same 26 universities. The cost of a "Junior Year Abroad" is about $2,400, and application should be made direct to the British university, not through the UCCA. Details are available from Educational Programs Abroad, 112 Dover Road, Williamsburg, Virginia 23185.British universities don't have summer schools, but various university departments do organize special summer courses. A list —"Short Courses and Summer Schools"—is available at no charge from the British Information Services, 845 Third Avenue, New York 10022. A new list is published each spring.

Postgraduate Study.   Your first step is to send off a letter of application to one of the following:

CRANFIELD INSTITUTE OF TECHNOLOGY: The Registrar;
HULL and NEWCASTLE universities: The Registrar;
UNIVERSITY OF LANCASTER: The Graduate Studies Officer;
LOUGHBOROUGH UNIVERSITY OF TECHNOLOGY: The Higher Awards Section;
ALL OTHERS: The Head of the Department.

List your references, explain how you propose to finance your study and your living expenses, and state how long you wish to remain at the university. (Count on two, possibly three, years if you plan to submit a thesis.)

The Polytechnics.   There are about 30 polytechnics, offering approximately 400 approved courses. They are not universities—but they do confer undergraduate and graduate degrees. (These are the CNAA degrees referred to earlier in this section.) An applicant for a course

[7]Aston, Bath, Birmingham, Bradford, Bristol, Durham, East Anglia, Exeter, Hull, Keele, Kent, Lancaster, Leeds, Leicester, Liverpool, London, Manchester, Newcastle, Nottingham, Reading, Sheffield, Southampton, Surrey, Sussex, Warwick, and York.

leading to a CNAA Bachelor's degree should address his inquiries directly to the polytechnic in which he's interested; an applicant for a higher degree course should address the CNAA, 3 Devonshire Street, London W1N 2BA. The CNAA will provide a list of courses and a résumé of their contents.

Specialized Training in the Arts. Many of the institutions devoted exclusively to instruction in the arts are affiliated with universities or polytechnics; otherwise, they would not be able to offer degree courses. The Royal Academy of Music, for example, offers courses leading to a B. Mus. degree conferred by the University of London; the Rose Bruford College of Speech and Drama offers preparatory courses for degrees conferred by the University of Kent. There are, of course, many other institutions which, although not affiliated with degree-conferring bodies, provide excellent training in music, art, and drama on a part-time or full-time basis. Some of these institutions offer diplomas and certificates that are recognized as being equivalent to degrees so far as qualification for performing or teaching is concerned. Two excellent publications contain listings of specialized institutions: *Schools 1972*, which may be examined at the New York offices of the British Information Services; and *Higher Education in the United Kingdom: A Handbook for Students from Overseas*, which may be ordered for $2.40 from Pendragon House, Inc., 220 University Avenue, Palo Alto, Cal. 94301.

U.S. Auditions. Two British institutions have facilities for auditioning prospective students in the United States:

THE ROYAL ACADEMY OF DRAMATIC ART: Auditions are held in New York in December, April, and September; information is available from the Institute of International Education, 809 United Nations Plaza, New York 10017; and

GUILDHALL SCHOOL OF MUSIC AND DRAMA: Auditions are held in December; details are available from Professor Elliot Seiden, Speech Theater, Long Island University, Brooklyn Center, Zeckendorf Campus, Brooklyn, N.Y. 11201.

British Scholarships and Fellowships

The British government does not want any young person who has the desire and the capacity for higher education to be denied an opportunity to attend a university or college. About 90 percent of the students at British institutions receive financial aid, either from private or public funds. The Education Act of 1962 made it the duty of local authorities to provide scholarships, the amounts to be determined according to the income of the students and that of their parents. These local-authority grants are intended for students who are normally residents of Britain—not for those who reside in Britain only while attending a further-education institution. It should be noted, also, that the 500 one-year scholarships awarded annually to graduates of overseas universities by the British Council, an organization whose goal is the promotion of cultural relations between Britain and other countries, are not available to U.S. students.

Many other awards, however, *are* available to Americans, and some of the more important ones are described below:

1. Twenty-four *Marshall scholarships* for study at any British university are offered to U.S. college or university graduates, male or female, under 26 years of age. A Marshall scholarship is awarded initially for a period of two academic years but may be extended for an additional year. Its monetary value is approximately £1,250. Letters of inquiry may be addressed to the Education Office, British Embassy, 3100 Massachusetts Avenue, N.W., Washington, D.C. 20008, and applications must be submitted by October 22 of the year preceding the year of award. Every year, four or five students are selected from each of five U.S. geographical regions: Mideast, Midwest, Northeast, Pacific, and South.

2. Of the sixty *Rhodes scholarships* available for study at Oxford, 32 are set aside for U.S. students. Like the Marshall scholarships, they are awarded initially for two years but may be extended for a third year. Rhodes scholars must be unmarried males between the ages of 18 and 24; they must have been domiciled in the United States for at least five years; and they must be in at least their third year at an accredited, degree-granting college or university. To distribute these scholarships equitably about the United States, four are awarded each year in each of eight geographical regions. A Rhodes scholarship pays full tuition plus £900 for living expenses. Inquiries may be addressed to the Rhodes Scholarship Office, Wesleyan University, Middletown, Conn. 06457.

3. A number of *Churchill scholarships,* each worth a minimum of $3,500, are awarded to U.S. students between the ages of 19 and 26 who have earned Bachelors' degrees from certain accredited American schools (about 30 have been designated) and who wish to study science or engineering at Cambridge's Churchill College. Details may be requested from Mr. Harold Epstein, Executive Director, the Winston Churchill Foundation of the U.S., Ltd., 1740 Broadway, New York 10019; applications must be filed with the campus representative of the Foundation by November 15 of the year preceding the year of study at Cambridge.

4. Under the *Fulbright-Hays* program (a reciprocal exchange program between the United Kingdom and the United States), grants are made to students under the age of 35 who wish to enroll at a British institution for a year of graduate study or research. Applications may be submitted between May and October of the year preceding award to the campus Fulbright Program Adviser or, if the applicant is not

currently enrolled in a college or university, to the Institute of International Education, 809 United Nations Plaza, New York 10017. A person who has spent three months of the preceding year in the United Kingdom is not eligible for a Fulbright.

5. A number of traineeships in engineering, architecture, agriculture, and the sciences are available to U.S. students at the sophomore level or above. The student pays for his own travel and receives only a nominal stipend from the company or institution with which he trains. These traineeships are generally for periods of eight to twelve weeks during summer vacations. Address your inquiry to IAESTE/US (International Association for the Exchange of Students for Technical Experience/U.S.), American City Building, Columbia, Md. 21044.

6. A worldwide program of work traineeships is operated by the *Association Internationale des Etudiants en Sciences Economiques et Commerciales* under which students receive stipends sufficient to cover living expenses from participating firms. Write to the Association at Suite 1110, 52 Vanderbilt Avenue, New York 10017.

About 75,000 foreign students (25,000 of them from outside the Commonwealth) are enrolled in British educational institutions, and many of them are recipients of awards, fellowships, and traineeships made available to them by the British Government and by various British foundations and corporations. A complete listing of British postgraduate awards is available for $3.50 (second class airmail) from the Association of Commonwealth Universities, 36 Gordon Square, London WC1H OPF. Ask for *Scholarships Guide for Commonwealth Postgraduate Students.*

Chapter XII contains some additional information about adult education that may be of special interest to retirees.

Chapter XI
LEISURE TIME

ART GALLERIES

Many English towns have art galleries with their own permanent collections of old masters and works of local artists, as well as temporary exhibits borrowed from larger galleries. In your travels around England you will be able to pick up brochures at newsstands or at local or regional tourist boards that will tell you the specific locations, visiting hours, and admission fees.

In London be sure to visit the Tate Gallery, Millbank, which houses the National Collection of British art; the Queen's Gallery in Buckingham Palace, with great paintings from the Royal Collection; the National Gallery in Trafalgar Square, which houses one of the finest collections of paintings in the world; the National Portrait Gallery at St. Martin's Place, where you can see portraits of famous British men and women from the Middle Ages to the present; the Wallace Collection of eighteenth-century pictures, at Hertford House in Manchester Square; the Dulwich Art Gallery on Gallery Road, with fine works by old masters; and the Hayward Gallery at Festival Hall, where constantly changing exhibits of modern paintings and sculpture provide a continuing source of pleasure while you're waiting for concert time at one of the neighboring auditoriums.

CASTLES

Any child with a fairy-tale book knows that where there are kings and queens there are castles; and England has had kings and queens for

hundreds of years. Castles are, of course—or were, originally—for-
tresses. Many of them were built with walls 12 feet thick and battlements and narrow slits for windows and moats with drawbridges. As
homes they must have been terribly cold and damp and somewhat
frightening and not at all cozy—but who can look at a castle without
being stirred by remembrances of childhood stories about intrigue and
romance and dragon-slaying knights?

And yet, today, there are people who would do away with England's
monarchy—just as there are educators and authors who believe our
children should read about drugs and divorce, not about kings and
castles and crown jewels. But while there may be, sadly enough, a real
need in our contemporary society for children's books about drugs and
divorce, the people who do not treasure England's monarchy are, I
think, simply uninformed; or perhaps they are members of a breed with
which we have become all too well acquainted in our own country in
recent years—the kind who cannot be content without denigrating and
destroying. These people—fortunately in the minority—perhaps do not
realize that England's monarchy is a constitutional, not an absolute,
monarchy and therefore is not to be feared; or maybe they do not know
that, far from being a tax burden to the English people, it is, in fact, a
profit-making establishment. Only a little more than one cent a year is
required from each person in the United Kingdom to pay the government's grant to the Queen, and that amount is repaid many times over
in revenues from the crown lands and in the more intangible benefits
that derive from the maintenance of tradition and the unifying loyalty
that the majority of English subjects have to their sovereign. But back
to the castles. . . . Be sure to see:

- In *Berkshire:* Windsor Castle, the principal residence of English sovereigns for 850
  years.
- In *Cornwall:* Tintagel Castle, thirteenth-century ruins believed by many to have
  belonged to King Arthur.
- In *Dorset:* Lulworth Castle, where Charles X of France took refuge.
- In *Durham:* Durham Castle, built as a defense against the Scots, standing next the
  magnificent Durham Cathedral; and the ruins of twelfth-century Barnard Castle on
  the River Tees.
- In *Gloucestershire:* Berkeley Castle, England's oldest inhabited castle, where Edward II was murdered in 1327; and Sudeley Castle, where Henry VIII's widow,
  Catherine Parr, lived with her second husband, Lord Seymour.
- In *Hampshire:* Portchester Castle, built by Henry II in the twelfth century and
  where Henry V put together the forces for his Agincourt expedition; and Winchester Castle's Great Hall (the rest of the castle is gone), where what is said to
  be King Arthur's Round Table hangs and where Sir Walter Raleigh was sentenced
  to death.

- In *Kent:* Hever Castle, once the home of the Boleyn family; Dover Castle, a magnificent Norman structure overlooking the town and the Straits of Dover; Lympne (pronounced "Lim") Castle, home of the Archdeacons of Canterbury for centuries; and Deal and Walmer Castles, both built by Henry VIII.
- In *Northumberland:* Alnwick (pronounced "Annick") Castle, home of the Percy family for centuries, a fascinating Norman structure with many ancient treasures including a Celtic sword from the second century A.D.; and Bamburgh Castle, with an imposing Norman keep.
- In *Oxfordshire:* Broughton Castle, dating from the fourteenth century.
- In *Somerset:* Dunster Castle, built about 1070 and occupied by the same family (the Luttrells) since 1376.
- In *Sussex:* Bodiam Castle, built in the fourteenth century for protection against French raiders, now only a picturesque shell surrounded by a lily-covered moat; and Arundel Castle, occupied at various times by William the Conqueror, King Harold, and Alfred the Great, and for the past 500 years the home of the Dukes of Norfolk.
- In *Warwickshire:* Warwick Castle, on the banks of the Avon River, perhaps the most beautiful of all England's castles.
- In *Yorkshire:* Skipton Castle, home of the Earls of Cumberland, a thirteenth-century fortification with a banquet hall, a dungeon, and a charming courtyard.

Ask at the Ministry of Public Buildings and Works, Lambeth Bridge House, London, S.E. 1, about a season (12-month) ticket that will admit you to all historic buildings as often as you like. It will cost you less than $2 ($1 for a child or an old-age pensioner.)

CATHEDRALS

England's cathedrals are among the most beautiful in the world, and they are noted not only for their superb architecture, their delicate ironwork and stained glass, and the richness of their ecclesiastical plate, but also for their high musical standards.

Outstanding in all respects are:

- In *Cambridgeshire:* Ely Cathedral, one of the loveliest, built in the eleventh century on the site of a seventh-century Benedictine Abbey. Ely Cathedral has an unusual octagonal tower.
- In *Devon:* Exeter Cathedral, a thirteenth-century Norman edifice built on the site of an earlier church founded by Athelstan in 932. Exeter has some outstanding examples of fourteenth-century sculpture.
- In *Durham:* Durham Cathedral, a fine and ornate building on the River Wear.
- In *Gloucestershire:* Gloucester Cathedral, one of the most impressive, the burial place of the Duke of Normandy (William the Conqueror's son) and of Edward II.
- In *Hampshire:* Winchester Cathedral, the longest in England, scene of many historic events when Winchester was England's capital.

- In *Herefordshire:* Hereford Cathedral, which houses books dating from the eighth and ninth centuries and the "Mappa Mundi," a large medieval map of Europe.
- In *Kent:* Canterbury Cathedral, begun in 1070, completed in 1503, burial place of Henry IV and of the Black Prince, and scene of Thomas à Becket's murder.
- In *Lincolnshire:* Lincoln Cathedral, considered by many to be England's finest church, noted for its three towers and its eleven statues of kings (William I to Edward III).
- In *Norfolk:* The Holy Trinity Cathedral at Norwich, a handsomely proportioned and majestic structure.
- In *Somerset:* The magnificent Wells Cathedral, noted for its 300 statues and its medieval clock.
- In *Sussex:* Chichester Cathedral, a Norman structure dating from the eleventh century.
- In *Warwickshire:* Coventry, a new and modern cathedral built to replace the one destroyed in World War II.
- In *Wiltshire:* Salisbury Cathedral, perhaps the most beautifully proportioned of all English cathedrals, and with the tallest spire.
- In *Yorkshire:* York Minster, a thirteenth-century Gothic church with outstanding stained glass.

There are also many fine old parish churches, abbeys, and priories. In fact, it would be difficult to go anywhere in England where there is not a church with some notable architectural feature or fine example of craftsmanship.

EATING OUT

Eating out in England is whatever you choose to make of it. All Englishmen seem to breakfast on bacon and eggs, cornflakes, and kippers. Lunches and dinners can be miserable if you try to save money, as we do (we'd rather buy concert tickets), by eating in cheap restaurants where lamb chops and fish are cooked on the same grill at the same time. But for those who attach more importance to eating, there are very fine restaurants that serve well-prepared traditional British meals of Welsh lamb and Scotch beef and York hams and Norfolk turkey and Aylesbury duckling; and when those begin to pall, you can always find a restaurant that specializes in French cuisine—or Greek, Indonesian, Italian, German, Danish, Chinese, or almost any other nationality you can think of. (British home cooking, which has never been a source of national pride, is improving as more and more British housewives holiday abroad and become interested in continental recipes.)

Have at least one great traditional English meal prepared for you at Inigo Jones, Rule's, Stone's Chop House, Jasper's Eating House, or Simpson's. Try a "pub lunch" or two of beer, crusty bread, and Cheshire cheese. When you visit Lancaster, order a Lancashire hot pot (a "reet good do" of lamb chops layered with potatoes and onions, simmered in a brown earthenware dish and served with pickled red cabbage). And whatever you do, don't miss a charming teatime of sandwiches, scones with strawberry jam, hot tea and fruitcake at Fortnum & Mason's, Her Majesty's grocers, where the assistant managers patrol the aisles in formal attire of frock coats and striped trousers.

FESTIVALS AND CEREMONIES

Britain's festivals and ceremonial rituals provide a year-round source of cultural entertainment, education, and just plain fun. If there's any excuse whatever for a show, the British will schedule one. There are sports festivals, music festivals, drama festivals, and art festivals. There are dog shows, horse shows, sheep shows, and flower shows. There's an Apple Pie Fayre in Devon, an Oyster Feast at Colchester, Morris dancing in Oxfordshire, and a Traction Engine Rally in Devon. There's a Beer Festival in Warwickshire and a Cider Festival in Hereford. There are May Day celebrations everywhere.

Rituals and ceremonies surround everything from locking the Tower at night to Trooping the Colour on the Queen's birthday. There are stately processions in October to mark the opening of the law courts and a royal procession in November for the opening of Parliament. Every evening, guards march solemnly past the Little Old Lady of Threadneedle Street (the Bank of England) because someone assaulted her in 1780. For more than 300 years, on January 30, bagpipes have been wailing in Charing Cross at the scene of Charles I's execution, while mourners leave flowers and pray for the King's soul. When the Queen wants to shop in London, she waits at the outskirts of the City in regal solemnity until the Lord Mayor graciously grants her permission to enter. And despite what must surely be their lingering sentiments about the American Revolution—or maybe they just can't pass up another chance for a ceremony—the British generously hoist the Stars and Stripes over George Washington's ancestral home on our first President's birthday.

England's arts festivals are particularly impressive. Special mention should certainly be made of the music festivals at Aldeburgh (founded by Benjamin Britten, opera and concerts from March through September); at Bath (ten days of orchestral and chamber music in the spring); at Glyndebourne (opera performances of the highest standard); and at Cheltenham (master classes, famous soloists, and new and commissioned music performed in early July by such renowned orchestras as St. Martin-in-the-Fields, the BBC Symphony, and the Royal Liverpool Orchestra). Also important are the Haslemere Festival of Early Music and Instruments; the Three Choirs Festival, with concerts of choral and orchestral music performed in successive years in the Hereford, Worcester, and Gloucester cathedrals; and the English Bach Festival, where fabulous performances of such works as the *B-minor Mass* and the *St. Matthew Passion,* as well as contemporary music, are performed in London from late April to early May and repeated in Oxford from early to mid-May. Other famous arts festivals (for example, the ones at Swansea, King's Lynn, Brighton, York, Newcastle, Norfolk, and Harrogate—to name only a few), are broader in scope, embracing not only music but also paintings, films, poetry, ballet, and drama.

Send 15*p* to the Arts Council Publications Office, 105 Piccadilly, London W1V OAU, for a comprehensive list of British Arts Festivals. Select the ones that interest you and then write to the Coordinator, British Arts Festivals Association, 33 Rufford Road, Sherwood, Nottingham NG5 2NQ, for details.

HISTORIC HOUSES

Because the English were for so long a rural people (and, by and large, still prefer the countryside to the city), England has many fine country estates. Many of them are worth visiting because of their architecture or their beautiful parklike grounds or their fine furnishings; others are noteworthy because they have housed eminent statesmen or writers or royalty. Some of these magnificent houses are still owned and occupied by the peerage; many others are now the property of the National Trust and are open to the public. Details about visiting hours and admission fees (if any) are available from the British Tourist Authority. Among those that should head up your list are:

- In *Bedfordshire:* Luton Hoo, which contains many fine paintings and porcelains and an outstanding collection of Russian jewelry; and Woburn Abbey, seat of the Duke of Bedford, which also contains an interesting collection of paintings.
- In *Buckinghamshire:* Cliveden, a fine mansion set in beautiful woods; Hughenden House, Disraeli's home; and Waddesdon Manor, the elegant home of the Rothschilds.
- In *Cornwall:* Cotehele House, a medieval mansion with fine tapestries; and Lanhydrock House, with a seventeenth-century gatehouse and a stately avenue of sycamore trees.
- In *Derbyshire:* Haddon Hall, home of the Duke of Rutland; and Chatsworth, home of the Duke of Devonshire, where Mary, Queen of Scots, spent much of her captivity.
- In *Hampshire:* Beaulieu Abbey and Palace House. The Abbey was founded in 1204 by King John; the Palace House is the residence of Lord Montagu.

- In *Herefordshire:* Hampton Court, begun in 1514 by Cardinal Wolsey and later given to Henry VIII.
- In *Hertfordshire:* Knebworth House, ancestral home of Sir Edward Bulwer-Lytton; Salisbury Hall, a moated manor house built during the reign of Charles II; and Hatfield House, where Elizabeth ! learned of her succession to the throne.
- In *Kent:* Knole House, a very large fifteenth-century estate, seat of the Sackville family; Penshurst Place, with a great hall dating from 1340 and a vaulted crypt; and Chartwell, which was occupied at one time by Sir Winston Churchill.
- In *Norfolk:* Sandringham, the Queen's country home, with magnificent gardens open to the public when the royal family is not in residence. The elaborate iron gates were a wedding gift from the City of Norwich to Edward VII.
- In *Northamptonshire:* Sulgrave Manor, sixteenth-century home of George Washington's ancestors.
- In *Oxfordshire:* Blenheim Palace, Churchill's birthplace; Chastleton House, a Jacobean manor in a lovely park; Mapledurham, a fine Tudor mansion; Rousham House, a seventeenth-century manor with Italian gardens; and Grey's Court, a fourteenth-century Jacobean home, now largely in ruins but with its fortifications and gardens still there to be enjoyed.
- In *Surrey:* The fine Elizabethan Losely House; and Polesden Lacey, where George VI and his bride honeymooned.
- In *Sussex:* Goodwood House, seat of the Duke of Richmond; and, on a steep hill near Chichester, the seventeenth-century Haremere Hall.
- In *Warwickshire:* Compton Wyngates, a spectacularly beautiful Tudor house, perhaps the most intriguing of them all, with hidden rooms and secret stairways, a Council Chamber, a Priest's Room, and a topiary garden.
- In *Wiltshire:* Longleat House, seat of the Marquess of Bath, a splendid example of early Renaissance architecture, with parks and a wildlife enclosure where the famous "Lions of Longleat" roam; Avebury, a sixteenth-century manor house; and Wilton, elegant home of the Earl of Pembroke.

KEEPING INFORMED

There are 142 daily and Sunday newspapers, 1211 weekly papers, and about 5000 periodicals published in Britain. Four of the daily papers and three of the Sunday papers have circulations in the millions. All English newspapers are free of government censorship.

In addition to its high per capita newspaper consumption, England's annual publication of *new* book titles works out to about one for every 1740 people. (In the U.S., the ratio is approximately 1 to 2760.) There are several thousand libraries, including the great national and university libraries as well as the public libraries with their more than 11,000 branches and 113 million books.

Two public organizations—the British Broadcasting Corporation (BBC) and the Independent Broadcasting Authority (IBA) operate networks of television and radio stations. BBC is financed largely by government grants based on revenues from receiving set licenses, and commercials are not permitted. IBA (or ITA, if you refer solely to the television network) is dependent on advertising for revenue, but its programs must meet certain minimum standards established by the Television Act and monitored by a board appointed by the Postmaster General.

MUSEUMS

Almost every English town of any importance has its museum, generally one with interest centered on the history, industry, or arts of the region in which it's located. The Dyson Perrins Museum in Worcester, for example, houses the finest collection of Worcester porcelain in the world. The Corinium Museum in Cirencester (Britain's second-oldest city) has a splendid collection of sculpture and mosaics dating from the Roman occupation, when the city was called "Corinium." The Royal Earlswood Hospital Museum at Redhill traces the history of medicine. The Museum of Science and Industry in Birmingham covers a wide range of scientific and industrial interests, including a fascinating collection of antique automobiles. The Chelmsford and Essex Museum in Oaklands Park has a magnificent collection of English birds and one of period costumes. The Tyrwhitt-Drake Museum in Maidstone specializes in carriages and carriage accessories. At the Verulamium Museum in St. Albans you can examine the Hypocaust (the Roman central heating system) and artifacts from the Verulamium excavations.

Museums in and around London are generally open from 10:00 A.M. to 5:00 or 6:00 P.M., Monday through Saturday, and on Sunday afternoons. Most of them close only on Christmas Day and Good Friday. Among the most renowned are: the British Museum on Great Russell Street, where you will see Magna Carta, the Rosetta Stone, Scott's Diary, Nelson's Log Book, and other treasures too numerous to mention; the London Museum at Kensington Palace, showing the history of London from earliest times and including a display of royal robes; the Bethnal Green Museum, Cambridge Heath Road, with collections of costumes, English silver, and dollhouses; the Public Record Office Museum, Chancery Lane, where you can look at the Domesday Book, Shakespeare's will, and Wellington's Waterloo dispatches; the Victoria and Albert Museum, Cromwell Road, South Kensington, with a beautifully displayed collection of arts including paintings and drawings by Constable; and, also in South Kensington, the Natural History Museum, with minerals and fossils of plants and animals from prehistoric times.

Anyone interested in literature will want to see the Brontë Parsonage

Museum at Haworth, Yorkshire; Jane Austen's home in Chawton, Hampshire; Dickens's Birthplace Museum in Portsmouth and Keats's house at Keats Grove (both in Hampshire); the properties administered by Shakespeare's Birthplace Trust in Stratford-upon-Avon; and, in London, Carlyle's house at 24 Cheyne Row, the Dickens house at 48 Doughty Street, and Dr. Johnson's house at 17 Gough Square. All of these homes have displays of the authors' manuscripts, letters, and personal effects.

Ship fanciers will be interested in the Cutty Sark and Gipsy Moth IV at Greenwich Pier; the H.M.S. *Discovery* at Victoria Embankment; the H.M.S. *Victory* at Portsmouth; the Maritime Museum at Buckler's Yard, Hampshire; and the National Maritime Museum at Greenwich.

There are many, many more—some of which may be more interesting to you than the ones named above. Ask for brochures at the British Tourist Authority, 64 St. James's Street, Piccadilly; at one of the London Transport Travel Enquiry offices; or at the Public Relations Office, 55 Broadway, Westminster.

MUSIC

In her delightful book *Here Is England,* Elizabeth Burton reminds us that when Old King Cole (see p. 55) called for his pipe and his bowl and his fiddlers three, he could not possibly have been preparing to enjoy a smoke while his musicians entertained him; in fact, tobacco wasn't heard of in England for another 1500 years. His pipe, she suggests, was a musical instrument—an early bagpipe or flute, perhaps—and what he really was calling for was a quartet rehearsal. (To Mrs. Burton's comments I add my own speculation that the bowl was filled with good cheer to help him maintain his merry old reputation in the unison passages.)

Old King Cole was a typically British king, and his idea of forming a musical ensemble was a typically British idea. Nowadays, England has many fine quartets and chamber orchestras and full symphony orchestras. In London alone, there are five major symphonies (the London Symphony, the London Philharmonic, the New Philharmonia, the Royal Philharmonic, and the BBC Symphony) and many smaller ensembles, including the London Mozart Players, the New London Ensemble, the London Brass Ensemble, the Park Lane Ensemble, the London String Orchestra, the London Soloists' Ensemble. There is at least one fine orchestra in each of the other major cities (for example, the Bournemouth Symphony, the Royal Liverpool Philharmonic, the Guildford Philharmonic, the City of Birmingham Symphony, the York Symphony, the Brighton Philharmonic, and Manchester's Hallé Orchestra); and smaller cities have good amateur symphonies, string orchestras, and choral groups. There is also an English Philharmonic Orchestra, an English National Orchestra, and an English Sinfonia Orchestra. The London suburb of Croydon has a symphony, and the London suburb of Camden has an excellent chamber orchestra. The orchestra of the Academy of St. Martin-in-the-Fields is exceptionally fine; and the greatest of all is the English Chamber Orchestra, which must surely be the most perfect musical ensemble this side of heaven.

As for choral music, London's Choral Society and its Bach Choir are particularly fine, and the great cathedrals all over England have their own splendid choirs. Attend Easter services at Coventry Cathedral for choral music you will not forget.

During the season (mid-September to early July), a music lover within commuting distance of London has his choice of two or three concerts every day of the week. In the summer, the many fine festivals throughout England, Wales, and Scotland, and the Henry Wood Promenade Concerts in Albert Hall keep his evenings pleasantly and excitingly filled.

Neither is there a shortage of pop music, jazz, and folk music; and as for rock—it has received as much enthusiastic response and innovative treatment in Britain as in America.

Most evening concerts start at 7:30, and refreshments are sold at intermissions ("intervals" in England). The average price of a balcony seat is 40 p. (Programs are sold separately, at the hall, and usually cost 10 p.) Tickets may be purchased in advance from any one of a number of official ticket agencies (in London, start with Ashton & Mitchell's Royal Agency, 50 New Bond Street, W. 1); but it is more fun to go to the box offices at the various concert halls. For a rundown of current attractions in London, pick up a copy of *What's On in London* (10 p) at any newsstand.

NIGHT LIFE

A newcomer's first impression of England's night life is that it is nonexistent, and, to a large extent, he's right. Concerts and plays begin at early hours, by American standards, and finish early. By 11:00 P.M. the halls are empty, cafés are dark, park gates are bolted shut, and subway trains are few and far between. The bartender at the neighborhood pub signals his customers that it's time to go home and the watchdog lying by the lager barrel assumes a menacing expression. By midnight, even the taxis make known their displeasure by raising their rates. This general early-closing habit very likely accounts in part for the safety of

England's streets: Where there is no one to mug, there are no muggers.

Behind closed doors, though, there are hotels and theatre restaurants with dancing and floor shows, elegant casinos, sophisticated nightclubs, and switched-on, beat-pounding discotheques where British reserve is abandoned behind clouds of cigarette smoke. The two weeklies, *What's On in London* and *Time Out,* will clue you in on the whereabouts of London's night life; and perhaps the best way to gain entrance initially is to join the Passport Club, 39 Sloane Street, where, for £10, you can buy a membership in 15 of the better clubs.

Two of the most exciting nightclubs are Churchill's, where there is an exceptionally good floor show, and Dietrich's favorite, the Blue Angel. For jazz, try Ronnie Scott's at 47 Frith Street and Café des Artistes on Fulham Road.

Outside of London, your best bet for nighttime swinging is probably at the beach resorts of Brighton, Blackpool, and Southend-on-Sea.

OUTDOOR FUN

It is difficult to find an Englishman who does not enjoy some type of sport, either as a participant or as a spectator, and if you do find one who is not enthusiastic about a particular sport for the sport's sake, you can be pretty sure he has at least placed a bet on a horse. Betting on sports is legal in England and very popular. When we first arrived in London and were interested in talking with real estate agents about the price of lots, we passed several establishments with signs that read "Turf Accountants." Naïve colonials that we are, we thought these must be dealers in land and were on the point of entering one such place when —fortunately in time to avoid embarrassment—we realized that we were about to address our inquiries to a couple of bookies. Horse racing, "the sport of kings," is only one of many kinds of racing that are enthusiastically applauded in England. The British apparently act on the assumption that if it has legs or wheels or can be propelled by wind or motor or manpower, it should be raced—and bet upon. If they aren't at the races, they are attending ball games—soccer, cricket, rugby football, tennis—or they're playing polo or golf. (England has 1600 golf courses, including some of the world's finest.) And when they grow too old and feeble to enjoy these sports in person, they stay home and watch them on the telly.

Topography and climate, of course, determine the favorite sports in various areas of England. The beaches on the eastern coast have a high rate of sunshine and are favorite amusement centers, not only for water sports and deep-sea fishing but for night life and kiddie attractions. The

Lake District and mountainous areas to the north provide ample opportunity for winter sports. The hills to the west and northwest are favorite spots for hiking and pony trekking. The New Forest is superb for following nature trails and observing wildlife. The Yorkshire moors are for those who enjoy solitary walks in the company of their own thoughts. The calm waters of the Norfolk Broads are popular for houseboat holidays. The rivers and streams of the Cotswolds are unexcelled for trout and salmon fishing. The southwestern peninsula (the "English Riviera") is for swimming and sailing in sunny warmth.

An Englishman's vacation (his "holiday") is very important to him. He plans and saves year round for his two weeks of fun, and when the great day arrives he's gone like a shot, cut off from the rest of the world, inaccessible, hidden behind a clump of reeds somewhere along England's 3000 miles of inland waterways, asleep by a haystack with his bicycle beside him, or tootling around Wales in his Mini. Don't even try to search him out; he'll be back at work on the appointed day, ready to start planning and saving for next year's holiday.

PARKS AND GARDENS

I think it is safe to say that the beauty of England's parks and gardens is unparalleled. A cool, damp climate and fertile soil provide the essential elements; but it is British pride and patience and recognition of beauty that use these elements to such advantage. Step across the street from Albert Hall into Hyde Park, and you will see that the placement of the flower beds and the heights and color combinations of the plants within them are chosen with the minutest attention to detail, that weeds have been carefully pulled and edges precisely trimmed by hand.

There are 5639 acres in the London area, which together comprise the Royal Parks (Bushy Park, Green Park, Greenwich Park, Hampton Court Park, Hyde Park, Kensington Gardens, Regent's Park, and St. James's Park), and there are many, many others all tended with the same pride and care.

One's inclination to think of England as a small country is dissipated when one tries to name all the parks and gardens worth visiting; there are far too many. Be sure to see the Royal Botanic Gardens at Kew, however; the Savill Gardens and Valley Garden at Windsor; the Westonbirt Arboretum at Tetbury, Gloucestershire; the beautifully landscaped grounds at Stourhead in Wiltshire; the Bicton Gardens at East Budleigh in Devon; Wisley Garden in Ripley, Surrey; and the University Botanic Gardens at Cambridge and Oxford.

PUBS

England's "pubs" come in all shapes and sizes (there are 6500 in London alone) and are famous the world over as places to enjoy good food and ale and camaraderie. Except for a two- or three-hour break in the afternoon, they are open from 11:00 A.M. to 11:00 P.M. on weekdays and from 6:30 P.M. to 11:00 P.M. on Sundays.

Among the best pubs in London are Ye Olde Cheshire Cheese in Fleet Street, where Dr. Johnson spent many hours, and, also in Fleet Street, the Cock Tavern, which was patronized by Dickens and Thackeray; the Londoner, on East India Dock Road, which serves up Cockney food and live music; the thirteenth-century Hoop and Grapes in Aldgate Street; the haunted Grenadier on Wilton Row; the Swan Tavern on Bayswater Road, with beautiful girls and good food; the theatrical hangouts of the Nag's Head in James Street and the Salisbury in St. Martin's Lane; the Chelsea Potter on King's Road, which is popular with young people, especially art students; and the Audley, which is a bit more sedate and dignified.

Pubs are not peculiar to London, of course. They are in every city and village of England, and they provide excellent places in which to enjoy the companionship of friends, to make new acquaintances, and to while away lonely hours. Hanging on a thatched inn in the village of West Stafford, there is a message that conveys the purpose of English pubs and describes, far better than I can, the atmosphere within them:

I trust no wise man will condemn
A cup of Genuine now and then.
When you are faint, your spirits low,
Your string relaxed, twill bend your bow,
Brace your drumhead and make you tight,
Wind up your watch and set you right.

SHOPPING

London is one of the world's most fascinating shopping centers. Every product imaginable is available, and every type of store. (At 140 Kensington Church Street, there's a bookstore that stocks only children's books; on Wormwood Street there's a spice shop—A. Abdullah & Sons; at 65 Beak Street there's a store whose entire stock is designed for left-handed customers.) There is excitement and adventure in every purchase, from a bouquet of roses at Covent Garden to a diamond necklace at Cartier's. If there is a problem at all with shopping in London, it's that the selection is so vast that one hardly knows where to begin. There are three things that will add to your shopping pleasure:

(1) wear comfortable shoes (it takes 30 minutes to cover the distance a Britisher describes as a "ten-minute walk"); (2) don't try to "do" more than one very small area in a day, with time out for a good lunch; and (3) before you start shopping at all, visit the Design Centre at 28 Haymarket, where there is a constantly changing exhibit of 1000 British-made items (and 9000 others listed in catalogs) with information on where you can buy them and how much they cost.

It would be impossible to name all of the good places to shop in London. Here are just a few of the best:

Department Stores
Oxford Street: Marks & Spencer; Bourne & Hollingsworth; D. H. Evans & Co.; Selfridge's; John Lewis
Regent Street: Dickens & Jones
Knightsbridge: Harrods, Ltd.
Kensington High Street: John Barker & Co.; Derry & Toms

Women's Sports Clothes
New Bond Street: Town & Country Clothes

Dresses
New Bond Street: Stewart & Spencer; Fenwick, Ltd.; Hunts

Children's Clothes
New Bond Street: The White House; Rowes

Women's Shoes
New Bond Street: Hutchings, Ltd.; Dolcis Shoe Company
Oxford Street: Babers

Scarves, Blouses, Ties
Regent Street: Liberty & Co.

Couturier Clothes
Bruton Street: Norman Hartnell (the Queen's dressmaker); Anne Gerrard
Royal Arcade, Bond Street: Annette

Suede and Sheepskin Garments
New Bond Street: Suedecraft
Oxford Street: The Sheepskin Shop

Woolen and Cashmere Sweaters
Regent Street: Estridge
Piccadilly: Jaye Kaye, Ltd.; W. & M. Lane
Burlington Arcade: N. Peal
Old Bond Street: Hunt & Winterbotham

Furs
S. Audley Street: Tico, Ltd.

Hanover Street: Lema Furs
Welbeck Street: Bradley's
Brompton Road: National Fur Company

Men's Suits
Savile Row: Anderson & Sheppard, Huntsman Sons

Men's Trousers
Regent Street: S & W Trousers

Haberdashery
Burlington Arcade: S. Fisher; David Berk; David L. Lord
Burlington Gardens: Hawes & Curtis

Men's Shoes
Dover Street: Alan McAfee, Ltd.
St. James's Street: John Lobb
Oxford Street: Babers

Rainwear
Haymarket Street: Burberrys, Ltd.

Woolens (for the whole family)
Regent Street: Jaeger

Plaids
Corner Knightsbridge and Brompton Road: The Scotch House

All Fabrics
Duke Street: Allans Fabrics

Leather Goods
Piccadilly: Swaine & Adeney
Bond Street: Jays

Perfumes
Grosvenor Street: Lancôme Salon
Sloane Street: Taylor of London

Silver
Chancery Lane: London Silver Vaults (50 merchants)

Jewelry
New Bond Street: Cartier's; Asprey's
Regent Street: Garrad & Co., Ltd.

Luggage
New Bond Street: Finnegan's, Ltd.

Porcelain
Curzon Street: Worcester Royal Porcelain Company
Burlington Arcade: Zelli's

Regent Street: Gered's
S. Audley Street: Thomas Goode and Company

Fine China and Glassware
Piccadilly: James Leather, Ltd.
Regent Street: Lawley's, Ltd.
Oxford Street: Chinacraft, Ltd.

Fine Furniture
Tottenham Court Road: Maple & Company, Ltd.

Antique Furniture
New Oxford Street: M. Harris & Sons

Modern Furniture
Tottenham Court Road: Heal's

Household Accessories
Sloane Street: The General Trading Company
Tottenham Court Road: Heal's

Household Linens
New Bond Street: The National Linen Co., Ltd.

Fine Antiques and Paintings
New Bond Street: Sotheby's auction rooms; Phillips Son & Neale, Ltd.
King Street: Christie's auction rooms

Phonograph Records and Sound Equipment
Oxford Street: Alfred Imhof, Ltd.
Shepherd Street: Discurio

Photographic Equipment
New Bond Street: Wallace Heaton
Old Bond Street: Dollond & Newcombe

Books
Charing Cross Road: Foyle's
Piccadilly: Hatchard's
Malet Street: Dillon's University Bookshop, Ltd.
Kensington Church Street: Children's Book Centre, Ltd.

Toys
Regent Street: Hamley's

Bargains

Phonograph records at The International Collectors' Agency in Newport Court, Charing Cross Road (reviewers' records at one-fourth the retail price)
Electrical appliances at Your Best Buys, 12 Earlham Street (10 percent to 20 percent discount)

China at the Reject China Shop, 33 Beauchamp Place (originally intended for export, sold at a fraction of its usual price)

All commodities at the January sales in the better London shops

For the fun of street-market shopping and, incidentally, some strange and comical sights, try Portobello Road and Petticoat Lane, as well as the Chelsea Antique Market in King's Road and the New Caledonian Market in Bermondsey Square. And young people, especially, will enjoy the boutiques of King's Road and Carnaby Street, where jeans can be made to the customer's design and measurements in an hour, rock music blares from every doorway, and the air is heavy with incense.

Because of its international flavor and its seemingly endless number of stores, London offers the shopper an excitement and variety that can't be matched elsewhere in Britain. Don't think that good merchandise is available only in London, however; there are many fine shopping centers in the smaller towns, and you will discover treasure troves of local craftsmanship wherever you go—from hand-carved walking sticks in Northumbria to old-fashioned hobby horses in Cornwall, and from paintings by local artists in the tiny fishing villages of the southwest to patchwork quilts in the Lake District.

THEATRE, OPERA, AND BALLET

With at least 30 theatrical productions going on in London at any given time, there is always a choice of light comedy, satirical revues, musicals, serious contemporary drama, and classical repertoire. Among the many theatres, the most renowned are the Old Vic (home of the National Theatre Company) and the Aldwych (Royal Shakespeare Company), and, for a charming evening of theatre and dining by the Thames, the Mermaid Theatre. Experimental theatre may be enjoyed at the New Arts Theatre Club and in Tottenham Court Road; and each year there is, at the Aldwych, a three-and-a-half-month festival program with about 16 different plays performed by the best foreign theatre companies. Open-air theatre in Regent's Park is popular in the summer. Evening performances in London start about 7:30 (unless there are two shows scheduled for the same evening), and there are frequent matinees. Gallery seats cost about 50p at the box offices. (You will pay a 20 percent commission if you buy from a ticket agent.)

British theatre is by no means confined to London, however. Many towns in the provinces have excellent repertory companies—some of them financed by the British Arts Council. Many famous actors (*e.g.*, Sir Laurence Olivier, Sir John Gielgud, and Sir Ralph Richardson) got their start in the provincial theatres. Perhaps the most famous playhouse in the world is the Royal Shakespeare Theatre at Stratford-upon-Avon, where five or more Shakespeare plays are produced each season (April to December). The Chichester Theatre in Sussex is also renowned for its fine summer performances (May to September). In addition, touring companies bring good theatre to the provinces. (One of the touring companies is the Royal Shakespeare Company, which performs all over England while foreign companies are performing at the Aldwych.) Theatrical performances are frequently a part of the British Arts Festivals, and two of the most unusual opportunities for summer theatre are the medieval mystery plays in York and the Minack Theatre performances on the cliffs at Penzance.

The Combined Theatre Libraries, Ltd., publishes weekly theatre listings that are available at the British Tourist Authority and at most London hotels. A monthly theatrical publication, *Plays and Players,* may be purchased for $35p$ at London bookstalls.

Opera and ballet programs may be obtained in advance from the D'Oyly Carte Opera (1 Savoy Hill, London, W.C. 2), Sadler's Wells Opera (London Coliseum, St. Martin's Lane, London WC2N 4ES), and the Royal Opera and Royal Ballet (Royal Opera House, Covent Garden, London WC2E 7QA). But perhaps the best opera in England is to be found at the Glyndebourne Opera Festival (May to July in Lewes, Sussex) and at the Aldeburgh Festival (March through September in Aldeburgh, Suffolk).

Ballet is especially good at Royal Festival Hall from Christmas to mid-January and from late July to mid-September.

London cinemas generally open at 12:30 noon, and they often show late Saturday night programs starting between 11:00 P.M. and midnight.

TRAVEL WITHIN BRITAIN

One of the most convenient things about England is that although there are so many things to see they are not far apart. There is a compactness to England that Americans are not accustomed to: Distance, as we think of it, does not exist. It takes seven days of hard, steady motoring to get from one end of the United States to the other; it takes less than a day to cross England. And yet, all the components of a large country are present: the rivers and forests, the peaks and meadows, the beaches and cities and country estates and cathedrals. So little travel time is expended in getting from one place to another that a trip can be at once short and broad, static and varied, economical and all-encompassing.

If you are motoring through England, you can find out about road conditions within 50 miles of London by dialing 246–8021. For other motoring information, inquire at the Automobile Association, Fanum House, Leicester Square, London, W.C. 2.

Of course, you needn't motor at all. There are so many rivers and canals that you can travel by water from Wales on the west coast to Norfolk on the east, or from Surrey in the south of England almost to Yorkshire in the north. You can travel by day on regularly scheduled luxury "hotel boats," or rent a camping boat with sleeping accommodations (with or without a skipper), or sail or canoe. Write to the Inland Waterways Association, Ltd., 144 Regent's Park Road, London, N.W. 1, or to the British Waterways Board, Melbury House, Melbury Terrace, London, N.W. 1.

If you like to cycle, the Cyclist's Touring Club and the Youth Hostels Association (which, incidentally, has no upper age limit) will plan your trips for you and provide you with maps, insurance, and advice. Write to the YHA, Trevelyan House, St. Albans.

British rail travel is fast and clean. Main-line diesel and electric locomotives travel at speeds up to 100 miles per hour. The coaches are soundproof and have comfortable seats, and restaurant cars offer everything from snacks to full meals at reasonable prices. Motorail service enables the passenger to take his car with him on the same train.

A network of internal air routes covers the whole country. Off-peak and night flights are available at low rates, and children and students travel at reduced fares.

Bus and coach service is available everywhere. (Although a bus and a coach look exactly alike, the British make a distinction: A "bus" is for local travel; a "coach" is for long distance.)

The British Tourist Authority will put you on to vacation bargain tours and special interest holidays where you can indulge your passion for music, bridge, archaeology, or even ghosts—or help you map your own routes through King Arthur country or Thomas Hardy country, or show you how to follow the trail of Charles Dickens or Mary, Queen of Scots.

As for where to stay in your travels: England has many fine hotels— as well as some modern motels, if you prefer the American way. But the really fun places are the charming little inns, many of them renowned for their associations with historical events and personages and no two of them alike except in their hospitable treatment of guests. Ask the British Tourist Authority for a list.

TRAVEL ABROAD

An American who heretofore has been able to spend only an occasional fortnight in Europe will thoroughly enjoy his new proximity to the

Continent. He can fly to Paris in an hour, Frankfurt in an hour and 20 minutes, Rome in two hours. He can take his car across the channel on a ferry and have it available for motoring all over Europe. He may eventually, in fact, be able to put his car on a train and send it across through the proposed "chunnel." Because he is already so close, he can more reasonably consider steamer trips across the North Sea and through the Norwegian fjords, or Mediterranean cruises with a turn around the Greek Islands and a stopover in Africa. He can rent a villa or an apartment in Spain and enjoy the sunny warmth of the Costa del Sol.

The list of places to go and things to see is endless, but it falls more properly within the province of the tourist-guide experts. There is no dearth of information: Start by ordering (for $4.95 plus 50 cents postage) *World's Best Travel Bargains Start in London* from Joyer Travel Report, Box 707, Corona del Mar, Cal. 92625. It will tell you where to find the best travel bargains after you are living in England.

IF YOU STILL CAN'T THINK OF ANYTHING . . .

Dial 246–8041 for a recital of the day's events in and around London; and if you'd like a little continental flavor added to your phone call, dial 246–8043 for a French reply, 246–8045 for a German one, 246–8047 for Spanish, 246–8049 for Italian.

Chapter XII
TIPS FOR RETIREES

FINANCIAL

"Over-80" Pensions

You may be entitled to a small pension from the British government, in addition to your other income, if you meet the following eligibility requirements: (1) you are age 80 or over; (2) you are a resident of Great Britain (*i.e.*, England, Scotland, or Wales), and you have lived in Great Britain or in Northern Ireland or the Isle of Man for ten of the twenty years preceding your eightieth birthday; (3) you are not a recipient of a National Insurance pension (and you probably won't be, because only people who have contributed to the British National Insurance Scheme during their working years are eligible for National Insurance pensions.)

At the post office you can pick up Leaflet N1 184, which tells you more about "Over-80" pensions and to which is attached a claim form to be completed and forwarded to the nearest office of the Department of Health and Social Security, together with your birth certificate and, if you are a woman and your husband is living, your marriage license. If you and your spouse are both eligible, pick up *two* claim forms. The post office will provide you with a stamped, addressed envelope if you are not certain where to mail the claim.

The amount of your pension will be £3.85 per week—unless you are a married woman whose husband is still living, in which case it will be £2.45 per week. Married couples who are both eligible, however, may both submit claims and collect a combined total of £6.30 per week. Your pension will be somewhat reduced if you spend 56 days in hospital, further reduced if you are hospitalized for a full year, and still further reduced after two years; it can never, however, fall below £1.35 per week.

When your claim is approved, you will be sent a book of "money orders," and you may cash one every Thursday at the post office; or, if you prefer, your "Over-80" pension can be paid directly into your bank account in quarterly installments. If you choose the quarterly plan, you won't have an order book to identify you as a pensioner, so ask the Social Security office to give you a pension card. This identification will entitle you to certain concessions (free or reduced-fee admissions, and so forth) offered by various organizations throughout England.

Income Tax

British tax laws provide certain benefits for people over 65, but it is unlikely that you will be able to profit from most of them. They are designed for people with extremely low incomes—incomes that are probably less than your American Social Security pension.

There are, however, a few minor "reliefs" that may help you. For example, if you maintain a daughter in your home to take care of you when you are incapacitated by age or illness, you may deduct an allowance of £55. If you have a resident female housekeeper for the same reason, you may deduct £100. You can't claim both, however, so list your daughter as your housekeeper and take the £100 deduction; this is legitimate.

Of course you already know that the personal exemption allowance on your U.S. tax return will double when you reach 65.

U.S. Social Security

I have mentioned that pension money is not, at present, taxed by Britain unless it is actually remitted to or received in Britain. A retiree who can spare all or part of his Social Security pension will, therefore, be well advised to keep that portion of his income in the United States, where (except for the interest it earns) it will not be taxable by either country. Unfortunately, after you have lived abroad for six months, the Social Security Administration may try to insist on mailing your checks to your British address. If you permit this to be done, you must pay income tax to Britain on the amounts even if you send the checks back to the United States for deposit.

There is no point in looking for some devious way—such as having your checks mailed to a friend or relative—to keep the money out of England: That sort of thing won't work. The checks must be made payable to the beneficiary, and the only way you can have them deposited to your U.S. bank account without first endorsing them yourself is to file a form SF–233 ("Power of Attorney by Individual to a Financial Organization for the Collection of Checks Drawn on the Treasurer of the United States") with the bank. (The bank will send a copy to the Social Security Administration.)

The Administration's manual, "Social Security Benefits outside the United States," states that after the beneficiary's first six months abroad the checks will be sent to his overseas address. No mention is made in the manual of the SF–233; in fact, it has been the practice of the Administration to deny the privilege of the SF–233 route to any beneficiary not in a continuous travel status or unable to prove a compelling need for having his checks sent to the bank. "Compelling need" has, in the past, been interpreted to mean something as serious as physical or mental incompetence. Now, however, I believe you will find that the Administration has relaxed its definition of "compelling need" and that it is willing to consider your desire to protect your pension from unnecessary taxation a sufficiently valid reason for asking that your checks be mailed to the bank.

When you apply for your pension and are asked to state your reason for wanting the checks mailed to the bank, don't hesitate to say that you wish to keep the money in a tax-free status. There is nothing illegal about this. England's Inland Revenue makes it quite clear that the Administration's practice of sending the checks overseas is not a British requirement and that England has no interest in your Social Security money if it stays in the United States. If the clerk in your local Social Security office is still going by the manual (which, as of this writing, has not been revised), stick to your guns: Officials higher up the Social Security ladder know that there are no laws, American or British, to prevent your having the pension checks mailed to the bank.

Those of you who are already living overseas may also arrange to have your checks sent to a bank if you wish. Write to the Director, Division of International Relations, Social Security Administration, P.O. Box 1756, Baltimore, Md. 21203, state your wishes, and ask that the SF–233 forms be forwarded to you.

Everyone who lives overseas and draws Social Security benefits is required (whether or not the checks are mailed overseas or held in the United States) to report changes in marital status, custody of children, employment—anything and everything that may affect his Social Security status. The handiest way to report such changes is on the Administration's preaddressed postcard form SSA–1425(f)—"Report to Social Security Administration by Persons Outside the United States." Pick up a handful of these forms at your local Social Security office and take them to England with you in your metal box.

Retirement Income Credit

There are a few instances when a retired person over 65 may receive, on his U.S. tax return, a credit of up to 15 percent of his retirement income. This credit is not generally available to someone who is eligible for Social Security benefits.

To determine whether you are eligible for retirement income credit, follow these steps:

Step 1.   Ascertain whether you meet the "prior earned income test" (and you probably will, because its only condition is that you have had more than $600 annual earned income for the past ten years).

Step 2.   Determine how much of your income qualifies as "retirement" income. To do this, include: (1) taxable income from pensions (including amounts received from a qualified trust, if you have been self-employed); (2) taxable income from annuities; (3) taxable income from interest and dividends (including your share of taxable income and dividends from estates and trusts); (4) income from rents (net profit after expenses, including depreciation); (5) income from U.S. retirement plan bonds.

Do *not* include: (1) disability annuities; (2) capital gains dividends from a mutual fund; (3) royalties from literary, musical, or artistic works, from patents on inventions, or from oil or mineral rights.

Step 3.   Determine which is the lesser of: (1) your retirement income received during the year (from Step 2, above); or (2) $1,524 (if you are single) or $2,286 (if you are a husband and wife filing jointly).

Step 4.   Then—and here's where the rub comes—using whichever of the figures in Step 3 is the lesser, subtract: (1) Social Security or railroad retirement payments (this will make most of us ineligible for credit); and (2) nontaxable pension or annuity payments (but *don't* count that portion which is nontaxable by virtue of its being a return of your contribution). Your "retirement income credit" is 15 percent of anything that may be left.

Capital Gains Tax on Sale of U.S. Home

If you are nearing the age of 65 when you decide to retire, it may pay you to delay the sale of your U.S. home until you have your sixty-fifth birthday. Once you reach 65, you are generally entitled to exclude from your gross income all or part of the capital gain realized from the sale *if* you have owned and occupied the property for five or more years out of the eight-year period ending on the date of sale.

If you are a married couple who own the property jointly and who file a joint return in the year of sale, it is not necessary that you both be 65 or that both of you have occupied the residence for five years; you will qualify for the over-65 tax break if either of you is eligible.

If you meet the age and residency requirements, and if the adjusted sale price of the home you sell is not more than $20,000, you will be totally exempt from the capital gains tax on the profit; but if the adjusted sale price is more than $20,000, you are exempt only from that portion of the capital gain which bears the same ratio to the total gain as $20,000 bears to the adjusted sale price. You can, however, postpone payment of tax on the balance of the gain if you buy or build another residence.

It works like this:

Line 4 (of form 2119)—Selling price of old residence	$32,500
Line 5—Less selling expenses	− 2,000
Line 6—Amount realized	30,500
Line 7—Less adjusted cost of old residence	−24,000
Line 8—Gain on sale	6,500
Line 9—Fix-up expenses	500
Line 10—Adjusted sale price (Line 6 minus Line 9)	30,000

Now if the amount on Line 10 were $20,000 or less, you could exclude the entire gain on Line 8 from your gross income; but it's not—so skip to that part of the form that pertains only to people over 65, and go on as follows:

Line 15—Divide the amount on Line 10 by $20,000 and
multiply the answer by the amount on Line 8. (In this example,
you will multiply 66 2/3 by $6,500) $4,333

(This $4,333 is the portion of the gain on which you are totally exempt.)

Line 16—Subtract the amount on Line 15 from the amount on
Line 8 ($6,500 minus $4,333) $2,167

(This $2,167 is the amount that is taxable in the year of the gain.)

But suppose you buy and occupy a new home (even one in England) within a year of the sale (or *build* and occupy one within 18 months), go ahead with your computation as follows:

Line 17—Cost of new residence	$24,500
Line 18—Gain taxable this year (Add the amount on Line 15 to the amount on Line 17, and subtract the total from the amount on Line 10.) In this example, $4,333 plus $24,500 equals $28,833; and $30,000 minus $28,833 equals	$1,167
Line 19—Gain on which tax may be postponed (Line 16 minus Line 18)	$1,000

The figure on Line 19 is transferred to Schedule D and then halved before it is combined with the other taxable income on your form 1040.

HEALTH

U.S. Medicare

Since Medicare will not pay for any services obtained outside the United States (except in the unlikely event that the patient requires service as the result of an emergency that occurs within the United States but the nearest hospital is outside the United States), there is no point in continuing to pay the premiums unless you plan to return eventually to the States. Be certain that you are going to stay in England, however, before you withdraw from Medicare.

After you have terminated your coverage, you can re-enroll in the Medicare program only once and that must be during the general enrollment periods (January through March of each year); 10 percent is added to the premium for each year during which you were eligible but not enrolled; and after three years you cannot get back into the program at all.

If you decide to drop Medicare, notify the Social Security Administration, P.O. Box 1756, Baltimore, Md. 21203, in writing, of your decision. Be sure to give your Social Security number, state clearly your wish to withdraw from Medicare, and ask that your monthly pension checks be increased by the amount normally withheld for your Medicare premiums. Your coverage should then terminate at the end of the calendar quarter following the quarter in which you have filed your notice of withdrawal.

British National Health Service

Health services available to you as a resident of Britain have already been discussed in Chapter VIII. The hospital and specialist services and the general practitioner services described there are all-encompassing and readily available to you. The local authority services, however, because of their widely divergent benefits in different areas of England, are more difficult to define.

Local authority (LHA) services for the benefit of the elderly are intended primarily for people with very low incomes; it is unlikely, therefore, that you will be eligible for most of them.

There is, however, one very valuable LHA service for which you *can* apply (although even that one was originally established for the benefit of maternity cases, not for elderly people)—the health visitor. A health visitor is a trained nurse who has had special instruction in social work. Nursing is not her primary duty. She is, however, skilled in recognizing health needs, and she can advise you about the various health services available in your area and can help you arrange to obtain them—if not without charge, at least for a reasonable fee. You can seek her out yourself by writing or phoning your local health authority or Citizens' Advice Bureau; or your family doctor may send her to see you, without your asking, if he thinks you need someone to look in on you occasionally. Her services are free.

A district nurse may also be available to you without cost through the LHA if your doctor recommends one. She (or he, though there are not many male district nurses) can administer injections prescribed by your doctor, change bandages, and perform other general nursing duties.

Vaccination and immunization, ambulance service, and sometimes the loan of a wheelchair are also available free of charge.

Among the LHA services for which a fee is charged are chiropody treatments, meals-on-wheels, and household help. Not all these services are available in all areas, however, and even where they are available there may be so many applicants that you will be placed on a waiting list.

You need not rely solely on the local health authorities, of course. There are voluntary organizations that can help you; or, if you can afford the rather expensive fees, you can engage a private nurse or apply for residence in a privately run nursing home.

The "health" sections of this book have attempted to give you some insight into the operation of the National Health Service and the facilities that will be at your disposal while you are living in England—things that you may not already have known. Your cheapest and best bet for a long and happy retirement is still, in England as in any country, the practice of preventive medicine: daily exercise, nutrition, adequate rest, good posture, low caloric intake and, above all, a life style that is characterized by physical and mental activity. Upon the first indication that, despite your preventive measures, the inevitable process of aging has begun to take its toll, do something about it without delay. If you feel you could benefit by wearing a hearing aid, for example, don't put off getting one; you might miss something.

RESIDENTIAL HOMES

Sometimes it's difficult to tell a residential home from a nursing home because the occupants of both are so often elderly and frail. A nursing home, however, has nursing as its primary function and is required to have a trained nurse on its staff; a residential home, if it is a good one, will put more emphasis on other aspects of care and cater more to the individual tastes of its occupants.

If you are not so ill that you require hospitalization or constant nursing, and if you can contribute physically to your own care, a residential home may be a less expensive and more satisfactory choice for you than a nursing home. It's difficult to generalize, however, because there is such a variance in the atmosphere of these homes and the services offered.

The prospect of having to enter a residential home for elderly people is, in any case, not a particularly enticing one; yet you should learn something about these homes in case loneliness and the infirmities of old age finally get the better of you and you have no relatives to whom you can turn.

Residential homes operated by the local authorities differ widely in their accommodations. They are administered by matrons or wardens, and many of them are housed in old-fashioned buildings that have no elevators. The residents sleep in wards to facilitate nursing care and must eat, sleep, and get up in the morning at specific hours to suit the convenience of the staff. The charge varies from £8 to £17 per week. Dismal though they sound, LHA homes are much in demand; if you apply for admission you will be placed on a waiting list and you may have to stay on the list for as long as a year. These homes are not all so terrible, of course; most of them have central heating, and some of the wealthier local authorities are trying to make their homes more comfortable and attractive than they used to be. Keep in mind, too, that your entering an LHA home need not be final; you can leave whenever you think of something better, and that's one consolation.

In addition to the LHA homes, there are homes for the elderly operated by voluntary secular and religious organizations. As a rule, these are smaller homes in heavily populated areas. Many of them are understaffed and will not keep residents after they become too old and infirm to take care of themselves. Generally, too, the residents must be all of one sex; it is not often that married couples will be accepted. Charges are established by the sponsoring organization and vary widely.

Privately run homes are in business for profit and are generally expensive but are more likely to be attractive and comfortable than either the LHA homes or those run by voluntary organizations. Most private homes are located around London or in the retirement areas along the south coast. They are, as a rule, small. Since you will pay well for the privilege of living in a privately run home (£10 to £30 a week), make your choice carefully. Visit the home and ask to be shown around, taking note of the proprietor's willingness to show you everything and of his courtesy (or lack of it) to his guests. Ask what specific items your fee will cover (some homes charge extra for such services as laundry and special diets). Find out if you may have a private room and whether there is a lounge where you can visit with the other residents. Make sure there is a way out in case of fire. And, most important of all, look at the faces of your prospective housemates to see if they appear happy and interested.

EMPLOYMENT

It is virtually impossible for an American to get a paying job with an English employer; that privilege is reserved, rightly, for the British citizen. Furthermore, an alien must not attempt to set himself up in any business, trade, or profession without first obtaining the consent of the Home Office, Immigration and Nationality Department. If you are one of those retirees who are so accustomed to getting up and going to work each morning that you cannot be happy without a job, therefore, you will probably have to settle for volunteer work—and even that, strange to say, is sometimes difficult to obtain.

You must, first of all, find an organization that uses volunteer help. That in itself is not too difficult because there are many charitable organizations that are totally dependent on volunteers. What will complicate things for you is the odds on finding one near your home that requires whatever particular talent you can contribute. If, for example, you have enjoyed a long and successful career as a highly respected but somewhat absent-minded history professor, and the charitable organization in your area requires a driver for its meals-on-wheels service— you will still be unemployed. Many volunteer organizations have rigid standards for the people they permit to help them, and some simply don't like to train new help if they can get along without it. You should keep in mind, too, that any job—even a volunteer job—is a commitment. Never undertake volunteer work unless you intend to stick with it long enough to be of real value to the organization you wish to serve. If there is the slightest suspicion in your mind that you may want to quit after a short try at it, or even take a few months off now and then to visit the Continent, be frank with your prospective employer; it is the only fair thing to do.

The best place to begin your search for a volunteer job is probably at your nearest Citizens' Advice Bureau. The CABs seem to have the answers to almost everything, and they will either have in their files lists of organizations that require help or they will be able to tell you where to find such lists. Other good sources of information are: The National Council of Social Service, 26 Bedford Square, London W.C. 1; and David Hobman's book, *A Guide to Voluntary Service*, which you can examine at your local library or order through your local bookstore.

If you *do* find and accept paid employment in England or if you become self-employed,[1] the amount of your Social Security pension may be affected. If your wages or your earnings through self-employment are *not* covered under the United States Social Security system, you will not receive a pension check for any month in which you work seven days, or parts of seven days, consecutive or nonconsecutive. If your earnings *are* covered under the United States Social Security system, your pension is subject to the same laws that would apply if you earned the money in the United States, *i.e.*, after you reach a certain earning level (the amount changes from time to time), your pension is decreased. Once you reach age 72, whether your earnings are covered by the United States Social Security system or not, you're home free: You will not be penalized no matter how much you earn.

ADULT EDUCATION

Adult education classes in a variety of subjects are offered in most localities. Some of these classes (*e.g.*, hobby classes and classes that provide information about retirement life) are designed especially for older people—though there is certainly no need to limit yourself to these. Most classes start in September and extend over three terms, ending in June. Most are held at night, a few during the day.

Some classes—especially the arts-and-crafts type—are sponsored by the local authorities. The roll is called, but beyond that there aren't many formalities. This is fun-and-games education, and while it's not exactly a part of academia it does have social value. Courses of a more scholarly nature with high teaching standards (and requiring homework) are offered by the university extensions. You will find that classes of both types provide an excellent way for you to meet other people of your age who share your interests. And, in addition to enjoying the social aspects, you might learn something. How about conversational French, for instance, so you can order a meal in a Parisian restaurant or ask how to get to the Eiffel Tower?

[1] The Social Security Administration's definition of "self-employment" includes not only business or professional operations that you conduct alone; it also includes those operations in which you are one of two or more partners, even if you yourself are not actively employed.

There are, in addition to the educational facilities available in your immediate vicinity, residential centers where schooling and holidays may be combined for periods as short as a weekend. Almost every conceivable subject is taught in one or another of these centers, from calligraphy to Egyptian archaeology, from heraldry to current events, from mime for the deaf to a listening course in J. S. Bach. The centers are generally housed in attractive country homes, and the cost of tuition plus board and room is, in some cases, as low as £1 a day.

Your local education authority can provide you with detailed information on adult education courses available in your area. The best source of information on the residential centers is The National Institute of Adult Education, 35 Queen Anne St., London W. 1.

KEEPING INFORMED ON RETIREMENT LEGISLATION

One of the best ways to keep abreast of U.S. legislation affecting retirees is to maintain your membership in professional organizations and trade unions. Some of these associations will not require payment of dues after retirement—but, whether they do or not, keep your membership active and make certain that you remain on the mailing list for newsletters and other association publications.

You should also join an association with interests devoted exclusively to retirees. Some of the better ones are:

American Association of Retired Persons (AARP)
1225 Connecticut Avenue, N.W.
Washington, D.C. 20036
    or
215 Long Beach Blvd.
Long Beach, Cal. 90801

National Retired Teachers Association (NRTA)
(same address as AARP, above)[2]

National Association of Retired Federal Employees
  (NARFE)
1533 New Hampshire Avenue, N.W.
Washington, D.C. 20036

[2]Bernard E. Nash, Executive Director of NRTA-AARP, has been elected president of the newly formed International Federation on Aging (headquarters in Washington, D.C.). It is IFA's goal to protect and promote the interests of the elderly.

RECREATION

England is big on spectator sports—cricket, soccer, rugby, hockey, tennis, horse racing. You can enjoy these in person (a seat at a ball game will cost you from $1.95 to $4.00) or watch them on television. There are other, less strenuous, sports—croquet, archery, golf—in which you can be an active participant. Many communities offer training facilities in conjunction with their recreational programs. Museums, concerts, theatres, travel—the opportunities for all of these diversions have been discussed in an earlier chapter; so, although they are every bit as relevant to retirees as to any other group of people, I won't bore you with repetition. And there is certainly no need to get into the usual bit about hobbies for retirees—not that I'm downgrading hobbies (they are pleasant and exciting and often eminently worthwhile), but there is nothing either peculiarly British or peculiarly American about them: The procedure for watching a European finch through your binoculars is very much the same as the procedure for watching an American woodpecker, and a goldfish requires the same amount of food in either country.

MAKING FRIENDS IN ENGLAND

Volunteer work and adult education classes, already discussed, are among the best ways to make new friends; but there are many other ways to meet people with whom you can share your leisure hours—through the churches, for example, or clubs, or holiday tours.

The Church of England is the "established" (you might even say "official") church in England. It is the one to which the sovereign belongs—the one to which her title, Defender of the Faith, refers. This does not mean, however, that you can't find a church of your own faith. Britain has churches of all denominations. Most of them arrange social activities in which you may participate, and many operate residential homes for the elderly and have volunteer visitor services for people who are too infirm to attend services and social gatherings. You can learn about London churches from a book called *London City Churches —A Brief Guide,* available at London Information Centre, St. Paul's Churchyard, E.C. 4, for about 60 cents.

England is also a country of clubs. There are women's clubs; Rotary clubs; clubs for people who share interests such as music, reading, drama, history; clubs whose purpose is to arrange group holidays; clubs for the elderly, where you can drop in for a chat and share a meal. Before you ever leave the States, you can ask at the nearest British

Consulate how to go about locating associations of people in England with interests similar to yours.

One of the best ways to make friends is to arrange to stay for a week or so with a British family. The British Tourist Authority, 64 St. James's Street, London, has a list of organizations that can help you make such arrangements. From BTA you can also get a booklet called *Farmhouse Accommodations,* which will tell you where you can have a pleasant visit and good home-cooked food in clean, simple surroundings among hospitable people. Bed and breakfast (and sometimes evening meals are included, too) will cost from $21 to $28 per week per person. If you want to stay with a family in the London area, you can write direct to the London Tourist Board, 4 Grosvenor Gardens, London SW1W ODU, stating the number of people who require accommodations and the proposed length of your visit. Allow a minimum of six weeks to complete your arrangements.

If none of these suggestions appeals to you, you can always go to the corner pub for a pint of bitters. After a few successive Saturday nights, the bartender will give you a nod of recognition—a signal to the rest of the patrons that you may now be accepted as one of the "regulars."

Americans have a tendency to picture the typical Englishman as a reserved and sometimes rather haughty individual. That's true, and all to the good, if by "reserve" you mean a reluctance to slap a total stranger on the back or poke him in the ribs while telling him an off-color story. You are mistaken, however, if you think you can't make friends in England. The British are a basically friendly people who will treat you with courtesy, respect, and sincere concern, and with whom you can spend many hours of delightful companionship. Don't bore your new acquaintances with tales of "how we did it in America"; instead, ask how it's done in England. Seek their advice on shopping, housing, gardening. After all, you had a choice: Tell them why you chose England—not in the overly effusive manner in which so many of us are accustomed to expressing our emotions, but with the quiet and rather understated sincerity that the British understand. They will shrug and laugh and pretend that they think you're crazy—but they'll like it.

Appendix A / Authorized Kennels and Carrying Agents

County	Kennel/Cattery	Animals Accepted
Bedfordshire	Four in Hand Kennels Sharnbrook, Beds. Mr. H. Bland Tel: Sharnbrook 431	Dogs and cats
Berkshire	Spire Ridge Kennels Bath Road, Midgham, nr Reading, Berks. Mrs. D. Gough, Mr. H. S. Gater Tel: Woolhampton 2187	Dogs only
	The Granary Kennels The Homestead, Hawkridge Wood, Frilsham, nr Newbury, Berks. Mrs. J. Nowell Tel: Yattendon 489	Dogs only
Buckinghamshire	The White House Belle Farm, Seven Hills Road, Iver Heath, Bucks. Mr. H. A. Scott Tel: 395 2497	Dogs only
Cheshire	Little Creek Kennels Kingswood Lane, Saughall, Ches. Mr. F. Cassidy Tel: Saughall 267	Dogs and cats

County	Kennel/Cattery	Animals Accepted
Devonshire	Elm Cottage Milehouse, Plymouth, Devon Messrs. Parkinson & Watson Tel: Plymouth 51522	Dogs and cats
Essex	Par Air Kennels & Cattery Warren Lane, Stanway, Colchester, Essex Mr. & Mrs. M. Parish Tel: Colchester 330 332	Dogs and cats
Gloucestershire	Kilcarken Kennels Newnham-on-Severn, Glos. Mr. & Mrs. E. Dudley Tel: Newnham 326	Dogs and cats
Hertfordshire	Barrimilne Kennels Great North Rd., Baldock, Herts. Mrs. M. Bastable Tel: Hitchin 730–221	Dogs only
Kent	International Quarantine Kennels, Ltd. Bridledown, West Hougham, Dover, Kent Mr. S. J. Scales Tel: Dover 1382	Dogs only
Norfolk	The Limes Acle, Norwich, Norfolk Mr. C. D. Hopkins Tel: Acle 616	Dogs and cats
Somerset	St. Giles Kennels Wrantage, Taunton, Somerset Mr. J. D. Cook Tel: North Curry 333	Dogs and cats
Suffolk	Millview Kennels Kelsale, Saxmundham, Suffolk Mr. J. C. Elwell Tel: 0728 2254	Dogs only
Sussex	Hazel House Elsted, Midhurst, Sussex Mr. R. G. Gwyer Tel: Midhurst 3616	Dogs and cats

County	Kennel/Cattery	Animals Accepted
	Arden Grange International Quarantine & Boarding Kennels London Road, Albourne, Hassocks, Sussex Mr. M. J. Streatfield Tel: Hurstpierpoint 2416	Dogs and cats
Yorkshire	Prospect Kennels Pannal Road, Follifoot, Harrogate, Yorks. Mr. & Mrs. I. R. Johnson Tel: Harrogate 81942	Dogs and cats

This material is British Crown copyright and is reproduced by permission of the Controller of Her Britannic Majesty's Stationery Office. There are frequent changes. For the most recent listing, write to the Ministry of Agriculture, Fisheries and Food, Government Bldgs., Hook Rise South, Tolworth, Surbiton, Surrey.

Appendix B / Principal Makes of British Cars

Make	Manufacturer and Address
A. C. Cars	A. C. Cars, Ltd., High St., Thames Ditton, Surrey
Aston Martin	Aston Martin Lagonda, Ltd., Newport Pagnell, Buckinghamshire
Austin Morris M.G. }	British Leyland Motor Corp., Longbridge, Birmingham, Warwickshire
Triumph	British Leyland Motor Corp., Canley, Coventry, Warwickshire
Daimler Jaguar }	British Leyland Motor Corp., Browns Lane, Allesley, Coventry, Warwickshire
Rover	British Leyland Motor Corp., Meteor Works, Lode Lane, Solihull, Warwickshire
Rolls Royce Bentley }	Rolls Royce, Ltd., Pyms Lane, Crewe, Cheshire
Hillman Humber Sunbeam }	Chrysler, Ltd., Devonshire House, Piccadilly, London, W. 1
Vauxhall	Vauxhall Motors, Ltd. (a subsidiary of General Motors), Kimpton Road, Luton, Bedfordshire
Bond Reliant }	Reliant Motor Company, Ltd., Watling St., Twogates, Tamworth, Staffordshire
Ford	Ford Motor Company, Ltd., Eagle Way, Warley, Brentwood, Essex
Lotus	Lotus Cars, Ltd., Hethel, Wymondham, Norwich, Norfolk

Appendix C / Steps Required to Become a Licensed "British" Driver

What to Do	Where	Cost	Prerequisites
1. Get international driving permit[1]	Any AAA office in U.S.A.	$3	2 passport-size photos Current U.S. driver's license
2. If you've imported a car, get it out of Customs	Port of Entry	None	Evidence of 12-month prior ownership/use
Obtain form C.&E. 386 from Customs Officer		10% V.A.T. 10% car tax 7½%–11% duty[2]	If unable to produce above evidence Data for Customs declaration (See p. 32)[2]
3. Obtain temporary insurance certificate	Port of entry or insurance agency	Varies (a portion of the premium)	Completed proposal form (form will be furnished by agent)
4. Get motor vehicle test certificate[3]	Any authorized examiner (ask Customs Officer or dealer to direct you)	£1.25	

What to do	Where	Cost	Prerequisites
5. Get motor vehicle license, registration number, and logbook	Motor Taxation Office of nearest County Council (ask Customs Officer or dealer to direct you)	£25/year, or £9.15 for 4 months	Form C.&E. 386 (Step 2), Insurance certificate (Step 3), Test certificate, if required (Step 4)
6. File application for driving test (DL 26/DL 26M)	Forms available at GPO.[4] Send to Traffic Area Office (address on form)	Amount shown on application form	
7. Enroll for driving lessons[5]	List of instructors at Traffic Area Office (Address on DL 26/26M. See Step 6)	Min. £1.50/hr. (£18 for 12 lessons)	International driving permit[1]
8. Order manuals	See p. 45	See p. 45	
9. Take test	At place shown on appointment card	£3.75	International driving permit[1] A car in good condition
10. File application for driver's license (D.L. 1)	Forms and filing instructions available at GPO[4]	£1	International driving permit[1] Test Pass Certificate if applying for substantive license (furnished after Step 9)
11. Buy plates	Garage or dealer	£2.50 to £4.50	Motor vehicle license and registration number (Step 5)

[1]Not mandatory if you have a current U.S. driver's license, but desirable.
[2]Rate of duty depends on place of manufacture (See p. 32).
[3]Required only if car is more than three years old.
[4]General Post Office.
[5]Recommended, not mandatory.

Appendix D / Tourist Information Centers

Head Office	4 Grosvenor Gardens London SW1W ODU
Northumbria Tourist Board	Prudential Building 140–150 Pilgrim Street Newcastle-upon-Tyne NE1 6TH
English Lakes Tourist Board	Ellerthwaite, Windermere Westmoreland
Yorkshire Tourist Board	312 Tadcaster Road York YO2 2HF
North West Tourist Board	119 The Piazza (1st Floor) Piccadilly Plaza Manchester M1 4AN
East Midlands Tourist Board	90 Bailgate Lincoln
West Midlands Tourist Board	1 Shaw Street Worcester WR1
East Anglia Tourist Board	14 Museum Street Ipswich IP1 1HU
Thames and Chilterns Tourist Board	c/o Tourist Information Office St. Aldates, Oxford
West Country Tourist Board	Trinity Court Southernhay East Exeter EX1 1QS
South East England Tourist Board	Cheviot House 4–6 Monson Road Tunbridge Wells, Kent

Appendix E / Compulsory Registration Areas

(With Year in Which Registration Became Compulsory)

Towns

Birkenhead (1965)
Birmingham (1966)
Blackburn (1962)
Bolton (1965)
Brighton (1965)
Bristol (1967)
Burnley (1965)
Bury (1965)
Canterbury (1958)
Chester (1966)
Coventry (1964)
Crewe (1967)
Darlington (1968)
Derby (1968)
Dudley (1967)
Durham City (1967)
Eastbourne (1926)
Gloucester (1967)
Greater London (1899–1967)
Hartlepool (1968)
Hastings (1929)
Huddersfield (1962)
Leeds (1970)
Leicester (1957)

Manchester (1961)
Northampton (1968)
Norwich (1968)
Oldham (1956)
Oxford (1954)
Preston (1965)
Reading (1962)
Rochdale (1963)
Salford (1961)
St. Helens (1967)
Sheffield (1970)
Solihull (1968)
Southend (1968)
Stockport (1965)
Stoke-on-Trent (1968)
Sunderland (1968)
Teesside (1970)
Wallasey (1965)
Walsall (1967)
Warley (1967)
Warrington (1966)
West Bromwich (1967)
Wolverhampton (1967)

Counties

Berkshire (1963)
Kent (1957–1961)
Surrey (1937 and 1952)

    and parts of

Cheshire (1967)	Lancashire (1965)
Gloucestershire (1967)	Sussex (1965 and 1966)
Hertfordshire (1937 and 1968)	Warwickshire (1965)

Reproduced from *The Legal Side of Buying a House,* with the permission of the publisher, Consumers' Association, 14 Buckingham Street, London WC2N 6DS.

Appendix F / Basis of Liability to United Kingdom Tax on Earned Income

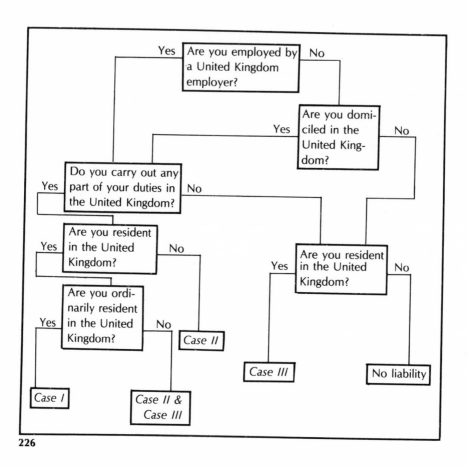

The income charged to tax for any year under the various Cases is as follows:

Case I: The full emoluments arising in the year (whether received in or remitted to the United Kingdom or not).

Case II: The emoluments payable in respect of duties carried out in the United Kingdom in the year (whether received in or remitted to the United Kingdom or not).

Case III: The emoluments received in or remitted to the United Kingdom in the year from earnings of the year, or of any other year in which you were resident in the United Kingdom, *plus* any advance payments for the year remitted to the United Kingdom in an earlier year.

Appendix G / Universities in England

University of Aston in Birmingham, Gosta Green, Birmingham B4 7ET
University of Bath, Claverton Down, Bath BA2 7AY
University of Birmingham, P.O. Box 363, Birmingham B15 2TT
University of Bradford, Bradford, Yorkshire BD7 1DP
University of Bristol, Senate House, Bristol BS8 1TH
Brunel University, Kingston Lane, Uxbridge, Middlesex
University of Cambridge, Cambridge CB2 1TN
The City University, St. John Street, London EC1V 4PB
University of Durham, Old Shire Hall, Durham DH1 3HP
University of East Anglia, Earlham Hall, Norwich NOR 88C
University of Essex, Wivenhoe Park, Colchester, Essex
University of Exeter, Northcote House, The Queen's Drive, Exeter EX4 4QJ
University of Hull, Hull HU6 7RX
University of Keele, Keele, Staffordshire ST5 5BG
University of Kent at Canterbury, Canterbury, Kent
University of Lancaster, University House, Bailrigg, Lancaster, Lancashire
University of Leeds, Leeds LS2 9JT
University of Leicester, University Road, Leicester LE1 7RH
University of Liverpool, P.O. Box 147, Liverpool L69 3BX
University of London, Senate House, London WC1E 7HU
Loughborough University of Technology, Loughborough, Leicestershire
University of Manchester, Oxford Road, Manchester M13 9PL
University of Newcastle-upon-Tyne, Newcastle-upon-Tyne NE1 7RU
University of Nottingham, University Park, Nottingham NG7 2RD
University of Oxford, Oxford
University of Reading, Whiteknights, Reading RG6 2AH

University of Salford, Salford M5 4WT
University of Sheffield, Sheffield S10 2TN
University of Southampton, Highfield, Southampton SO9 5NH
University of Surrey, Guildford, Surrey
University of Sussex, Falmer, Brighton BN1 9QQ
University of Warwick, Coventry CV4 7AL
University of York, Heslington, York YO1 5DD

Reproduced from Bulletin RL–44, *Study in Britain,* by permission of the British Information Services, New York.

Appendix H / Conversion Tables

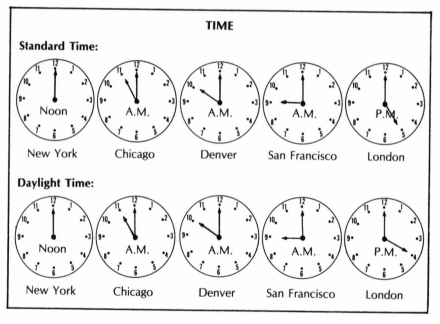

TIME

Standard Time:

New York	Chicago	Denver	San Francisco	London
Noon	A.M.	A.M.	A.M.	P.M.

Daylight Time:

New York	Chicago	Denver	San Francisco	London
Noon	A.M.	A.M.	A.M.	P.M.

You will note that Britain has advanced its time by one hour throughout the year.

HOLIDAYS

Good Friday
Easter Monday
Spring Bank Holiday (last Monday in May)
August Bank Holiday (last Monday in August)
Christmas Day
Boxing Day (the day after Christmas)

CURRENCY

British Coins		Value in $
Halfpenny	(½ p)	$ .0125
Penny	(1 p)	.025
Twopence	(2 p)	.05
Fivepence	(5 p)	.125
Tenpence	(10 p)	.25
Fifty-pence	(50 p)	1.25

British Paper Currency

£1 note (= 100 pence)	$ 2.50
£5 note	12.50
£10 note	25.00
£20 note	50.00

Britain introduced the decimal monetary system in February 1971; the old coins (not shown above) are being phased out.

The above figures are based on *average* exchange rate of $2.50 to the pound. The exchange rate fluctuates from day to day.

Temperature

°C		°F
100		212
90		194
80		176
70		158
60		140
50		122
40		104
30		86
20		68
10		50
0		32
−10		14
−20		−4
−30		−22

Speed/Distance

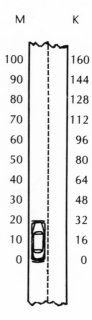

M		K
100		160
90		144
80		128
70		112
60		96
50		80
40		64
30		48
20		32
10		16
0		0

To convert Centigrade to Fahrenheit, multiply by 9, divide by 5, and add 32°.

To convert Fahrenheit to Centigrade, subtract 32°, multiply by 5, and divide by 9.

1 kilometer = 3280.8 feet (approx. ⅝ mile)

MEASUREMENTS

British Standard Measurements

Volume

1 British fluid ounce = 0.961 U.S. fluid ounce
1 British quart   = 1.201 U.S. liquid quarts (1 1/5)
1 British gallon   = 1.20094 U.S. gallons (1 1/5)
1 British bushel   = 1.032 U.S. bushels
1 British quarter   = 8.256 U.S. bushels

Distance

1 kilometer   =   0.621 mile
1 furlong   = 660 feet
1 land league =   3 miles
1 chain   =   66 feet
1 hand   =   4 inches
1 mile   =   1.609 kilometers

Weight

1 stone =   14 pounds
1 cwt   = 112 pounds

Metric Measurements

Liquids

1 gram   = 15.432 grains
1 liter   =   1.0567 quarts
3.785 liters =   1 gallon

Distance

1 kilometer   = 0.621 mile
1 meter   = 39.37 inches
1 centimeter = 0.3937 inch

Weight

1 gram   =   0.03527 ounce
1 kilogram   =   2.2046 pounds
1 metric ton =   1.102 English tons
1 ounce   = 28.35 grams
1 pound   =   0.4536 kilogram

CLOTHING SIZES

Ladies' Clothing	U. S.	England
Stockings	(no difference)	
Shoes	6	4½
	7	5½
	8	6½
	9	7½
Blouses and Sweaters	(no difference)	
Gloves	(no difference)	
Hats	——	(made to order)
Dresses	8	10 (or 30)
	10	12 (or 32)
	12	14 (or 34)
	14	16 (or 36)
	16	18 (or 38)
	18	20 (or 40)

Men's Clothing

	U. S.	England
Socks	(no difference)	
Shoes	(no difference)	
Shirts	(no difference)	
Sweaters	S	34
	M	36–38
	L	40
	XL	42–44
Gloves	(no difference)	
Hats	6¾	6⅝
	7	6⅞
	7¼	7⅛
Suits and Coats	(no difference)	

INDEX

Oakley, 70
Ockham, 85
Ockley, 90
Old Basing. *See* Basing
Olney, 68
Opera, 7–8, 187, 199–200
Ophthalmic services, 141–142
Orpington, 79
Otford, 80
Outdoor fun, 193–194
Oxford (city), 65, 188, 194
Oxfordshire (co.), 56, 64–66, 185, 187, 189

Pangbourne, 67
Parks and gardens, 6–7, 194
Passports, 13–14
Pavenham, 70
Penshurst, 79
Pensions
  British, for people over 80, 203–204
  documentary evidence of, for entry, 12
  payment of taxes on, 17–18, 149, 204–205
  U.S. government, exemption from British income tax, 149
Peperharow, 90
Periodicals, 189
  for information on entertainment, 193, 200
  for real estate advertisements, 103 n.
Petersfield, 94
Pets, shipment and quarantining of, 33–36, 217–219
Petworth, 83
Pharmaceutical services, 142–143
Pirbright, 92
Potton, 71
Prescriptions, 142–143
Preston Candover, 93
Princes Risborough, 69
Publications, 8, 189
  See also Newspapers; Periodicals
Pubs, 195
Pulborough, 83
Puttenham, 87

Radio, 189–190
Rates (property tax), 8 n., 114, 159
Rayleigh, 63
Reading, 56, 66
Reciprocal taxation agreement. *See*

Double Taxation Conventions
Redhill, 90, 190
Regional tourist boards, 48 n., 223
Reigate. *See* Redhill
Rents, 96–98
Residency
  Exchange Control regulations, 16–17
  health benefits, 137
  liability to capital gains tax, 152
  liability to income tax, 147–150
  See also Domicile
Residential homes. *See* Retirees, residential homes for
Retirees
  adult education courses for, 212–213
  associations of, 213
  employment opportunities for, 211–212
  entry requirements for, 12
  financial tips for, 201–208
  health tips for, 208–209
  leisure-time pursuits for, 214–215
  residential homes for, 210–211
Retirement income credit, 206
Rickmansworth, 74
Ripley, 85, 194
Rochester, 79
Rochford, 63
Rodings, The, 61
Romford, 61
Rotherfield, 80
Royal Tunbridge Wells, 80
  See also Tunbridge Wells
Royston, 74
Rutland (co.), 53

Safe deposit boxes, 19, 24–25
Saffron Walden, 61
Saint Albans, 74, 190
Sandy, 71
Schools (pre-college)
  admission to, 176
  examinations required by, 176
  independently maintained, 172–173
  middle, 175
  nursery, 174
  primary, 174–175
  publicly maintained, 173–176
  secondary, 175
  special, 175–176

TOWNS AND CITIES WITHIN COMMUTING DISTANCE OF LONDON

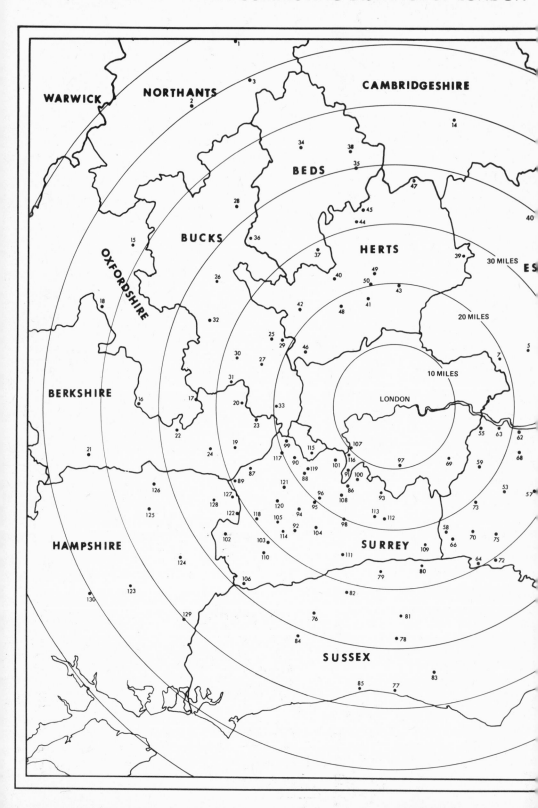